Continuing to Care

The organization of midwifery services in the UK: a structured review of the evidence

Josephine M Green
Penny Curtis
Helene Price
Mary J Renfrew

Books for Midwives Press
an imprint of Hochland & Hochland Ltd

Published by Books for Midwives Press, 174a Ashley Road, Hale, Cheshire, WA15 9SF, England.

© 1998 Green, Curtis, Price and Renfrew

First edition

ISBN 1-898507-69-4

British Library Cataloguing in Publication Data
A catalogue record for this book is available from the British Library

Printed in Great Britain by Cromwell Press Ltd, Trowbridge, Wiltshire.

Contents

Acknowledgements

We are particularly grateful to the Advisory Group for steering the project initially: Tony Dowell, Janet Hirst, Jenny Jefferson, Liz Kernohan and Kathy Marfell, and to Saira Dunnakey for help with devising the initial literature search.

Over the summer of 1997 eight stalwart individuals devoted considerable time and effort to a critical reading of an earlier draft of this report. Their contributions cannot be underestimated. Our thanks to: Rosemary Currell, Jo Garcia, Janet Hirst, Kate Jackson, Kathie Marfell, Mary Newburn, Jim Thornton and Ulla Waldenström. James Piercy also read and commented on Chapter 14. Every effort has been made to incorporate their comments and criticisms, but the views expressed in this report are, of course, our own.

We would also like to thank Jenny Clarke, Limota Vaughan and Charlotte Tomkies for secretarial support.

Staff at Hochland and Hochland have, as ever, been cheerfully supportive.

Helene Price's work on the project was funded by the Yorkshire Collaborating Centre for Health Services Research.

CHAPTER ONE

Introduction

The past decade has seen fundamental changes in the organization of the maternity services. These changes have accelerated in the years since the publication of the House of Commons' Select Committee's Inquiry into Maternity Services in 1992, and the report of the Expert Maternity Group, 'Changing Childbirth' in 1993. These reports made recommendations for changes in the maternity services, and 'Changing Childbirth' identified specific indicators by which success may be judged. Across the country, health authorities and trusts have responded to these recommendations in different ways. There is now a wide diversity in the types of care being offered to childbearing women and their families. This diversity may be beneficial, in that it may foster services geared to local needs but it may also be confusing for caregivers, planners, purchasers and service users alike.

Published descriptions of innovations in this area sometimes seem to suggest conflicting results. It is difficult for commissioners, providers and women to know which studies to rely on, and what is the best way to organize their services. There is a pressing need to assess the evidence that exists in a systematic way, to provide information to commissioners, providers, policy makers, service users and researchers.

In this study, we review the evidence relating to the organization of midwifery services, to help inform the provision and purchasing of services, and the need for future research. Our remit was to focus on midwifery services, rather than maternity services more generally. We recognize that this is problematic; midwifery services do not exist in a vacuum, but are intimately connected with other areas of the maternity services such as obstetrics and general practice, as well as with the location of care, especially the shift to community-based care. The evidence, therefore, rarely relates exclusively to the organization of midwifery services. Rather, it is just one element of a changing kaleidoscope. We discuss this issue in relevant sections of the report.

CHAPTER TWO

Context and Background

Two powerful reports in the past five years have recommended fundamental changes to the way in which the maternity services are organized; the report of the House of Commons Select Committee on Health (the Winterton Report, House of Commons 1992) and 'Changing Childbirth' (Department of Health, 1993). Although we will focus specifically on the changes recommended by these reports, it is important that they are seen within their historical context, and in relation to changes in the wider social context, and other policy directions. Appendix A describes the historical and social context, and related changes which have had an impact on thinking about the maternity services. In summary, recent decades have seen increased consumer involvement and empowerment, the use of research evidence in practice and an emphasis on cost effectiveness.

Many of these wide social issues and policy directions are reflected in the 'Winterton Report' and 'Changing Childbirth'. The impetus for both of these reports arose from concerns voiced by women, health professionals and consumer organizations such as the National Childbirth Trust (NCT), Association for the Improvement in Maternity Services (AIMS), Maternity Services Liaison Committees and Community Health Councils. Ninety recommendations were made as a result of the findings of the Winterton Report. The key elements included the need for women to have continuity of care, choice of place of birth, involvement in decisions about their care, and, for women having a normal pregnancy, care from a midwife. The Committee also concluded that the policy of encouraging all women to give birth in hospital could not be justified on grounds of safety.

In response to the Winterton Report, the government established an Expert Group, chaired by Baroness Cumberlege. The remit of the group was to review the current policy on maternity care provided for women during childbirth and to make recommendations for change. Their report, 'Changing Childbirth', recommended that women should become actively involved in the planning and delivery of maternity care, and that a flexible service be provided to meet their needs. The concept that care should become 'woman centred' is the underlying principle. The provision of appropriate, accurate and unbiased information based on research was emphasized. This process was intended to allow and encourage women and their families to make informed choices in relation to their care. Multidisciplinary team working was also emphasized.

Based on these principles, 'Changing Childbirth' identified ten indicators of success that should be achieved within five years (Department of Health, 1993, p. 70):

1. all women should be entitled to carry their own notes;

2. every woman should know one midwife who ensures continuity of her midwifery care;

3. at least 30% of women should have the midwife as the lead professional;

4. every woman should know the lead professional who has a key role in the planning and provision of her care;

5. at least 75% of women should know the person who cares for them during their delivery;

6. midwives should have direct access to some beds in all maternity units;

7. at least 30% of women delivered in a maternity unit should be admitted under the management of a midwife;

8. the total number of antenatal visits for women with uncomplicated pregnancies should have been reviewed in the light of available evidence and the RCOG guidelines;

9. all front-line ambulances should have a paramedic able to support the midwife who needs to transfer a woman to hospital in an emergency and;

10. all women should have access to information about the services available in their locality.

Purchasers and providers across the country have been working towards achieving these indicators. There has been wide variation in ways of doing this, perhaps especially in achieving continuity of caregiver (indicators 2 and 5). Questions have been raised by purchasers and by providers about the extent of structural change that may be needed to achieve progress towards these indicators or, at the least, towards enacting the principles of continuity described in 'Changing Childbirth'. Some Trusts have introduced extensive changes to the structure of the services, for example by introducing team midwifery or caseload working for midwives. Others have carried out changes within the existing structure, for example by setting up 'Home from Home' schemes, or by increasing the amount of community-based care.

This structured review was commissioned by a group of purchasers who were seeking evidence-based information about the best way to organize local midwifery services. Research studies in this area have used a wide range of methods and have examined very different forms of care. It is difficult for purchasers, providers and women to know which studies to rely on, and what is the best way to organize services. There is a pressing need to assess the evidence that exists in a systematic way.

Aim of the study

The aim of this study is to review the evidence relating to the organization of midwifery services, to help inform the commissioning and provision of services, and the need for future research.

Our remit was to examine midwifery services, rather than maternity services more generally. Midwifery services, of course, do not exist in a vacuum, but are intimately connected with other areas of the maternity services such as obstetrics and general practice, and with the location of care, especially the shift to community-based care. This has been a challenge in deciding which studies to include and which to exclude. We have had to make pragmatic decisions about the limitations to this review, and we discuss our decisions in the relevant sections of the report.

This report will:

a)   review the evidence relating to the organization of midwifery services including a critique of research methods used,
b)   make recommendations for practice, and
c)   make recommendations for research.

CHAPTER THREE

Some Methodological Issues

Secondary research

The present report is the result of secondary research, that is to say that it is based on accounts written by others. This is in contrast to primary research studies, that is studies which have gone directly to the sources of data, such as women themselves, midwives, or maternity records. When conducting secondary research, the researcher can choose which questions to ask, but the answers may not be there. They may not be there because the primary researchers did not ask the appropriate questions, or because the original research design did not permit an unambiguous interpretation of the data. One of the functions of this report is to draw attention to the answers which are not there as well as those that are.

Randomized controlled trials

Random allocation

Data which permit unambiguous interpretation are the researcher's holy grail. It is for this reason that the randomized controlled trial (RCT) is seen as the 'gold standard' when assessing evidence of effectiveness. Without random allocation to study groups, and the inclusion of a control group, we cannot be confident that observed differences between groups are not a result of the groups being different to start with. It may be that those choosing, or being chosen for, one form of treatment are older or more articulate, or less anxious, or they may differ in other systematic ways that we have not even thought of. These problems are seen clearly, for example, in the debate about home versus hospital birth, where random allocation has not been carried out, but the same issues arise in less obvious cases. Wherever study groups have arisen in a non-random way, there is a strong possibility that there will be systematic differences between them, and that these systematic differences may be related to the outcomes of interest. When participants in a study have been randomized using a secure technique, we can assume that pre-existing differences between the groups balance out and differences in the outcomes of interest are a result of the experimental practice or treatment.

There are few RCTs in this field. It is difficult to organize a randomized controlled trial in an area of care where this would involve major changes to the way in which large numbers of caregivers work. Without randomization, however, interpretation of the results of studies is very difficult as they may result simply from pre-existing differences. This will be discussed in more depth when individual studies are examined in the Results section.

Large enough studies

If a study is too small, observed differences between groups may result from chance variation. A study needs to be large enough to rule out the play of chance. When reading reports of RCTs, therefore, it is essential to check that randomization has been secure and that the sample size has been calculated in advance, based on an assessment of the differences expected in the main outcomes. The measurement of outcomes such as women's views, or satisfaction with care, or some clinical outcomes, such as method of delivery, require a reasonably small sample size, as all women will have such outcomes. Rare outcomes, such as perinatal death or serious morbidity, require a much larger sample size, and are often not measured. Where they are measured, they are difficult to interpret as the play of chance cannot be ruled out.

In our area of interest in this report, the numbers of women studied in RCTs have not been large enough to really inform the debate about important, rarer outcomes. Much of the evidence presented therefore relates to women's views and feelings. Caregivers and women will also want to know about the relative safety of different forms of care. Without much larger trials being available, we are limited in what we can say about these outcomes.

Intention to treat analysis

If RCTs are not analysed on an 'intention to treat' basis, that is, analysing the groups as allocated regardless of whether or not the participants received the treatment, the strength of unbiased, random allocation is lost. This is the basis of the 'pragmatic' trial which examines the 'real life' effect of the policy to carry out a particular treatment or practice, even if people end up receiving a different treatment from the one that they were allocated to receive. For example, a woman may be randomized to receive care in a midwifery-led unit, but then may develop problems and be transferred to the consultant unit in labour. Analysing the results as if she were in the consultant unit group removes the benefits of randomization and would tell us little about the real-life effects of a policy to provide midwife-led care. Instead, the transfer should be seen as an outcome of that policy, and the number of such transfers is of interest in itself. In the context of the questions asked in this report, however, this results in some problems of interpretation.

Preference

Another common problem arises from people's preference for one treatment rather than another. Whenever a new treatment is compared with an existing one, there is an in-built asymmetry such that those who favour the new treatment will enter the trial if that is their only opportunity to get their preference met, but those who favour the old treatment will opt out because the treatment that they want is automatically available to anyone not in the trial.

Thus, the group of women included in the trial is already likely to be biased towards the new-style treatment. Even if there are no real differences between the treatments, those who get allocated to the new treatment are likely to be more satisfied because their preference was met and, conversely, those allocated to the old treatment, less satisfied. This problem can introduce substantial bias into any trial where most potential recruits have a preference and only one of the treatments is available outside of the trial, and is especially important to consider where 'satisfaction' is a key outcome (Green, 1994).

An additional problem is that the control group might react adversely to feeling that they were being deprived of the new form of care. Conversely, initial preference aside, people may feel more positive about an intervention just because it is something new, even if it is not in any way objectively better (the 'Hawthorne' effect). We must, therefore, always bear in mind the possibility that differences in psychological outcomes between groups in an RCT contain such elements. In other words, the 'new care' group may express more satisfaction just because they have had something new, rather than because the care is better, and, where women in a control group know that they did not get allocated to a new form of care, they may feel relatively more negative for this reason, rather than because their care was any worse. This possibility obviously has implications for questions of sustainability of new models of care. It could be that once they become standard care women will be less positive about them.

Yet another problem that can arise is when a substantial number of potential recruits prefer not to be in the trial at all. This is relatively common in situations where both treatments are available outside the trial and people tend to have a preference for one or the other (for example, home versus hospital birth). Here one could find that those who are willing to be randomized are not representative of the whole group – they may, for example, be more apathetic or more compliant, and this can have serious implications for the generalizability of the results.

For further information about the design of clinical trials, see Meinert (1986) and Chalmers et al. (1989).

Evidence from sources other than RCTs

The advantages of randomized controlled trials should not lead us to reject evidence from other sources. Whatever the study design, appraisal of the results must include consideration of how the sample was selected and how generalizable the results might be. Some RCTs are in fact so restrictive in their entry criteria that little can be said about generalizability to a more heterogeneous population.

Studies may be **descriptive** or **comparative/experimental.** Descriptive studies tell us what has occurred, or is occurring, and the 'description' may be in words (qualitative) or numbers (quantitative). Comparative or experimental studies look at differences between groups where group members receive different forms of care or treatments. Again, the data may be qualitative or quantitative, but if tests of statistical significance are used to tell us how likely it is that a particular difference between groups may have occurred by chance, then some data must be in a numerical form. Descriptive studies can be very valuable, but they are necessarily limited – we may know that x% of women are satisfied with their care under the new scheme, but we do not know whether that is more or less or the same as would have been satisfied with some other form of care. A comparative study is generally (but not always) more informative than an evaluation that does not involve any comparison group. The necessary caveat concerns how similar the comparison group is.

If we think that we are comparing like with like, but we are mistaken, then the results could be seriously misleading. Such a study design could, in fact, result in a false confidence that the study was 'controlled'.

Audit and evaluation

We will distinguish these two terms as others have (e.g. Campbell and Garcia, 1997). We will use 'evaluation' to mean finding out if something is of value, and 'audit' to mean finding out if what *should* be happening *is* happening.

CHAPTER FOUR

Terminology Used

Discussion of the organization of midwifery services is hampered by the lack of consistency in the use of some of the most commonly used terms. Further confusion is caused by some misnomers; for example in 'GP units', deliveries are mainly the responsibility of midwives. Systems of 'midwife led care' or 'consultant care' do not exclude other professionals (Meldrum et al., 1994). In fact, virtually all women in the United Kingdom have a large proportion of their care provided by midwives, whatever the setting and whatever complications the woman has.

A consistent vocabulary is needed to ensure a common understanding of the evidence provided in this report, and commissioners, providers and users need to be clear that they each understand the terms they use.

For the benefit of readers of this report we have provided a definition of some of the most commonly used terms. In compiling these definitions, we have drawn on the work of Meldrum et al. (1994), modified and added to by our own research team.

Definition of terms
Caseload/caseload midwifery:
A caseload is a specified number of women for whom a midwife is responsible, thus caseload midwifery is a system in which midwives take responsibility in this way. The number of women specified in a caseload varies. These terms are also sometimes used in the context of a team caseload i.e. the specified number of women are the responsibility of a group of midwives rather than individuals.

Community-led care:
Care provided by general practitioners and midwives working in the community, where hospital visits are kept to a minimum.

Continuity of care:
This is used to describe a situation where all the professionals involved share common ways of working and a common philosophy. The aim is to reduce the conflicting advice experienced by women.

Continuity of carer:

The same health professional(s) providing care throughout the childbearing period. It can also be used to indicate the same caregiver throughout a specific episode of care, such as during labour and birth.

Domino scheme (Domiciliary In and Out):

Care is provided by community midwives. They carry out the majority of antenatal and postnatal care, and also care for the women in hospital during labour and birth. In some areas the midwife will assess the woman in early labour in her own home before transfer to the hospital for delivery. The woman is usually discharged from hospital 6–24 hours after birth.

Early discharge/transfer:

Women and their babies are transferred from hospital 6–48 hours after birth. In fact, this is becoming the norm, rather than 'early'.

General Practitioner care:

Care provided primarily at the GP's surgery/health centre by the community midwife and GP. The woman is usually booked to give birth in the hospital, and the community midwife and GP may or may not be present. The GP will visit the woman and her baby at home after birth, and postnatal care is provided by the community midwife.

General Practitioner units:

Units where women go to give birth, where they are cared for by community midwives and GPs. Such units may be free-standing, for example in rural areas, or they may be an integral part of a hospital maternity unit.

Home birth (planned):

The mother plans to give birth at home, under the care of a community midwife. Usually two midwives are present for the birth. The GP may or may not be involved in the care, and may or may not be present for birth.

Independent midwife:

A midwife who works on a self-employed basis, contracting either with NHS Trust/s or directly with individual women for her services. Services may include total care throughout the childbearing period, including birth at home and antenatal and postnatal care. She may also provide components of that care, for example, antenatal and postnatal care, with the woman giving birth with midwives in hospital. Independent midwives, like all midwives, are responsible to their local supervisor of midwives, notify their intention to practice, and adhere to the *Midwives Rules* and *Code of Practice*.

Integrated care:

Care provided in the appropriate setting, depending on the needs of the woman, including in her own home, the GP's surgery, health centre or hospital.

Lead professional:

Defined by 'Changing Childbirth' as 'the professional who will give a substantial part of the care personally *and* who is responsible for ensuring that the woman has access to care from other professionals, as appropriate'. This term is not always used in precisely this way in practice.

Low-risk/high-risk:

These terms are widely used, in spite of the lack of an agreed system for classifying women into different levels of risk. We suggest that 'low risk' is usually used to mean women with no obvious physical, psychological or social problems, either before or during childbearing – what might be described as 'uncomplicated'. 'High risk', therefore, is likely to mean anyone not covered by that term.

Midwife-led care:

A system of care where the midwife is the health professional who takes responsibility for planning and providing care for the woman and her baby throughout the childbearing cycle. This will include the woman being able to book directly with the midwife.

Midwifery units:

Units in which women give birth, staffed only by midwives, possibly with some input from GPs. These may be free-standing, or part of an existing hospital facility.

Named midwife:

A woman is assigned to a specific midwife who is responsible for the co-ordination of her care, even if she does not provide all of it herself.

Shared care:

Usually an agreed arrangement between the GP and the obstetrician. The majority of antenatal care takes place at the GP's surgery/health centre, where care is provided by the midwife and GP. The woman usually gives birth in hospital and after discharge is cared for by the community midwife. The GP is likely to visit during the postnatal period. In some units, shared care is shared between the obstetrician and the midwife.

Selective postnatal visiting:

Until recently, it was expected that all women would receive a daily visit from the midwife until 10 days after birth, and occasionally less frequent visits up until 28 days. In recent years, midwives have been visiting women on less of a routine basis, and more according to the midwife's assessment of the woman's needs, and the woman's wishes.

Specialist obstetrician care:

Women with medical and obstetric complications are offered regular visits to the obstetrician. Some or all of their antenatal care, and their birth, will probably take place in the hospital. Midwives and medical staff will provide care in labour and at birth and after birth in hospital, and care will be provided by the community midwives at home.

Standard care:

This term, or its alternative, 'traditional care', is sometimes used to define the care received by the control group in a study, to contrast it with the new form of care given to the experimental group. Its meaning can vary widely, as it will depend on what standard care was in that locality at the time of the study. Interpreting the results of a study which uses this term will depend on how well the 'standard' form of care is described.

Team midwifery:

A defined group of midwives working closely together provide care for a specific group of women throughout the childbearing cycle. They usually work in a clearly defined geographic area, and work both in hospital and in the community. (However, see Chapter 8, 'Mapping team midwifery' p. 37). Sometimes contrasted with 'caseload midwifery', but sometimes used interchangeably.

Woman-centred:

The needs of the woman provide the focus for the planning, organizing and delivery of maternity services.

CHAPTER FIVE

Methods of the Review

This study was a structured literature review that followed some of the conventions of a systematic review. Funding did not allow time for a full systematic review, and there may be areas of literature that have not been fully covered. We have done our best to identify all the relevant studies in this field. We know, however, that it is possible that we have missed some studies. We would welcome information from readers who know of research studies that have not been included.

Advisory group and critical readers

At an early stage it was recognized that this review was challenging because the literature in this area is extensive, and clear decisions were needed to establish limits to the material to be included. An advisory group was therefore established to advise on the study protocol. Members of the group had backgrounds in midwifery, general practice and commissioning. In addition, a group of critical readers, including researchers in the field, consumers, managers and practitioners, agreed to read and critique the review.

Inclusion/exclusion criteria

The last 15–20 years has seen a wide variety of attempts to meet the goals of improved services for women and enhanced job satisfaction for midwives. New schemes[1] have spawned others and the added impetus of 'Changing Childbirth' has resulted in a plethora of variations. Unfortunately, many of these schemes have not been subject to any rigorous evaluation or audit. As this report is concerned with evaluating evidence, our focus must necessarily be on those schemes which have been evaluated. We have, therefore, not included any reports which are simply a description of a way of organizing a service.

Only the English language literature was searched. The searches identified research studies published from 1980 to 1996, although some key studies from before 1980 and after 1996 are included. Studies have been included regardless of the research method used. Only studies from the United Kingdom have been included, as the organization and content of care provided by midwives varies widely from country to country.

---

1. To avoid confusions of nomenclature, we will refer to any of these new ways of organizing services as a 'scheme'.

The review focuses on research studies which examine the organization of midwifery services, rather than the content of care, although these are not always easily separated. We have included studies which examined provision of care both to the general population and to women of 'low risk'.

Schemes that targeted women with special needs were felt to introduce so many additional variables as to need a review in their own right, and have therefore been excluded. Studies which examined the setting of care for birth such as birth centres and home birth have been excluded, on the grounds that this includes much more than the work of midwives; women giving birth in different settings differ also in their access to obstetric, anaesthetic and paediatric services.

Search strategy

The initial search was devised with the help of Saira Dunnakey from the National Health Service Centre for Reviews and Dissemination, University of York. Both electronic and hand searches were carried out. We also wrote to organizers of schemes that we had heard of through informal networks. Repeat electronic searches were carried out in May 1997 to ensure that we had full details of all relevant studies published to that date. Full details of the search strategy are given in Appendix B.

Categorization of studies

Core comparative studies

The publications which were central to this review were research studies that had the organization of midwifery services as their main independent variable. Within these, as we saw in Chapter 3, the most informative studies are likely to be those that have compared an innovative form of care with 'standard' or 'traditional' care. Accordingly, the review focused on the relatively small number of studies which had built in such a comparison. The criteria for inclusion as a core comparative study were:

- the scheme had been evaluated;

- the evaluation included a comparison between the innovative form of care and some alternative;

- a written report of the scheme and its evaluation was available;

- the evaluation included process and outcome data and the views of women. These were considered a minimum requirement for addressing our key questions.

We use the term '*core* comparative study' to distinguish these from other comparative studies that did not have the organization of midwifery services as their main independent variable.

Multi-scheme descriptive studies

Although comparative studies were considered central, descriptive studies can also be very valuable, particularly if more than one scheme was studied. We, therefore, also considered as core descriptive multi-scheme studies. These studies have rarely been able to compare directly with standard care, but they are still of considerable value to this report in that they provide a breadth which is necessarily missing from studies that have looked only at a single scheme.

Other studies

Studies which were neither core comparative nor multi-scheme descriptive were included under this heading if they had had the organization of midwifery services as the main independent variable, or if they otherwise yielded data relevant to the review.

The review intentionally focused on schemes that changed some aspect of the way in which midwives worked with the aim of increasing the satisfaction of mothers and midwives through a less-fragmented, more user-friendly service. The stringency of our criteria for inclusion as a core study has meant that certain studies are not given the attention that some readers might expect. This is principally because they did not meet the criterion of having the organization of midwifery services as the main independent variable. Sikorski et al.'s (1996) randomized controlled trial of a reduced schedule of antenatal visits is one example. These are important studies, but they do not give us direct evidence which would help us choose between different ways of organizing midwifery services. The majority of studies that were not considered as core were single-scheme descriptive studies. These other studies have still been included in the report, as some help to shed light on some details of care, and there is much to learn from reading them. They are used to inform discussion, and to allow readers to assess relevant topics and research methods used for themselves. Details of these studies can be found in Appendix C.

CHAPTER SIX

Results of the Search

Papers identified

Over 600 publications were identified through the search, but only a small proportion of these were empirical studies which had the organization of midwifery services as a major independent variable. A selected Bibliography of useful background reading based on the search is presented in Appendix D.

Of the papers identified, seven met the criteria for core comparative studies (five of which were randomized controlled trials) and four were multi-scheme descriptive studies. A further three studies were identified which seemed likely to meet core comparative criteria (Birmingham, Kidlington and Sidcup), but for which we were unable to obtain a written report of the study in time for inclusion in the review.

Only research studies which had the organization of midwifery services as their main independent variable have been included as key sources of evidence in the Results section. We have, however, drawn on other studies where appropriate, particularly in considering women's views of their maternity care. Other published material, including policy documents and discussion papers, have been used in discussion and are cited in the references.

In the last four years, a number of new research studies have been set up to examine some of the implications of 'Changing Childbirth'. Final results of many of these are not available at the time of writing this report. It is anticipated that many of these studies will contribute to the debate on the organization of midwifery care, and some contact names of researchers are included in Appendix E.

Preparation of material

All research studies were read by the research team. A structured format was prepared to summarize all studies that met the entry criteria and HP prepared summary tables for all studies in consultation with JMG and MJR.

These were summarized using the following headings:

- Authors
- Date
- Full citation
- Intervention assessed (where relevant)

- Evaluation
- Number of women studied
- Main outcomes
- Results

The core comparative studies were expanded into two sets of summary tables by PC in consultation with JMG: the first table for each (A) summarizes the characteristics of the scheme:

- Name of the scheme
- Authors of the evaluation and date
- Organization of midwifery service
- Aim of scheme and pattern of care provided
- Number of midwives involved in the scheme
- Midwives grades
- Number of women cared for per annum

The second table (B) summarizes the evaluation and the results of the study:

- Name of the scheme
- Authors of the evaluation and date
- Aim of the evaluation
- Methods and outcomes
- Number of midwives in the evaluation
- Number of women involved in the evaluation
- Results

These tables relating to the core comparative studies and to other studies are presented in Appendix C.

Resources did not allow systematic assessment of the methodological quality of each of the non-core studies. Readers can assess the quality for themselves by reading the summary of methods used in each table. In addition, methodological quality is discussed in the text where this is relevant.

Presentation of findings
Tables
The tables in Appendix C contain structured descriptions of all core comparative studies and other relevant empirical studies identified by the search. Tables have not been included for the multi-scheme descriptive studies because self-contained descriptions exist in an easily accessed format in the text (Chapter 8).

The tables in Appendix C are numbered sequentially. Tables 1 to 7 (presented as 1A, 1B, 2A, 2B etc. as defined in the previous section) are the core comparative studies. Subsequent numbers are for other studies in the order that they appear in the text. Tables are presented only for those studies which are particularly pertinent. Thus, a study may be referred to in the text but not have a summary table. For those studies that do have tables in Appendix C, the appropriate number will be given in the text in square brackets [ ] whenever the study is referred to so that the reader knows where to find further information, including the full reference(s) to the study. More detailed tables relating to the core comparative studies are also presented in the text in Chapter 7.

Text

- Chapter 7 will describe the core comparative studies, how they were evaluated, and a discussion of specific methodological issues.

- Chapter 8 will describe the multi-scheme descriptive studies. These studies have not been tabulated in Appendix C and so subsequent references to these studies are not accompanied by a number in square brackets. Instead both the descriptions of the studies and their results are covered in some depth in the text.

SIX KEY QUESTIONS

The presentation of our findings will be structured around six key questions in Chapters 9–14 inclusive. These questions arise from the broader literature, including policy documents and the stated aims of many of the schemes.

The questions are:

1. Are new ways of organizing services achieving greater continuity of carer?

2. Are they associated with different clinical outcomes?

3. What are women's views and experiences of these alternative ways of organizing midwifery services?

4. What are the views and experiences of the midwives who work in the schemes?

5. What are the views and experiences of other healthcare workers?

6. What are the costs?

In addressing these questions, we will draw principally on the findings from the core comparative studies described in Chapter 7, since it is these studies that can tell us how the new schemes compare with other forms of care. However, in many cases further understanding can be gained from thorough descriptive studies (such as the multi-scheme studies described in Chapter 8) or from studies that have not had the organization of midwifery services as their main independent variable. These additional studies, many of which are summarized in Appendix C, will be drawn on as appropriate. For each question we will be seeking to define what is *not* known, as well as what is.

CHAPTER SEVEN

Description of Core Comparative Studies

The seven schemes which met the criteria of 'Core comparative studies' (Chapter 5, p. 14) were:

♦ The Know-Your-Midwife scheme (KYM) [1] (Flint and Poulengeris, 1987)

♦ The Leicester Home-from-Home scheme [2] (MacVicar et al., 1993)

♦ The Aberdeen Midwives Unit [3] (Hundley et al., 1994, 1995a, 1995b)

♦ The Glasgow Midwifery Development Unit (MDU) [4] (Turnbull et al., 1995a, 1995b, 1995c, 1996; Cheyne et al., 1995)

♦ One-to-One Midwifery Practice [5] (McCourt and Page, 1996; Piercy et al., 1996)

♦ Midwifery Teams in West Essex [6] (Farquhar et al., 1996)

♦ The Scottish Antenatal Care Trial [7] (Tucker et al., 1996)

All of these schemes had reorganized their midwifery service with the aim of providing some or all of the following:

• a service which is less fragmented

• a service which is more 'user-friendly' and 'woman-centred'

• a service which minimizes duplication of tasks

• a service which minimizes obstetric contacts for women with no obstetric problems

• a service which utilizes midwives' skills.

Four of the schemes [1], [4], [5], [6], included the additional aim of having an individual or a small group of midwives who look after a woman throughout the whole process from booking to postnatal discharge. This means that, unlike other ways of organizing midwifery services, there is the potential for total continuity of carer. We will refer to such schemes as 'start-to-finish' schemes.

The next section describes the seven schemes. This is followed by a structured description of the studies which evaluated them. Finally, methodological issues will be discussed.

Core comparative studies: description of the schemes

A tabulated summary of the main features of the seven schemes is given in Tables 7.1 to 7.4.

Know-Your-Midwife (KYM) [1]

One of the earliest documented attempts at reorganizing the way in which midwifery services were delivered was the Know-Your-Midwife scheme at St George's Hospital, Tooting in South London. As the title of the scheme indicates, the principal motivation was to reduce fragmentation of care by allowing women to get to know a small group of midwives who would provide most of their care. There was a single team of four carefully selected midwives. Women were eligible if they were low-risk and were planning to have all their antenatal care at the hospital; most women at St George's, in fact, had shared care. All other midwives in the area continued to work as they always had done. The team cared for 250 women per annum. Separate KYM antenatal clinics were held at the hospital. The aim was that a woman would get to know all four members of the team and that these four midwives would deliver the bulk of her care, including delivery. At any one time there would be one KYM midwife on call, and they would be on-call for 24 hours at a time carrying a long-range bleep. Midwives worked a nominal 150 hours per four-week period (37½ hours per week). Women had midwives' home phone numbers to call when labour started. Originally, women in early labour were visited at home and did not come to hospital until they were in established labour, but it was decided that this was not covered by the hospital's protocol, and was discontinued. Thereafter, the KYM midwife would meet the woman on the delivery suite. In the postnatal ward women were cared for by the ward staff plus KYM midwives who would come in each morning and usually visit again between four and seven in the evening. After discharge, postnatal care at home was given by KYM midwives unless the woman lived outside the area in which case she was transferred to the community midwife.

Home-from-Home [2]

The Leicester 'Home-from-Home' scheme was proposed and set up jointly by obstetricians and midwives. It covered antenatal and intrapartum hospital care, but not postnatal care. Low-risk women's hospital contacts were exclusively with the scheme midwives, both in the antenatal clinic and intrapartum unless consultant advice was sought. The delivery rooms were three rooms adjacent to the delivery suite with homely furnishing. Staffing consisted of two midwifery sisters and eight staff midwives. All had volunteered to work on the scheme and were already working in the hospital. There were thus no overall increases in staff costs, although some other areas may have been left short-staffed. The working day was organized in three shifts.

Scheme midwives were not usually involved in the care of non-scheme women. Initially there were two antenatal clinics per week, but this needed to be increased to three.

Women were seen at these clinics at 26, 36 and 41 weeks, and had normal shared care in the community given by their GP and/or community midwife in between. Referral to the consultant was mandatory after 41 weeks. Midwives who wanted an obstetric opinion in labour called the registrar, who decided whether the woman should be transferred.

Aberdeen Midwives Unit [3]

This scheme delivered midwife-only intrapartum care, in a separate midwife-managed delivery unit with no medical input, 20 yards from the hospital consultant unit. The unit had five rooms which all had a 'homely' environment. The philosophy was one of minimal intervention and moving around during labour was encouraged. The aim was to offer women choice, participation and control in their labour. The scheme was for low-risk women only.

The midwives worked only in the hospital and were allocated 'throughout the delivery suite according to clinical need'. In other words there was a common pool of midwives who might be working in either the Consultant Unit or the Midwifery Unit. In practice, however, the tendency was for F grades to be allocated to the Midwifery Unit and E grades to Consultant Unit because of the extra responsibility that the Midwifery Unit entailed.

Glasgow Midwifery Development Unit (MDU) [4]

The Glasgow MDU was a midwife-managed unit within the Glasgow Royal Infirmary. The scheme started in January 1993 and was preceded by stakeholder analysis and involvement of midwives in planning. Five hundred and seventy five women were cared for in the first year. Only low-risk women booking before 16 weeks and living in the north east of the city were eligible. This was a very socially disadvantaged population. Midwives had their own caseloads. Each midwife had a partner with whom she alternated clinics and other responsibilities. The concept of 'team midwifery' was rejected in favour of 'primary midwifery' where the midwife is lead provider. The term 'named midwife care' was also used. However, the service specification was that a healthy woman being cared for by the MDU could expect to be cared for by the named midwife and *up to three associates*, it having been decided that care delivered by only one or two midwives was unrealistic. These midwives delivered all the woman's care from start-to-finish whether in the hospital or the community. Thus, unlike the previous two schemes just described, these hospital-based midwives also provided all postnatal care both in the hospital and at home. The location of antenatal care (a recommended total of eight visits) was by negotiation between the midwife and the woman and could be hospital, home or community clinic. There were designated labour ward rooms for MDU clients which were more homely, but there was no separate unit as such.

There was a designated MDU area of the postnatal ward (eight beds). Women were referred to an obstetrician only when there was a deviation from normal, and transfer to obstetric care could be permanent or temporary. MDU midwives had direct access to senior doctors without going through the Senior House Officer. They could also seek midwifery advice from any appropriate midwife in the clinical area. The labour ward had full obstetric cover and a 24 hour epidural service.

Twenty midwives worked in the unit at the time of the evaluation. Twenty-one were chosen from 23 volunteers. They had to work full-time and to have completed at least one year post-registration rotation through all midwifery care areas. Four were G grade and 17 were E grade. One left before the start. The saved funding allowed upgrading of E midwives to F grade in recognition of the responsibility of caseload holding. Midwives were not 'on-call' but there was a fortnightly (75 hours) self-rostered rotation schedule through all areas of care designed to maximize the likelihood of a woman being delivered by her named-midwife or an associate. Forty-eight per cent of on-duty time was on the labour ward (3 x 12 hour shifts), 30 per cent was ward-based (3 x 8 hour), 17 per cent was in the community (2 x 5 hour + one 4½ hour community/outpatients) and 5 per cent in the hospital antenatal clinic (1 x 4 hour).

One-to-One [5]

This scheme started in November 1993 and covered all women in two London postal districts, irrespective of risk status. As its name suggests, the principle was for each woman to have a relationship with a named midwife, rather than a team. Each midwife had a caseload of approximately 40 women per annum. Each midwife had a partner who was her back-up if she was not available. Women had the mobile phone numbers of both the named midwife and her partner. Each partnership consisted of one F and one G grade midwife. Each partnership was part of a larger group – the group was the next line of back-up. Twenty midwives already employed by the Trust were appointed to the project after 'a rigorous process of selection'. Implementation was preceded by 18 months of planning and was 'a longed for dream for many of the midwives and the implementation group' (p. 18).

Booking was usually at the woman's home. Women covered by the scheme came under two hospitals: Hammersmith (HH) and Queen Charlotte's and Chelsea (QCCH). Women had hospital antenatal visits at 12 weeks (HH) or 15 weeks (QCCH), at 19–21 weeks for a scan, and at 41 weeks to review management. Other antenatal care was usually at home. The named midwife or her partner was on-call for women going into labour, and women were visited at home in early labour. The named midwife or her partner provided postnatal care at home and transfer home within 24 hours if there were no problems. While women were on the postnatal ward they typically received only one visit per day from their named midwife. High-risk women had an obstetrician as lead professional but the named midwife still provided care and support.

Each midwife pair worked out their own preferred way of working e.g. being on call for their 'own' women in labour in office hours but sharing night and weekend calls.

West Essex [6]

This study reported on an entire Health District (West Essex) where there had been a major shift to team working by a total of seven teams, each consisting of seven whole time equivalent midwives. The full scheme started in April 1994, preceded by a pilot scheme in 1992. The number of midwives per team had been increased from six to seven as result of the pilot. The caseload per team was theoretically no more than 350 per annum. There were a total of 55 community-based midwives and 37 hospital-based (core staff). One hospital-based team, with its own ward, was for women who lived in the adjacent health district and had their community-based care from that district's midwives. Midwives had been asked to choose whether they wanted to work in a community-based team, hospital core staff or the hospital-based team. There had not been enough volunteers for community teams, so some who had given it as second choice were allocated there.

Antenatal booking was by the named midwife in the woman's home or at the GP's surgery. The named midwife was responsible for organizing any hospital appointments that were needed. If the woman was high-risk she had shared care between the obstetrician, GP and midwife. Low-risk women had shared care from midwife and GP. Antenatal appointments were usually at clinics attached to GP surgeries. If a woman was admitted to hospital antenatally she was cared for by core midwives but team midwives would make social visits. During the pilot study, team midwives had delivered both antenatal and postnatal in-patient care, but the workload was found to be too great.

Women contacted the labour ward once in established labour and the on-call midwife for her team would meet her there. If more than one woman from a team was in labour at the same time, care was taken over by core midwives or midwives from another team. Team midwives also covered emergency caesarean sections. Postnatal ward care was from core staff although the team midwife might visit. The team took over care again after discharge home.

The Scottish Antenatal Care Trial [7]

Following on from earlier studies of antenatal care in Scotland (Tucker et al., 1994; Hall et al., 1980), this scheme was devised as a multi-centre study to answer the question 'Should obstetricians see women with normal pregnancies?'. The model of care being tested was that women at low-risk of pregnancy complications could receive their routine antenatal care in primary care settings from general practitioners and midwives only. Unlike the other schemes considered here, this did not involve individual midwives in taking on substantially new roles although presumably the midwives concerned (all of whom were community midwives) took on greater responsibility as a result of the scheme. Detailed care plans and protocols were defined for both arms of the trial after discussion with obstetricians, GPs and midwives. The clinical content was determined by expert consensus and proposed fewer visits for multiparous women than for primiparas. The care protocols were based on the Grampian integrated antenatal care schedule (Grampian Area Maternity Services Committee, 1989).

In order to assist the reader in understanding the diversity of the services offered by these seven schemes and the nature of the workload for midwives, Tables 7.1 to 7.4 give summary information about the seven schemes.

Table 7.1: Risk status and aspects of care covered by the scheme

	All women or low-risk only?	antenatal	intrapartum	postnatal, hospital	postnatal, community
Know-Your-Midwife [1]	low-risk	✓	✓	some	some
Home-from-Home [2]	low-risk	some	✓	X	X
Aberdeen Midwives Unit [3]	low-risk	X	✓	X	X
Glasgow MDU [4]	low-risk	✓	✓	✓	✓
One-to-One [5]	all	✓	✓	some	✓
West Essex [6]	all	✓	✓	X	✓
Scottish Antenatal Care Trial [7]	low-risk	✓	X	X	X

Table 7.2: Location of routine antenatal care in each of the seven schemes

Know-Your-Midwife [1]	Hospital
Home-from-Home [2]	Antenatal care from the scheme midwives at hospital at 26,36 & 41 weeks. Remainder of antenatal care from GP and community midwife.
Aberdeen Midwife Unit [3]	N/A (intrapartum care only)
Glasgow MDU [4]	By negotiation between the midwife and the woman and could be hospital, home or community clinic (usually hospital).
One-to-One [5]	Usually the woman's home
West Essex [6]	Booking usually at home. Other visits usually at clinic attached to GP surgery.
The Scottish Antenatal Care Trial [7]	All routine investigations, including scans, undertaken in primary care.

Table 7.3: Number of women cared for per annum, number of midwives in the scheme and involvement of other health professionals in providing maternity care in the seven schemes

	Number of women per annum	Number of scheme midwives	Other maternity caregivers
Know-Your-Midwife [1]	250	4	Obstetric team routine appointments at: booking; 36 wks and 41 wks. Core midwives provide back-up on delivery suite and wards; postnatal home care from community midwife if woman not close to the hospital.
Home-from-Home [2]	Number not given. 1,586 bookings and 802 deliveries per annum (calculated from numbers in trial)	10	Obstetric team routine appointments at: booking and 41 wks. Most antenatal care given by GP and community midwife. Scheme midwives did not give postnatal care.
Aberdeen Midwives Unit [3]	Number not given. 696 deliveries per annum (calculated from numbers in the trial)	There was a common pool of midwives who might be working in either the consultant unit or the midwife unit	The scheme only covered intrapartum care in the midwives unit, therefore, all other care was by other caregivers.
Glasgow MDU [4]	575 cared for in 1st year. Midwives had their own caseloads	20	None, unless GP involvement requested by woman or GP. No routine obstetric appointments.
One-to-One [5]	728 in the study year. Planned caseload of 40 per midwife per annum	20	Obstetric team routine appointments at: 12 or 15 wks and 41 wks and anomaly scan at 19-21 wks. Core midwives provided back-up on delivery suite and wards.
West Essex [6]	2,400, plus antenatal and postnatal care for women delivering out of area and 600 delivering in the area but having other care elsewhere. Planned maximum caseload of 350 per team, though higher for one of the teams	7 teams, each consisting of 7 whole time equivalent midwives	Antenatal care shared with GPs. No routine obstetric appointments for low-risk women. Core midwives for antenatal and postnatal hospital care. (During pilot study team midwives had delivered both ante- & postnatal in-patient care, but the workload was found to be too great). Back-up delivery suite cover from core midwives or midwives from another team. Team midwives covered emergency sections.
Scottish Antenatal Care Trial [7]	Number not given. 1,857 eligible per annum (calculated from study numbers)	45 community midwives	Antenatal care shared with GPs (N=224). No routine obstetric appointments for low-risk women. Scheme only covered antenatal care, therefore, all other care was by other caregivers.

Table 7.4: On-call arrangements in each of the seven schemes

Know-Your-Midwife [1]	On-call for 24 hours at a time for all the team's women.
Home-from-Home [2]	No on-call. Midwives worked a three-shift per day system delivering antenatal and intrapartum care to scheme women only.
Aberdeen Midwives Unit [3]	No on-call. All midwives rotated between the Midwives' unit and the labour ward, therefore, no 'scheme midwives' as such.
Glasgow MDU [4]	Midwives not 'on-call' but there was a fortnightly (75 hours) self-rostered rotation schedule through all areas of care designed to maximize the likelihood of a woman being delivered by her named-midwife or an associate. Forty-eight per cent of on-duty time was on the labour ward (3 x 12 hour shifts), 30% was ward-based (3 x 8 hour); 17% in the community (2 x 5 hour + one 4½ hour community/outpatients); and 5% in the hospital antenatal clinic (1 x 4 hour).
One-to-One [5]	Each midwife pair worked out their own preferred way of working e.g. being on call for their own women in labour in office hours but sharing night and weekend calls. 'Midwives work flexibly and have developed skills in time management'.
West Essex [6]	Duty rosters included a period of being 'on-call' for the delivery suite for the whole team. Otherwise varied from team to team.
The Scottish Antenatal Care Trial [7]	Not applicable – antenatal care only.

Core comparative studies: The evaluations

The seven schemes were all the subjects of comparative evaluations, but details of the evaluations vary. They are summarized here and in Appendix C. The main outcomes considered in each evaluation are summarized in Table 7.5.

Know-Your-Midwife (KYM) [1]

- *Date of evaluation:* April 1983–August 1985.

- *Comparison with:* Hospital-based, consultant-led care

- *Method:* Randomized controlled trial. Analysis was by intention to treat (including women who declined to take part of the trial) and also by subgroups, for example, acceptors versus refusers.

- *Eligibility criteria:* Low-risk women who were intending to have hospital-based antenatal care (the majority of women at St George's at that time had shared care).

- *Number of eligible women/number consenting/numbers per group:* 498 women were randomized to the control group and 503 were randomized to Know-Your-Midwife, 43 of whom (8.5%) declined. Women were randomized *before* being asked to consent to being in the study and consent was sought only from the group randomized to the Know-Your-Midwife scheme. Thus, the control group did not know that they were part of a study.

- *Rationale for sample size:* Pragmatic – 250 women per year was thought to be the optimum number for four midwives to care for.

- *Comparability of comparison groups:* The control group was found to contain significantly more Asian and fewer European women. It also had a smaller percentage of smokers and a smaller percentage of women with higher education.

- *Data sources:* Patient satisfaction questionnaires at 37 weeks, and at two days and six weeks after birth; the General Health Questionnaire was sent with the six week questionnaire. An obstetric record sheet was completed for every woman randomized into the study (whether she accepted or not). Some data were taken from the booking notes.

- *Evaluation carried out by:* The scheme's instigator and a researcher who worked with the team.

- *Other:* Comparison data were also collected on 577 women booked to receive shared care between the Spring of 1983 and the Spring of 1985. This group were not randomized, but were comparable in terms of age, parity, marital status and social class.

Home-from-Home [2]

- *Date:* 1 March 1989–6 July 1990.

- *Comparison with:* 'Standard care' (mainly shared care between consultant/GP/community midwife).

- *Method:* Randomized controlled trial. Randomization was in a 2:1 ratio because it was anticipated that approximately half the Home-from-Home women would be transferred.

  Only the Home-from-Home group were told about the trial, and this information was only given after randomization. The control group had the care that they would have had anyway and did not know that they were part of a trial. Analysis was by intention to treat.

- *Eligibility criteria:* Low-risk. All women were seen and examined by a consultant at their first appointment and the decision made regarding suitability for the trial.

- *Number of eligible women:* Of the 7,906 pregnant women presenting during the study period, 3,510 (44%) were considered suitable for the study.

- *Number consenting/numbers per group:* 2,304 (66%) were allocated to Home-from-Home, 189 (8%) of whom refused consent. 1,206 were randomized to the control group (33%).

- *Rationale for sample size:* 1,000 women in each group would have adequate power to detect significant changes such as induction rates or the incidence of perineal tears whose levels were around 15–20%.

- *Comparability of the groups:* The control group had significantly more women who smoked. Other variables were similar.

- *Data sources:* Case notes and postal questionnaires sent to women postnatally.

- *Evaluation carried out by:* The scheme's instigators with input from a Research Assistant and Medical Statistician.

- *Other:* The Home-from-Home group were told that continuous electronic fetal monitoring and epidurals were not available. Those who refused consent at this stage were still included in the group for analysis purposes.

Aberdeen Midwives Unit [3]

- *Date:* Bookings between October 1991–December 1992. All women had given birth by August 1993.

- *Comparison with:* Consultant unit delivery. Antenatal care was identical for the two groups.

- *Method:* Randomized controlled trial. Twice as many women were allocated to midwife care as to the consultant unit because of anticipated transfers. Intention-to-treat analysis.

- *Eligibility criteria:* Low-risk. Women who requested DOMINO deliveries were excluded.

- *Number of eligible women:* 3,451

- *Number consenting/numbers per group:* 2,844 (82%) agreed to take part. 1900 women were randomized to the Midwifery Unit and 944 to the consultant unit.

- *Rationale for sample size:* Target sample size of 2,700 was designed to yield 80 per cent power of detecting, at the 5 per cent significance level, a difference of 5 per cent in perinatal morbidity e.g. from 25 per cent to 30 per cent.

- *Comparability of the groups:* Comparable.

- *Data sources:* A staff questionnaire completed as soon as possible after each delivery, a woman's questionnaire completed after discharge home; interviews with a random 400 women from the study population; case note review; SMR2 (the Scottish Morbidity Register) forms; and the Aberdeen maternity and neonatal data bank.

- *Evaluation carried out by:* Researchers based in the University of Aberdeen's department of Obstetrics and Gynaecology at Aberdeen Maternity Hospital, with additional input from the Health Services Research Unit and Health Economics Research Unit at the University.

Glasgow Midwifery Development Unit (MDU) [4]

- *Date:* Recruitment was from 11 January 1993–25 February 1994.

- *Comparison with:* Shared care (combination of obstetricians/GPs/midwives).

- *Method:* Randomized controlled trial. Intention-to-treat analysis.

- *Eligibility criteria:* Booked within 16 completed weeks of pregnancy at a non-specialist hospital-based consultant clinic, had no significant complications and lived in the catchment area (a socially deprived area of Glasgow).

- *Number of eligible women:* 1,586

- *Number consenting/ numbers per group:* 1,299. 648 allocated to the Glasgow MDU and 651 to shared care.

- *Rationale for sample size:* The target sample of 1,400 had 80 per cent power to detect, at the 5 per cent significance level, a difference of 5 per cent between the two groups, if the characteristic occurred in at most 10 per cent of the women overall.

- *Comparability of the groups:* Comparable.

- *Data sources:* Case note review; questionnaires to women at 34/35 weeks, seven weeks postnatally and seven months. Also audit of service specification; questionnaires to scheme and non-scheme midwives; interviews/questionnaires to obstetricians.

- *Evaluation carried out by:* A multi-disciplinary research team based in the unit but not involved in providing care.

One-to-One [5]

- *Date:* Expected date of birth between 15 August 1994 and 14 August 1995.

- *Comparison with:* 'Traditional care' (usually shared care).

29

- *Method:* Women living in the two London postal districts (W3 and W12) served by the One-to-One scheme were compared with women living in two neighbouring districts (W4 and W6) served by the same hospitals.

- *Eligibility criteria:* All women living in the study area except those who moved in or out of the area during pregnancy or who gave birth or miscarried before 28 weeks.

- *Number of eligible women/number consenting/numbers per group:* 728 in the study area and 675 in the comparison area.

- *Rationale for sample size:* Not given.

- *Comparability of the groups:* Women in the One-to-One group were considerably more socially disadvantaged and included more women from ethnic minorities.

- *Data sources:* Ethnographic study of the organizational change (interviews, focus groups, participant observation, documentary analysis); women's responses to care (questionnaires at 35 weeks, and two weeks and 13 weeks postnatally; interviews, focus groups); clinical audit; economic evaluation.

- *Evaluation carried out by:* The scheme's instigator and a researcher, with some additional input from independent evaluators.

West Essex [6]

- *Date:* Births between 1st January 1995 and 30th June 1995.

- *Comparison with:* Comparison was between 'study women' i.e. those receiving all their care in the area and giving birth either at home or at the District General Hospital, and three other groups. These three groups were naturally occurring:

  Control I lived in a neighbouring district, had all of their antenatal and postnatal care from community midwives in that district but gave birth in the study district's District General Hospital.

  Control II were in the reverse situation: they received all of their antenatal and postnatal community care from the study district's non-team community midwives but gave birth in an out-of-area hospital.

  Control III were in a similar situation to Control II except that their antenatal and postnatal care was given by one West Essex team, although they also gave birth out-of-area.

- *Method:* Retrospective data collection from staff, women and case notes.

- *Eligibility criteria:* All women who met the definition for the study group or one of the control groups.

- *Number of eligible women:* 1,520

- *Number consenting/numbers per group:* Study group = 1,077 (88% response); Control I = 272 (89%); Control II = 133 (90%); Control III = 38 (82%).

- *Rationale for sample size:* Not given.

- *Comparability of the groups:* Women in the study group were younger and more likely to live in rented local authority accommodation. Control women were better educated than study women.

- *Data sources:* Case study; staff satisfaction survey (interviews and questionnaires); user survey (questionnaire 10 days after birth); collection of process and outcome data; audit of midwifery contacts.

- *Evaluation carried out by:* An independent group of researchers from the Institute of Public Health at the University of Cambridge.

The Scottish Antenatal Care Trial [7]

- *Date:* Bookings between February 1993–March 1994.

- *Comparison with:* Consultant-led shared antenatal care.

- *Method:* Randomized controlled trial. Intention-to-treat analysis.

- *Eligibility criteria:* Low-risk. <19 weeks at booking. Had not seen an obstetrician prior to seeing the research midwife.

- *Number of eligible women:* Of 2,642 low-risk women referred by participating GPs, 2,167 were still eligible after booking.

- *Number consenting/numbers per group:* 1,765 (82%) agreed to take part. Nine withdrew but were included in the follow-up. Data missing for 91 women. Evaluation data therefore presented for 1,674 cases (834 in the midwife/GP group and 840 in the shared care group).

- *Rationale for sample size:* Target sample size was 1,640 which would be large enough to detect a difference of, for example, transient hypertension of 6 per cent in one group versus 12 per cent in the other, and a difference in maternal satisfaction of 60 per cent versus 70 per cent, at the 5 per cent significance level with 90 per cent power.

- *Comparability of the groups:* Comparable

- *Data sources:* Record of the booking visit, medical records, shared care cards, midwifery records. Specially collected data on all antenatal contacts. Questionnaire to women six weeks postpartum. Also measures of staff satisfaction and economic analysis (not reported).

- *Evaluation carried out by:* A research fellow in the Department of Epidemiology and Public Health at the University of Dundee, with input from a number of other researchers and obstetricians across Scotland.

- *Other:* The study involved 51 GP practices and nine hospital centres in Scotland. The centres together provide maternity care for 38 per cent of the Scottish maternity population.

Core comparative evaluations: summary information

Tables 7.5 and 7.6 present summary information from the seven core comparative evaluations.

Table 7.5: Outcomes considered in the seven comparative evaluation studies

	Continuity of carer	Process & outcome data	Women's views	Midwives' views	Other staff's views	Costs
Know-Your-Midwife [1]	✓	✓	✓	✓	✓	surrogate measures
Home-from-Home [2]	X	✓	✓ but not fully published	X	X	X
Aberdeen Midwives Unit [3]	✓	✓	✓ but not fully published	of individual deliveries	X	✓
Glasgow MDU [4]	✓	✓	✓	✓	✓	✓
One-to-One [5]	✓	✓	✓	✓	✓	✓ but not fully published
West Essex [6]	✓	✓	✓	✓	✓	X
Scottish Antenatal Care Trial [7]	✓	✓	✓	✓ but not published	✓ but not published	✓ but not published

Table 7.6: Summary of eligibility criteria and refusal rates for the five RCTs

	Eligibility criteria	% refusal
Know-Your-Midwife [1]	Low-risk women* intending to have all their antenatal care at the hospital (i.e. not planning shared care, which was the norm)	8.5% of those allocated to Know-Your-Midwife
Home-from-Home [2]	Low-risk women*	8% of those allocated to Home-from-Home
Aberdeen Midwives Unit [3]	Low-risk women* (those satisfying existing guidelines for GP unit care) excluding those requesting a DOMINO delivery	18% of eligible women
Glasgow MDU [4]	Low-risk women* booked within 16 completed weeks of pregnancy; living in the catchment area (a socially deprived area of Glasgow)	18% of eligible women
Scottish Antenatal Care Trial [7]	Low-risk women*; <19 weeks pregnant at booking; not already seen an obstetrician	18% of eligible women

*the definition of low-risk, and who made the assessment, varied somewhat from study to study

The evaluations: methodological issues

Randomization and consent

The schemes that we have examined in this chapter have been chosen because a comparative evaluation had been undertaken, that is to say that the new way of working has been compared with another form of care. Five were evaluated by means of a randomized controlled trial (RCT), which is generally considered to be the best method of ensuring that the intervention group and the control group are comparable (see Chapter 3). Even in the RCTs, however, methodological issues arise which are inevitable in studies where the views of the participants are an outcome of central importance. In two of the RCTs (Know-Your-Midwife [1] and Home-from-Home [2]), randomization took place before women were asked to take part in the study, and consent was sought only from the intervention group. This is known as the Zelen method (Zelen, 1979). In the other three RCTs, consent was sought before randomization. Both approaches have their problems.

In the Glasgow MDU [4] study, 1,586 women were eligible for the trial. Consent was sought before randomization and 287 (18%) refused. The most common reason for refusing consent (71% of reasons given) was wanting old style care. As we have already pointed out (Chapter 3, p. 6 'Preference'), this is a typical situation for any RCT which seeks to compare a new treatment with an existing one, and means that the group of women included in the trial are already likely to be biased towards the new-style treatment.

The Zelen method can be seen as an attempt at addressing this problem. It is also based on the rationale that the control group might react adversely to feeling that they were being deprived of the new form of care. To avoid this, it is argued, there is no need to tell them what another group are getting since no change is being made to their own care, and, to all intents and purposes, they are not themselves part of an experiment. Some people might object to the ethics of this, but the issue that is being addressed is a real one. An equivalent problem is the 'Hawthorne effect' – people feeling more positive about an intervention just because it is something new, even if it is not in any way objectively better. We must, therefore, always bear in mind the possibility that differences in psychological outcomes between groups in an RCT contain such an element. Currell (1990) raises this issue with regard to the Know-Your-Midwife [1] study with the observation that women invited to be in the Know-Your-Midwife group received a letter that said '...we shall be seeing only a small number of women and we hope that you will get to know us as friends and that we shall get to know you well'. She suggests that this in itself will make women think that they are getting a superior and more personal service. (It could, of course, also be argued that the letter is part of the package that constitutes the intervention, rather than an outside 'distractor'.)

Seeking consent only from the intervention group introduces a bias into the RCT design, because people have the opportunity to decline to take part if they are allocated to the intervention group, but not if they are allocated to the control group. Some sub-groups of people are less likely to agree to take part in research than others. Thus, by not allowing equal opportunity to the two groups for declining to take part, groups will be created that are likely to differ in some of their basic characteristics. The Know-Your-Midwife study [1] sought to overcome this by defining its groups in terms of initial allocation, whether or not the women consented. Although this will help to overcome the problem to some extent, it is not altogether satisfactory. Firstly it introduces 'noise' into the system by including in the treatment group women who did not have the treatment, and secondly, whatever the *intention* of the analysis, data cannot be included if they are not available. Since many of those refusing to be in the trial will also refuse to fill in questionnaires, the data will be missing. This probably explains why there were significantly more Asian women and fewer European women in the control group than in the intervention group in the Know-Your-Midwife study [1]. The extent to which this matters will vary from one study to another. As we have said, if participation in the study involves the woman's active co-operation, such as filling in a questionnaire, then it is likely that those who were deprived of the chance of saying that they did not want to take part, will 'vote with their feet' at this stage and withdraw themselves from the study. This was evident in the Know-Your-Midwife study [1] where the number of women who 'seemed to vanish mysteriously when the Research Assistant or Secretary approached' was six in the Know-Your-Midwife group but 17 in the controls (Flint and Poulengeris, 1987, p. 12).

In the Home-from-Home study [2], which also used the Zelen method, the intervention group had to be told that continuous electronic fetal monitoring (EFM) and epidurals would not be available. Those who refused consent at this stage were still included in the group for analysis purposes. This was intended to overcome the problem just described in the Know-Your-Midwife study [1], and the rationale given for this was that this was a 'pragmatic trial', that is, a trial that sought to establish what would happen in 'real life' rather than under ideal conditions. While this is an appropriate aim, it is actually being misapplied in this case. In the real world, these women would not have been allocated to Home-from-Home. The correct procedure would have been only to include in the trial women to whom the Home-from-Home package would have been acceptable.

So, for any RCT it is necessary to be aware of who was and was not in the trial and thus the likely sub-populations of women to whom the findings may generalize. For the five RCTs considered here, the rates and eligibility criteria are shown in Table 7.6. There are, in fact, virtually identical refusal rates between studies which took the same approaches to randomization and consent. Note, however, that the refusal rate in the Know-Your-Midwife [1] and Home-from-Home [2] studies is less than half that of the other three. This may indicate that the new styles of care on offer were generally acceptable. However, it will also be partly because in the three Scottish studies consent was being sought to take part in a *randomized trial*, whereas in Know-Your-Midwife [1] and Home-from-Home [2] the consent was only to accept *a new form of care*. Thus some people will have refused consent in the former cases because they did not want their care determined at random rather than because they objected to the new form of care (e.g. the 29% in Glasgow MDU study [4] whose reason for refusal was *not* that they wanted old style care).

Non-randomized comparisons

One-to-One [5] was evaluated using a prospective comparative design, i.e. the study was designed to compare women from different postal districts that were all served by Queen Charlotte's and (to a lesser extent) the Hammersmith Hospitals. Building in such a comparison is generally considered to be better than having nothing to compare with, but it does lead to some difficulties in interpreting the data. It may even mislead the reader more than a simple descriptive study, as there may be a sense of reassurance that there has been a 'control' group. There are particular difficulties when there are pre-existing differences between the groups, as occurred in this case. Women having One-to-One care were considerably more socially disadvantaged than the comparison group, so one might expect across the board worse outcomes, which was not the case. Lack of difference in outcomes could then be interpreted as 'success' for One-to-One in overcoming the disadvantages. However, comparative historical data for the same postal districts before the study suggest that some of the differences in outcomes found between the two study groups (e.g. fewer epidurals and episiotomies) were pre-existing. This is a typical problem of data interpretation when groups are not equivalent. This case is only unusual in that the differences between the two groups were so apparent. An additional problem was that there were considerable differences between the two hospitals, but very few control women were booked at the Hammersmith Hospital. This means that data had to be analysed separately for the two hospitals, and the effective sample size for comparison purposes is reduced to those booking at QCCH.

The study of midwifery teams in West Essex [6] is an evaluation by outsiders, whose lack of involvement allowed them to question aspects of the system that many others would have taken for granted. There were no built in comparisons as there would be in an RCT or as there was for One-to-One [5]. Instead, the researchers took advantage of the naturally occurring sub-groups created by cross-boundary flows to identify comparison groups of local women receiving different patterns of midwifery care. While this is an ingenious and pragmatic solution, we have to be cautious in interpreting between-group differences when we have no reason to believe that the groups are equivalent in the first place. Although the women all lived in or near the same health district, that still covers a considerable demographic range, and the data presented show that study women were younger and less well educated than controls. This is likely to account for some of the differences found.

Whereas all five RCTs were restricted to low-risk women, this was not the case for either of these non-randomized studies. Also, in both cases the form of organization of midwifery service that a woman received was determined entirely by where she lived, and she had little opportunity to opt in or out. We should bear these differences in mind when comparing results of the studies.

Sub-samples within studies and statistical power

In all of the studies considered, some data come from a sub-sample. This is invariably the case when data are collected by questionnaires, because not everyone will return the questionnaires. However, in some of the studies, case note analysis was also based on sub-samples. In the Glasgow MDU study [4], for example, continuity was assessed from notes of a random sample of 180 women per group three months into the trial. In the Know-Your-Midwife study [1], data on the number of caregivers seen came from examination of the notes of a sub-group of 101 women due in September/ October 1984. In the same study, the questionnaires given to women were not introduced until over a third of the women had given birth. We need to be aware, therefore, that even if the full study groups are comparable and are large enough to give the study the required statistical power, the sub-samples may not be. Results from the seven comparative studies are presented in Chapters 9–14.

CHAPTER EIGHT

Multi-Scheme Descriptive Studies

The four studies to be presented in this chapter are methodologically very different from the comparative studies described in Chapter 7, and from each other. For this reason each study will be presented as a whole, including the study's findings, rather than in the format used for the comparative studies.

Mapping team midwifery (Wraight et al., 1993)

In 1993 Wraight, Ball, Seccombe and Stock from the Institute for Manpower Studies at the University of Sussex produced a report for the Department of Health called 'Mapping team midwifery'. This is a recommended introduction for those wishing to understand some of the varied ways in which midwifery services may be organized, and a warning on the pitfalls of ambiguous terminology. The report gives a historical context to the enthusiasm for 'team midwifery' and draws attention to the considerable variation in the services supplied under that heading in 12 individual schemes. It then goes on to report findings from a national survey of heads of midwifery focusing on 'team midwifery'. That this survey achieved a 95 per cent response rate may be taken as a measure of the topic's salience.

Respondents offered a variety of definitions of team midwifery, a selection of which are shown in Box 1. What is striking is the range of key features that different respondents saw as important: some highlighted aims, some the community-based nature of the scheme, others stressed organizational components.

Box 1: Defining team midwifery
'A group of midwives working together to reduce the number of professionals involved in a woman's care, to ensure that each woman will meet the same midwives throughout her pregnancy'
'A community-based system which involves midwives working flexible hours and delivering their women in hospital'
'A small group of midwives providing total midwifery care to a defined number of women. There is a named midwife who is the main carer, when she is not available the care is provided by another team member'
'Being on call 24 hours a day'
'A team of midwives with an allocated workload from a particular geographical area or GP practice' *from Wraight et al., 1993 (p. 37)*

One hundred respondents (37%) said that they had a team midwifery scheme. Another 16 units had had teams but had discontinued them. Reasons for introducing schemes are shown in Box 2.

Box 2: Reasons for introducing teams
•   Improve continuity of care
•   Reduce the fragmentation of care
•   Improve client satisfaction
•   Better identify the individual needs of women
•   Offer consistent advice to clients
•   Enhance the learning environment for students
•   Improve recruitment of midwives
•   Allow midwives to retain and develop a wider range of midwifery skills
•   Improve job satisfaction of midwives
•   Create a more efficient and effective service
from Wraight et al., 1993 (p. 15)

Clearly, different solutions may be appropriate to meet different aims.

A small number of schemes (mainly in Wales) had been running since the mid-1970s, but nearly three-quarters of the schemes had been set up since 1987. The figures given indicate that one quarter of all midwives represented in the survey were working in teams, but this varied considerably from Region to Region. Thirty-one ongoing schemes were hospital-based, 24 community-based and 45 covered both hospital and community. Thirty-seven of the latter cared for a caseload of women wherever they were and whatever the situation – in other words the majority of team schemes did not aim to provide a start-to-finish service across hospital and community. The number of teams per unit and the number of midwives per team were highly variable, as was the grade mix. Community teams tended to have more higher grade midwives than hospital teams. Integrated teams (i.e. hospital and community) fell between the two. The basis for allocation of women to teams was also highly variable: for example geographical factors, having booked with a particular GP or consultant, or being 'low risk'.

The study found very positive attitudes from respondents towards team midwifery but contains important advice:

> 'The impression gained during the interviews was that midwives working within all models of team midwifery are of a similar opinion, that to make this system of care a success, they need to be fully committed and confident in their own ability and skills. Senior midwives need to be able to devolve responsibility down to junior midwives in the team and the whole team must work together. In one unit visited, sessions on 'team building' had been organised by a specialist consultancy firm prior to the introduction of the team approach to facilitate the changeover. They believe that ideally a team should consist of no more than six midwives to achieve continuity of care and carer.' (Wraight et al., 1993, p. 65)

The report also draws attention to the lack of evaluation of team schemes: only 40 per cent had had some form of evaluation and many of these were methodologically weak. Only ten per cent had audited team midwifery and only five per cent had evaluated costs. The authors point out that they found no evidence either to support or deny the Health Committee's claim (House of Commons, 1992, paragraph 339) that teams provide better value for money. All midwifery managers were asked if it was possible to identify the proportion of women delivered by a known midwife. In all, only 26 per cent of respondents said that they were able to do so, but many of these were estimates and not accurately measured. For those operating teams the proportion was 35 per cent and in GP units, 44 per cent. Among those who said that they could supply this information, the figures given were approximately 60 per cent for teams, 40 per cent for consultant and combined units and 80 per cent in GP Units.

The researchers carrying out this valuable study also visited a number of schemes, both ongoing and discontinued. A surprisingly large proportion of the more recently started schemes had been discontinued after a short period. For example, 27 per cent of schemes started in 1990 had been discontinued by 1991. Reasons given for discontinuing schemes are shown quantitatively in Table 8.1 with examples in Box 3.

Table 8.1: Reasons why schemes discontinued

	N	%
Not liked by midwives	7	44
Aims not achieved	6	38
Insufficient staff	6	38
Change in unit structure	3	19
Other	4	25

from Wraight et al., 1993 (p. 107)

Box 3: Examples of reasons why team midwifery was discontinued

'Postnatal wards were continually disrupted because midwives were being called away. We did not find that mothers were being delivered by their own midwife'

'Lack of adequate staffing in the community and a lack of commitment from some team members'

'The mothers said they were unable to identify their midwife and the midwives found it unsatisfactory in practice'

'Due to the pressure of work, high levels of long term sickness and a large number of maternity leavers we had too few midwives to run the teams effectively'

'There were not enough midwives in each team to cover wards, clinics and the labour suite. Clinics were frequently not serviced and ward areas depleted. There were high levels of stress among the team leaders'

'Due to a very old building operating on four floors which did not lend itself to team midwifery'

from Wraight et al., 1993 (p. 108)

The authors identify features of the schemes examined that may be scored to give an indicator of the extent to which they achieve what they believe 'Changing Childbirth' to have envisaged as 'genuine' team midwifery.

The key features were:

- team consists of no more than six midwives

- each team has a defined caseload

- team provides total care for that caseload

- team works in all areas according to client need

- 50 per cent or more women are delivered by a midwife known to her.

Just one community-based and three community/hospital-based schemes of the 80 considered achieved the optimal rating.

Developing continuity of care in maternity services: the implications for midwives (Stock and Wraight, 1993)

This report was commissioned by the Royal College of Midwives following the publication of the study 'Mapping team midwifery' described above. The study focused upon the implications of team working for midwives. Specific concerns included:

- the role of part-time midwives

- changes to shift patterns

- the use of flexible hours and on-call arrangements

- the impact of unsocial working hours

- the impact on professional development

- the impact on the deployment of core and team midwives.

In addition, the study considered processes involved in the introduction of team midwifery, including an examination of the appropriateness of the grading structure. Five units were identified which were either delivering or developing continuity of care for childbearing women through team working. Case studies for the following are described:

- Chelsea and Westminster Hospital, where hospital-based midwifery group practices had been introduced alongside existing community practices.

- Leicester Royal Infirmary, where a 'home from home' scheme evolved into linked hospital-based and community-based teams serving geographical areas. The unit was then beginning the process of integrating the hospital and community teams.

- Rhondda/Taff Ely District where teams began as 'Know-Your-Midwife' schemes.

- Whipps Cross Hospital, where a pilot integrated team was set up as a research project. The project was to run for one year, and the results from the mothers cared for by the team compared with a control group.

- Scunthorpe and Goole Hospitals, where the process of developing integrated teams had been developing over three years, and was extended to cover the whole of a large predominantly rural district.

Jobs, grades and responsibilities: Stock and Wraight (1993) suggest that 'there was little indication that the units started off with a clear distinction between what was expected of midwives in the different grades' and considerable variability in grading within teams is highlighted. Grades E, F, G and H were variably represented in team schemes. Team leaders were encountered in H and G grades. Midwives carrying responsibility for a defined caseload were identified in F, G and H grades. In some schemes, a greater number of F grades were employed than was the case in many units in the past and the report notes that some midwives felt that team midwifery had been introduced specifically to downgrade posts. In most of the units visited by the research team, the implementation of team working had coincided with a 'realignment' of posts and the disestablishment of a number of hospital and community-based G grades.

While E grades were identified in two units, as 'development posts' for newly qualified midwives, the report suggests that the role of E grades had fundamentally changed in other units. E grade midwives may be required to exercise considerable organizational and administrative skills and there is the potential within teams for E grade midwives to be called upon to 'act up' and to take sole charge of an area for their team. Not surprisingly, midwives in E and F grades were particularly likely to feel that their grading did not reflect the level of responsibility they carried.

Hours, shifts and part-time working: The contractual hours of both hospital and community midwives remained unaltered. However, while hospital-based midwives continued to have their work organized on a shift basis, midwives working in the community and those providing an integrated service were required to exercise considerable flexibility within their contracted working hours. In some units, where on-call arrangements had been developed, the frequency and length of on-call commitments were regarded as the biggest single difficulty of team working. Although midwives recognized that increased flexibility in work patterns also had positive benefits, notably increased autonomy and enhanced job satisfaction, they also highlighted the fact that not all midwives would or could make the commitment required for team working.

Part-time workers account for a substantial, and growing, minority of the midwifery workforce. UKCC figures at the time of the report indicated that 40 per cent of the 35,000 midwives registered to practice worked part-time. The report highlights the contradictory position of part-time midwives. Most managers agreed that part-time workers frustrated the delivery of continuity of carer, on the other hand the managers recognized that part-time hours must be available for women if they are to remain within the workforce. Different units placed a different value on their part-time workforce, viewing them either as a useful, flexible resource that could fulfil the important function of 'topping-up' the service, or merely accommodating part-time midwives whose use was seen to be extremely limited.

Team working for part-time midwives was perceived to be particularly problematic. Specific difficulties included:

- on-call working which could be inconvenient to women who had chosen their working hours to suit their personal circumstances

- practical issues (such as the additional costs of child care) which may dissuade part-time midwives from team working

- staff (often part-time) who have home commitments which mean that they are not able to work during the day, may have particular difficulties in teams which require members to work both days and nights.

Personal and professional development, and career progression: Generally, midwives felt very positive about team working believing that this enabled better use of midwifery skills and facilitated personal development. The report does, however, raise important issues concerning the potential for the development of individuals within teams, particularly in smaller teams in which all members ostensibly carry the same professional responsibilities.

'Them' and 'Us' attitudes between core and team midwives were alluded to, as were concerns about the potential for the development of two tiers of midwives, with different grading and different opportunities for development.

Job satisfaction: Midwives reported increased job satisfaction linked to greater utilization of skills and greater autonomy in practice. In addition, many midwives reported improved relationships between midwives and medical staff.

The report's conclusions were:

- costs: 'There is little evidence yet that team midwifery is any more or less expensive than other forms of midwifery care'.

- continuity of care: 'If we consider all units which provide care under the name "Team Midwifery" there is little evidence that all such schemes achieve higher levels of continuity of carer, although there is agreement amongst midwives that continuity of care, and quality of care, is enhanced'.

- team size: the extent to which team midwifery delivers continuity of care directly relates to the number of midwives, the team and the caseloads served – the smaller the team, the more effective it is likely to be in this respect.

- small teams demand significantly more flexibility from team members.

The report includes advice to other units considering commencing team midwifery, taken from one of the schemes involved (see Box 4).

Box 4: Advice to other units considering commencing team midwifery

---

- assess the needs of women and the restrictions and adapt to meet those needs

- planning takes time and needs time (approximately 18 months before implementation)

- clinical midwives must be included in the planning from day one

- introduce team midwifery in stages and pilot in an area where the midwives and GPs are keen to try the scheme

- consult all carers and medical staff but remember that this is a change in the delivery of midwifery care and is therefore a midwifery decision

- meet frequently, evaluate and alter as necessary as the teams develop

- offer continuous support to all grades of staff.

Source: Scunthorpe and Goole Hospitals Team Midwifery Information Pack, cited by Stock and Wraight, 1993

Changing Midwifery Care – the scope for evaluation (Garcia et al., 1996)

Another very valuable study is that recently completed by a team co-ordinated by Jo Garcia at the National Perinatal Epidemiology Unit in Oxford. Their report is concerned with the very important topic of how one should assess these differing forms of care, and the study has also led to a book 'The Organization of Maternity Care – A Guide to Evaluation' (Campbell and Garcia, 1997). The study involved three anonymous maternity units with differing ways of organizing their services. We reproduce one of their tables overleaf to underline the variety of parameters that may differ between schemes.

The schemes are referred to as A, B and C. For each, the study used surveys and data from case records and other locally available sources to:

- describe patterns of care

- audit the process of care

- investigate the views and experiences of women and midwives

- study the costs of the systems of care

Table 8.2: Aspects of midwifery care in three schemes (A, B and C)

Aspects of care	A	B	C
All women booked to deliver are assigned to a team	✓	✓	
All team midwives work across hospital and community	✓		
Some team midwives work across hospital and community		✓	✓
Core midwifery staff in labour ward	✓		✓
Core midwifery staff in postnatal ward	✓		✓
Some teams providing care in hospital only		✓	✓
Teams for women with special needs		✓	✓
Teams providing antenatal or postnatal care to women who deliver elsewhere	✓	✓	✓
All G grade for teams working in community	✓		✓

from Garcia et al., 1996, (p. 5)

The changes in care were being brought about in different ways: in scheme B, care was changing slowly and new teams were only being set up at the request of midwives who wanted to form teams. In the other two services, teams were being implemented across the service following successful pilots.

Postal surveys of the mothers in the three areas yielded responses of 66 per cent (231/350), 62 per cent (185/300) and 41 per cent (123/300).

This report proposes five criteria by which a maternity service should be judged. It should be:

- effective and safe

- acceptable to women and families

- sustainable

- efficient

- accessible and equitable.

These headings are used to organize the presentation of the study's findings. They emerged from the findings of the study rather than being part of the original plan.

Effectiveness and safety

The main worries about safety arising specifically from the new patterns of care concerned four topics:

- core staffing in hospital

- extending the midwife's role in clinical care

- the acquisition and maintenance of midwifery skills for acute care

- safe levels of staffing and grading for the various ways of working and concern about pressure on funding.

These issues are very similar issues to those that raised by Wraight et al., (1993) in 'Mapping team midwifery'.

Acceptability to women

The wide-ranging questionnaire tackled various aspects of acceptability. Given the emphasis of the schemes on continuity of care, a number of questions were concerned with 'knowing your midwife'. Table 8.3 shows that schemes A and B were within five per cent of the 'Changing Childbirth' target of 75 per cent of women being cared for in labour by a known midwife. Note, however, the considerable difference between the two in terms of the proportion of women cared for by someone that they 'knew well' as opposed to 'had met'. In scheme C, the majority of respondents were not cared for by the team midwives and the figures show considerably less likelihood of a woman having a known carer.

Table 8.3 : Continuity of carer in labour reported in three schemes

The midwives caring for a woman in labour:	A N=173 %	B N=215 %	C N=112 %
– I knew one or more of them well	50	35	21
– I had met one or more of them before	31	35	14
– I had not met any of them before	20	30	64

from Garcia et al., 1996, (p. 13)

Women gave generally positive answers to questions about their care. There were, however, some responses which gave cause for concern. For example, 24 per cent of women from scheme C said that they had been left alone in labour at a time when it worried them to be left alone.

The greatest dissatisfaction was found with respect to postnatal hospital care: there was a strong perception, especially in schemes B and C, that midwives were often too busy and 41 per cent of women in schemes B and C (28% in A) reported being confused or worried by conflicting advice. These findings do not seem to be linked to continuity of carer: Only 31 per cent of women at A had postnatal hospital care from a known midwife, compared with 67 per cent of women at B and 24 per cent at C. Women at B particularly felt that they lacked advice or teaching about baby care. Midwives at B were aware of the same issues that women raised. They ascribed these to lack of core staffing and an overall shortage of staff that meant that midwives were often taken away from postnatal care to acute areas – an issue also raised by Wraight et al., (1993) in 'Mapping team midwifery'.

The schemes differed in their approach to providing postnatal care at home, although women's reactions were broadly similar. For example, scheme A provided almost complete continuity of postnatal midwifery care at home; 51 per cent of women said that they knew one or more of the visiting midwives well and a further 47 per cent said that they had met them before but did not know them well. In contrast, 50 per cent and 65 per cent of women in the other two places had not met any of the midwives who visited them at home after the birth. This may have arisen because of the differing proportions of women from outside the catchment area who delivered at each unit. Yet in all three places, the percentages of women saying that the midwives' visits were 'always' or 'sometimes' helpful was over 97 per cent. The proportions of women who said that they were confused or worried by conflicting advice at home were far lower than for care in hospital, ranging from 29 per cent to 12 per cent. The lowest figure was for scheme A, the place with the best continuity, which was, however, also the place where women were likely to see far more midwives in total at home after birth (75% saw three or more, compared to around 40% in the other two places).

Ratings of importance: Women in all services were asked to rate various characteristics of care as very important, fairly important or not very important. Skilled staff, being given information and being treated kindly and respectfully were all rated as 'very important' by over 80 per cent of the women in all three services. Being convenient and letting the woman herself make the decisions were both rated as 'very important' by between two-thirds and three-quarters of the women. The characteristic rated as 'very important' by the smallest proportion of women (between a third and a half) was 'care from someone you know'.

Sustainability

(i) economic evaluation:

A full economic evaluation of the sorts of services being considered here would be complex and costly since routinely collected data offer limited information.

All hospitals are required to maintain a Minimum Data Set (MDS) which contains basic hospital episode information. This allowed basic cross-tabulations of information such as length of stay by method of delivery. However it tells us nothing about the process or intensity of care, nor about community activity. Attempts were made to obtain cost information relating to: wards, delivery suite, outpatients and community; each broken down into fixed, semi-fixed and variable costs. This information was made available by only one of the services in the study. This revealed that 95 per cent of costs were fixed or semi-fixed, which means that marginal changes such as the closure of one or two beds in a ward would not release much in terms of costs or resources freed for other uses. The savings would be much less than the average cost per case per bed as identified from top-down costing alone. This is of importance when considering transfer of resources from hospital to community settings.

(ii) effects on midwives

Questionnaires were sent to all 352 midwives in the three services and replies were received from 220 (63%). The majority (53%) of respondents defined themselves as hospital-based. Just ten per cent were community-based and 35 per cent described themselves as both. Sixty-four per cent said that they were in a team, which included hospital-based 'core' teams. Seventy-eight per cent worked full-time and just over half the sample said that they did 'on-call' work – primarily those working in teams. Most 'team midwives' (91%) worked in teams of five to seven, and most felt that this was the right number. The caseload was nearly always for the group as a whole and was typically 200–250 women per year.

Team midwives were much more likely than non-team to say that they felt that they were using their midwifery skills to the full, and to make positive comments about professional development, although disadvantages were also mentioned. They were also more likely to describe their job as 'satisfying' or 'very satisfying' (60% compared to 39%). There were some demographic differences between team and non-team midwives: team midwives were less likely to be over 35, or to be single parents. They were also slightly less likely to have dependants. Team midwives were more likely to report an adverse effect of their job on the rest of their life, but the differences were not large. There was also little difference in reported stress – overall 30 per cent of respondents said that their job was very stressful most of the time.

Efficiency

The study's findings on efficiency came from audits and studies of midwives' work-patterns and travel times already carried out by the services being studied. In order to know whether a system of care is working efficiently, it is necessary to record accurate and relevant information. Two of the services studied had specialist computer information systems for maternity and the third was in the process of looking for such a system. The report points out that accuracy of data entry and analysis would be improved if more results were regularly fed back to midwives and managers in an interesting way, and that it is essential to have a midwife whose sole responsibility is computing and audit. Midwives need to have a clear idea of what they want to get out of the information system.

Accessibility and equitability

One of the issues that arose in all three services was that of cross-border flow. Women may receive hospital intrapartum care from one service and community antenatal and postnatal care from another. This may result in fragmentation of care and poor communication between the professionals involved. One of the services had set up a scheme specifically for women who needed extra support during the childbearing period. This scheme raised a number of questions such as: the needs of midwives for extra training for such circumstances; how the resources should be equitably divided if the scheme cannot cope with all those who want it; and how midwives can set limits to protect themselves from demands which are too great for them to cope with. There are also more general questions, for example, about the equity of selective home-visiting.

The report concludes that:

•   New models of care can enhance the satisfaction and professional development of many midwives.

•   Some midwives, however, may not be able to work in the new ways because of home responsibilities. Their skills should continue to be used by thoughtful planning of work patterns.

•   New ways of working in midwifery are very varied at present, and the details of a scheme may have a substantial effect on the quality of care for mothers and the impact on staff. For example, larger teams may not give women the opportunity to get to know the midwives as well as they did in some of the traditional patterns of care.

•   Continuity of carer is only one of the important aspects of care. It should not be given priority *at the expense* of other things that are crucial to women like good communication and adequate staffing.

•   Evaluation of different models of care is worth doing, but has some practical and 'political' difficulties. Any new system is likely to have benefits and disadvantages and evaluation can help to document these and aid the process of decision-making.

•   Locally, services often need expert advice on maternity information systems, audit techniques, costing methods and other aspects of evaluation.

•   It is crucial to bring together and weigh up the accumulating research evidence about different models of care so that everyone can benefit from the results.

A leading role for midwives? (Allen et al., 1997)

This recently published study is a very valuable independent evaluation of the three midwifery group practices (MGPs) that successfully tendered as pilot projects in the South East Thames Regional Health Authority (SETRHA). They were launched in January 1994 and consisted of:

- Lewisham Maternity Focus (Lewisham Hospital)

- The JACANES Midwifery Group, Ashford, Kent (William Harvey Hospital)

- The South East London Midwifery Group Practice based in Deptford and made up of self employed midwives operating within the NHS.

The report gives a very detailed account of the individual differences between the schemes in terms of, for example, the background and grades of the midwives involved, how they came to be working together, and their previous local knowledge and contacts.

The Lewisham scheme had seven midwives for an estimated 240 births per anum, was attached to three GP practices and cared for both high and low risk women.

The Ashford team (four full-time and three part-time; six whole time equivalent) had intended to provide midwifery services for 500 women per annum of all risks, with start-to-finish continuity of carer for approximately 200 women with uncomplicated pregnancies. This proved to be over-ambitious and a second team had to be created for high risk women (JACANES II), who were not part of this study. The scheme was based on five GP practices. They covered an area of 120 square miles.

Deptford was a self-managed midwifery group practice whose aims included continuity of care through a partnership of two named midwives. There were no formal links with GP practices or with a specific hospital. Their remit included targeting certain groups of women who were often denied choice, who might require intensive care and support or who had particular socio-economic factors in their lives which had been identified as placing their babies more at risk. The MGP was not, in fact, successful in reaching these groups and attracted a predominantly middle-class clientele. There were seven midwives, six full-time, one part-time, plus a practice manager. Three of the original midwives left in March/April 1995 and there was one new part-timer from May 1995. The scheme used rented offices in the community centre as a drop-in information centre as well as for consultations. The proposal was to care for 200 women per annum.

The performance of the midwifery group practices was monitored by the study team from the Policy Studies Institute (PSI) over 18 months from April 1994 to September 1995 using quantitative and qualitative methods. Midwives completed activity forms on all consultations and diaries for two weeks. Interviews were carried out with 180 women during pregnancy, 117 of whom were also interviewed postnatally. Midwives and managers were interviewed at the beginning and end of the monitoring period and interviews were also carried out with GPs and obstetricians. The PSI evaluation did not include clinical audit – this was carried out by the project staff themselves.

The evaluation identified a major mismatch between the planned and actual numbers of women booking with the schemes (Table 8.4), with consequent workload implications.

Table 8.4: Planned and actual number of bookings in three midwifery group practices

	Planned per month	Actual per month	Per midwife per annum
Lewisham	20	28	48 (range 42–55)
Ashford	42 (17 full care)	35 (1st year) 23 (last 6 months)	70 (1st year) 46 (last 6 months)
Deptford	17	6.5 (1st year) 15 (last 6 months)	12 (1st year) 27.7 (last 6 months)

(constructed from data in Allen et al., 1997)

In Ashford, midwives were attached to individual GPs and the number of women per individual midwife was largely determined by the numbers coming through each GP and was not under the midwives' control. One midwife had 114 bookings over the 18 months (average 6.33 per month) and another 108 (average 6.0 per month). Deptford bookings were very slow initially and financial difficulties led them to stop taking bookings for one month. The contract was renegotiated and they then booked 91 women in the last six months, but this was still much less than the other midwifery group practices.

The report draws attention to the problem of considering 'workload' as equal to 'deliveries', because not all bookings resulted in deliveries in that scheme. In Lewisham, women who chose to deliver at another hospital would not be delivered by the midwifery group practice midwife but would still have antenatal and postnatal care from her. The proportion choosing to deliver in other hospitals dropped over the study period – clearly such a trend has implications for workload.

The report goes into some detail about the characteristics of the women served by the schemes. These prove relevant to interpreting other differences between the schemes. In Deptford, for example, women were older and more likely to be multiparous. They often had transferred to the scheme late in pregnancy – ten per cent after 36 weeks. Ashford women, in contrast, booked early. This also had implications for the amount of work the midwife had to do.

There were a number of differences between schemes, such as the average length of consultations, which reflect the characteristics of the women and affect the workload. There were also differences between the schemes in labour, delivery and postnatal outcomes, many again attributable to differences in the populations served. For example, 63 per cent of Deptford women had chosen a home birth (compared to 16% in Lewisham and 7% in Ashford). This partly accounted for differences in the likelihood of the named midwife, or other MGP midwife attending the birth. Lower rates for Ashford midwives were partly because they started off giving antenatal care to women that they were unlikely to deliver because they were being transferred to consultant-led care.

Table 8.5: Presence of named midwife in first stage of labour and at delivery

scheme:	Lewisham (N=314)		Ashford (N=287)		Deptford (N=102)	
	1st stage	Delivery	1st stage	Delivery	1st stage	Delivery
Named midwife (alone or with others)	57%	61%	47%	42%	90%	95%
Other MGP midwife	28%	31%	20%	26%	3%	3%
Not MGP midwife	5%	6%	21%	30%	–	1%
Not applicable (e.g. no labour)	9%	2%	11%	–	7%	–

(constructed from data in Allen et al., 1997)

Detailed data are presented from interviews with mothers, and generally confirm the data from the midwives' records. In all the schemes, most antenatal consultations were with the named midwife. In Deptford, nearly three-quarters of the women had also been seen by another team midwife at some point in pregnancy (because the Deptford team often had two midwives present) but in Ashford the figure was only 20 per cent and in Lewisham 23 per cent. Although such a high level of one-to-one care is in keeping with the schemes' aims, it does mean that in Ashford and Lewisham women were not getting to know other members of the team. The majority of women in all areas said that they did not mind seeing other midwives. One Deptford woman said:

> 'I actually find the idea of a pair of midwives caring for me reassuring. If it were just one I would be anxious about what would happen if she were called away.' (ibid., p. 112)

Women in all the schemes were very positive about their midwife – they could talk to her, she explained things clearly and respected their wishes. Women valued being treated as individuals and as adults, and having a relationship with someone they trusted and who would act as their advocate. However, a quarter of women in Deptford, a fifth in Lewisham and nine per cent in Ashford said that the professionals involved in their care (including, for example, GPs) did not work effectively as a team.

Some women had had care from the same midwife in previous pregnancies. The authors commented that:

> 'It is noteworthy that, despite the introduction of a new model of care, most women who were treated by the same midwife as in previous pregnancies felt that there was no difference between past and present care... This point is important in relation to the issue of sustainable practice and replicability, because if the new model of care was, in effect, "more of the same" from a few midwifery group practice midwives, it is possible that the model itself may not have been sufficiently tested.' (ibid., p. 122)

Women who had seen their named midwife in labour were generally very positive about this, but most women who did not get their named midwife said that it did not matter – fewer than one in ten of them said that they were disappointed.

Some women reported overt tension between scheme and hospital midwives and poor communication. This was particularly true at Ashford – one woman in labour was told 'we really shouldn't be dealing with you because you're JACANES' – but there were also accounts from Lewisham women of neglect by hospital staff because they were on the scheme.

> 'I thought that maybe because I was on the scheme they were giving me no attention. I felt very neglected in that hospital. No-one else in there was on the scheme, and I think that was the reason.' (ibid., p. 136)

Many women clearly formed close relationships with their midwife. The main sources of satisfaction with care overall were the high professional standards of the midwives and their friendliness. However, a number of women did not feel that they had had a choice regarding GP involvement and would have preferred shared care.

The interviews with the midwives are also illuminating. They had generally joined the scheme because of disaffection with their old way of working, wanting more autonomy and wanting to work with a team that had a shared philosophy.

A number of points emerged from interviews with midwives:

- Group dynamics: Support from the group was cited as a major benefit but six midwives (two from Lewisham and four from Deptford) identified this as the most challenging aspect of the work. Overall the group was seen as a positive factor so long as communication was good.

- Demands of the job: Midwives had initial reservations about the commitment, the unsocial hours, tiredness affecting safety and the effect on their private lives and relationships. They subsequently reported that these were indeed areas of difficulty. Most in Lewisham and Ashford and half in Deptford found the work rota and on-call arrangements demanding. There were social costs, and also childcare costs. In Ashford, changes had been made to on-call arrangements which some midwives thought had helped: 'We were getting too tired. We were too ambitious. We took it literally – 24 hour cover'.

- Continuity/one-to-one care: At the start of the study, midwives tended to emphasize continuity of carer but by the end there was more emphasis on continuity of care by the group. This was mainly for logistical reasons. Some commented on feeling that they should be on-call for 'their' women at all times, and they experienced difficulty in saying 'no' when they were not on duty.

This attitude clearly caused some tensions. A midwife in the Lewisham practice said:

> 'I'm not sure that all the midwives understand totally what a group practice is. I've delivered some [women that] I don't know. We should be a group of seven midwives delivering care to women. We began being retentive of our women. It changed over time. I never say I will deliver your baby – rather the group practice will. I don't think it has to be the same midwife. We need to stop feeling guilty.'

The same midwife argued:

> 'Continuity of care can be achieved without continuity of carer. Continuity of carer does not mean good quality care. That's not the end of it. It has to be something deeper.'

Some disadvantages of a close one-to-one relationship were noted, such as women becoming dependent on one individual or 'treating us like social workers or psychologists'. Some found the depth of the relationship with women potentially overwhelming.

- Job satisfaction: Several midwives felt more in control working in the MGP because they had a known caseload and the support of colleagues. One commented that being on-call to a small number of known women was much better than a larger number of unknown ones: 'I know when the phone rings who is likely to have gone into labour and what is likely to happen'. This draws attention to the important point that not all on-call work is the same, which we will return to later. One midwife drew attention to the benefit of giving start-to-finish care in giving her feedback – in the hospital system she 'never saw how women gained or not from what I did'. Although job satisfaction was high, there were reservations in all the midwifery group practices about the replicability of the scheme because they thought that other midwives would not wish to work this way.

- Experience with other professionals: All midwifery group practices had some problems with GPs, especially Deptford. When the midwife had already been attached to the practice before the scheme, this helped. Relationships with hospital midwives were the most difficult and were universally reported as a problem.

The report goes on to give the views of GPs and consultant obstetricians. There was evidently concern by GPs that they were being excluded. This was felt to be bad for the woman – the GP would not know what had been going on if a woman developed a problem – and bad for the GPs too in that they were losing their skills. Some thought that there should have been more GP input initially and more ongoing communication: '… a lot of goodwill on the part of the GPs has evaporated, possibly beyond repair'. In Deptford, there were specific concerns that the midwives encouraged anti-doctor and anti-immunization views amongst their clients.

The GPs listed the following provisos regarding the replicability of the schemes:

- there should be better communication between midwives and GPs

- there should be appropriate and effective management of the midwifery group practices in place

- the respective roles and responsibilities of GPs, midwives and consultant obstetricians should be laid down in protocols and agreed in advance

- there should be checks on whether protocols were being followed

- there should be less stress and overload on the midwives

- it needed highly dedicated and committed midwives who might not be universally available

- it should be properly funded

- it should be adapted to local needs

- it might not be possible to ensure a known midwife at delivery

- it might not be possible to replicate evening home visits

- it was recognized that it was an expensive model of care

- it could lead to fragmentation of care if GPs were not in favour of it

- it might only be suitable for deprived areas with special needs

- duplication of effort should be avoided

- it could produce a two-tier service.

The chapter on 'Contracts, purchasing and funding arrangements' has many caveats concerning the accuracy of data, and the difficulty of obtaining the requisite information. This will be discussed further in Chapter 14.

The final Discussion chapter makes a number of points including:

> 'Women were not as concerned about continuity of carer throughout as some of the midwives were. Women laid more stress on the quality of the care which they received from the midwifery group practices in general and were usually happy to receive care from any member of the team.' (ibid., p. 233)

and also

> '… many of the comments made by women about their previous maternity care relate more to inadequacies in the organisation of hospital or community practice rather than to the need for a completely innovative system of working with all the potential resource implications. Many of the criticisms we heard from women of previous care described poor practice, poor interpersonal skills on the part of staff and poor organisation. It should not be assumed that continuity of care and carer will solve problems like these.' (ibid., p. 233)

Finally, they note as cause for concern that it was only their own independent evaluation that demonstrated the severe caseload problems experienced by two of the schemes – nothing was being done otherwise either to monitor it or to change it.

Summary of the multi-scheme descriptive studies

The four studies that we have just described varied considerably in their aims, methodology and style. The first report from the Institute of Manpower Studies considered the national picture, as well as visiting 16 sites, including four that had discontinued team midwifery schemes. This helps to set the parameters for subsequent discussion. Their second report:

> 'took a step back from the clearly laudable (and sometimes realized) aims of providing greater continuity of care and continuity of carer, and an improved service, and examined the implications for midwives of providing such continuity.' (Stock and Wraight, 1993, p. 2)

These reports give valuable indicators of what is going on at a local level: many of these schemes would not be known about otherwise.

The other two studies considered in this Chapter have each been concerned with only three schemes, but have considered a much wider range of outcomes; indeed the Garcia et al. (1996) study was specifically addressing the question of how such schemes can and should be evaluated. The study from the Policy Studies Institute (Allen et al., 1997) is unusual in the level of detail investigated. Both of these studies included a survey of women's views, as well as those of both scheme midwives and other staff. The presentation of results from each of these studies was, however, purely descriptive.

CHAPTER NINE

Are New Ways of Organizing Services Achieving Greater Continuity of Carer?

'Throughout her pregnancy, and most particularly during labour, the woman should be cared for by people who are familiar to her…' (Changing Childbirth, section 2.3)

Being attended in labour by a known midwife

Evidence from the seven comparative studies

Table 9.1 shows the different ways in which 'continuity' was assessed in the seven studies, and Table 9.2 their findings. 'Continuity of carer' is often taken to mean being delivered by a known midwife. However, we found that this outcome was not always easy to identify in the study reports. The Scottish Antenatal Care Trial [7] did not provide intrapartum care, and the Aberdeen Midwives Unit [3] did not provide antenatal care, so neither provides this information. In the Home-from-Home study [2], no continuity data are presented at all. In the Know-Your-Midwife study [1], the information was produced from case-note analysis only for a subgroup of 101 women, 52 randomized to KYM (one declined) and 49 to the control group. All KYM women saw someone in labour who they had met before (except one who had been transferred to consultant care at 24 weeks). In contrast, only nine control women saw someone in labour who they had met before and these were all doctors rather than midwives. The women themselves were not asked whether they knew their intrapartum carers. In the Glasgow MDU study [4], the only relevant data appear in the Discussion and refer only to a selected subgroup (women randomized to receive MDU care who had a spontaneous vertex delivery), 14 per cent of whom were delivered by the named midwife. Thus, in none of the five RCTs are data available for all women in the trial comparing the numbers in each group who were attended in labour by a known midwife. This seems an extraordinary omission given the centrality that this measure of continuity has had in the debate.

Both of the non-randomized comparative studies also relied more heavily on audit data than on women's accounts to answer this question. The One-to-One study [5], based on a subsample of study group women, showed a rate close to the 'Changing Childbirth' target of 75 per cent of women being attended in labour by their named midwife, although, interestingly, a small proportion of women had not previously met

Table 9.1: Measures of continuity of carer used in seven comparative studies

Know-Your-Midwife [1]	*based on the case notes of 101 women* • number of antenatal caregivers • number of intrapartum caregivers • being seen in labour by someone seen antenatally These were all subdivided as doctors or midwives. The only data pertaining to the whole sample were women's estimates of the number of antenatal caregivers.
Home-from-Home [2]	not assessed
Aberdeen Midwives Unit [3]	*Data from forms completed by the midwife after each delivery* • number of caregivers in labour • length of time that the midwife had cared for the woman before the birth (i.e during labour) • was suturing carried out by the midwife who delivered? • after the birth, did the midwife stay with the woman through to transfer to the postnatal ward?
Glasgow MDU [4]	• Total number of caregivers (*assessed from notes of random sample of 180 women per group 3 months into the trial. Women were also asked in the 7-month postnatal questionnaire*) • Number of MDU midwives involved in care from booking to discharge (*collected from audit of service specification – this was only for the MDU group, and drew data both from case-notes and questionnaires from 118 women*).
One-to-One [5]	*From 'Record of Carers' audit based on 185 women at QCCH and 85 at Hammersmith hospital* • attended in labour by named midwife • attended in labour by midwives woman had seen before • number of caregivers overall (including ultrasonographers, and students) for low-risk women *From women's questionnaires* • similar questions to those above • no. of midwives seen at home postnatally & how many known • assessment of relationship with their midwife.
West Essex [6]	*From women's questionnaires:* • number of midwives seen in pregnancy • woman's perception that she had formed a relationship with her midwife • known midwife in labour • number of midwives seen postnatally at home, and whether these met before *From audit of contacts for 919 study group women:* • mean number of midwives seen • mean number of times booking midwife met again • known midwife in labour.
Scottish Antenatal Care Trial [7]	*From signatures on notes:* • number of caregivers seen in pregnancy.

Table 9.2: Findings re continuity of carer used in the seven comparative studies

Know-Your-Midwife [1]	*From 101 case-notes:* • Antenatally, KYM women saw fewer doctors (75% saw only 1 or 2 cf 16% of control group), but more midwives – 81% saw 5 (although none saw more than 5) whereas only 28% of control women saw 5 or more. • In labour, the number of doctors seen was fairly similar but KYM women saw fewer midwives – 69% saw 1 or 2 cf 48% of control group. All KYM women saw someone in labour who they had met before (except one who had been transferred to consultant care at 24 weeks). In contrast, only 9 control women saw someone in labour who they had met before and these were all doctors rather than midwives. *From women's accounts:* • Data are not presented in a comparable format but the suggestion is that, in contrast to the case-note data, control women saw more midwives than KYM (note that this was asked at 37 weeks, while the case-note analysis covered all of pregnancy) *Women having shared care* • Data from these women's questionnaires (N=123) indicate that antenatally they saw fewer midwives than either KYM or the control group (63% had not seen one at all), and the same number of doctors as the KYM group.
Home-from-Home [2]	Not assessed, although the authors suggest that with only ten midwives in the unit a woman has an increased chance of having previously met the midwife who delivers her.
Aberdeen Midwives Unit [3]	There were no differences between the groups in the number of of caregivers in labour. In both groups the midwife at the birth was the only midwife responsible for the woman in labour in 50% of cases. The median number of additional midwives was one. The median length of time that the midwife had cared for the woman before the birth was just over 2½ hours in each case. Women allocated to the Midwives unit who needed suturing were more likely to be stitched by the midwife who delivered them than women allocated to the consultant unit (53% cf 47%), and more likely to have that midwife stay with them through to transfer to the postnatal ward (49% versus 44%).
Glasgow MDU [4]	• MDU women saw a mean of 10 providers (including MDU midwives, doctors and non-MDU midwives) cf 17 for control group. • 54% of the audit women saw <5 MDU midwives and 91% saw <7. • The Discussion (p71) says that 14% of women randomized to receive MDU care who had a spontaneous vertex delivery were delivered by the named midwife. Of those who were delivered by an MDU midwife and who had a spontaneous vertex delivery, 18% were delivered by the named midwife.

Table 9.2: Findings re continuity of carer in the seven comparative studies (cont)

One-to-One [5]	• At HH, 77% of One-to-One women were attended in labour by a known named midwife (66% at QCCH). • Overall, 88%(HH) and 82%(QCCH) were attended by midwives they had seen before - 23%(HH) and 18% (QCCH) were also attended by midwives they had not met before. • The target that low-risk women should be looked after by no more than 6 staff during pregnancy was not met (48% achieved this at HH and 44% at QCCH). • Compared to control group, One-to-One women saw fewer staff and knew more of them. The median number of individuals seen overall at QCCH was 16 compared to 24. (These figures come from the audit but are broadly the same from the women's questionnaires, except that women mentioned fewer carers). • One-to-One women saw fewer midwives at home postnatally • 71% of One-to-One women at QCCH knew all of these midwives before but only 7% of those in the comparison group • One-to-One women were more likely to say that they had got to know their principal antenatal caregiver 'quite' or 'very' well
West Essex [6]	*From women's questionnaires:* • Over three-quarters of the study group reported seeing a different midwife each time whereas Control II just saw one or two. Control II women were most likely to have a named midwife, most likely to have formed a relationship with her • 34% of study group women had previously met all the midwives who cared for them in labour, 36% had met some, and 30% had met none. Control groups were less likely to have met any of them. • Postnatally at home, Control II women saw the smallest number of midwives and the study group the largest number. Less than half of the study group had met all of these midwives before *From audit of contacts:* Mean number of midwives seen in pregnancy was 6. Mean number of times booking midwife met again was 2.2. Mismatch between women's report and audit on presence of a known midwife in labour: audit says 87% of study women attended in labour by a midwife they had met before, but women's report was 70%.
Scottish Antenatal Care Trial [7]	Study group saw significantly fewer antenatal caregivers: a median of 5 cf 7.

her. Although women were asked a number of questions related to continuity, the question asked postnatally appears to be whether the person delivering most *postnatal* care was present at the birth. Thus, it does not necessarily address the question of whether there was a known midwife present at the birth, because the person giving postnatal care may not have been known antenatally. Fortunately, women were also asked how many of the midwives delivering their postnatal care had been known to them antenatally and the answer was 'all' from over 70 per cent of the One-to-One women, but only 7 per cent for the comparison group. Thus, from both data sources, the One-to-One study does demonstrate a high rate of continuity for study group women.

In the West Essex study [6], audit data, based on the notes of nearly all study group women, indicated that 87 per cent were attended in labour by a midwife they had met before. However, when women themselves were asked the same question, the answer given was only 70 per cent. For the three comparison groups the rates were 13 per cent, 5 per cent and 16 per cent. The mismatch between women's reports and the findings from the audit for study group women raises interesting questions. Continuity data based on case-note analysis generally relies on matching signatures to determine whether or not a midwife present during labour was 'known'. In this case it was possible to match records between the two sources and this demonstrates that the difference seems to have arisen because women did not necessarily remember a midwife that they had only met once before. This is an important finding, relating to the question of what it means to 'know' your midwife. We will return to this point below.

Evidence from the four multi-scheme descriptive studies

As we have already seen in Chapter 8, the multi-scheme descriptive studies also presented data on this subject. In Wraight et al.'s (1993) study, only 26 per cent of midwifery managers said that it was possible to identify the proportion of women who were attended in labour by a known midwife, and in many cases these were estimates and not accurately measured. For those operating teams, the proportion was 35 per cent and in GP units, 44 per cent. Among those who said that they could supply this information, the figures given were approximately 60 per cent for teams, 40 per cent for consultant and combined units and 80 per cent in GP Units. Stock and Wraight (1993) concluded that: 'If we consider all units which provide care under the name "Team Midwifery" there is little evidence that all such schemes achieve higher levels of continuity of carer, although there is agreement amongst midwives that continuity of care, and quality of care, is enhanced'.

Garcia et al.'s (1996) study is particularly useful because it does address the difference between having 'met' someone and 'knowing' them. In two of the schemes studied 81 per cent and 70 per cent of women were cared for in labour by a known midwife (that is, someone that they had met). However, the proportion saying that they were cared for by someone that they 'knew well' as opposed to 'had met' were 50 per cent and 35 per cent. In the third service studied, the majority of respondents were not cared for by the team midwives and the figures show considerably less likelihood of a woman having a known carer (35%, including 21% 'knew well').

Finally we have the evidence from the study by Allen et al. (1997). This study reported that over 90 per cent of women in one scheme were delivered by their named midwife, the figures for the other two schemes being 61 per cent and 42 per cent. The proportions being delivered by a member of their team (who may or may not have been met before) were 98 per cent, 92 per cent and 68 per cent. The lower proportion in this last case was because the team had the care of women who were planned to deliver elsewhere or to transfer to consultant care.

In summary

The assessment of the proportion of women who were attended in labour by a known midwife was incomplete in all the comparative studies. Despite this, the evidence from three comparative studies (Know-Your-Midwife [1], One-to-One [5], West Essex [6]), and two multi-scheme descriptive studies (Garcia et al., 1996 and Allen et al., 1997) is that it is possible to deliver a service in which a high proportion of women will be attended in labour by someone that they have met before, although that is not to say that they will necessarily know them well. In the other two comparative studies where this was relevant (Home-from-Home [2] and Glasgow MDU [4]), the limited evidence supplied does not suggest that study group women are any more likely to be attended in labour by someone that they have met before. Thus we must conclude that alternative ways of organizing midwifery services can lead to a high proportion of women being attended in labour by someone that they have met before, but that this is not true for all schemes.

Other definitions of continuity of carer

Number of caregivers

EVIDENCE FROM THE SEVEN COMPARATIVE STUDIES

Being attended in labour by someone that has been met before is only one way of interpreting 'continuity of carer'. Most of the comparative studies in fact chose to assess it in other ways, as Table 9.1 shows. One alternative measure is the total number of caregivers seen during some specified aspect of maternity care, and this was assessed in some way by six of the seven studies. However they varied in terms of the definition of 'caregiver' (e.g. midwives only; students included), and the time period under consideration (e.g. intrapartum only, start-to-finish, excluding hospital postnatal care). Thus, comparison across studies is very difficult. Within studies, there is conflicting data in the Know-Your-Midwife [1] study as to whether study group or control group women saw more midwives antenatally. The non-randomized shared-care comparison group saw the smallest number – 63 per cent had not seen a midwife at all by 37 weeks. KYM women saw fewer midwives during labour. In the Aberdeen midwives unit study [3], there was no difference between the groups in the number of intrapartum caregivers seen. In the Glasgow MDU [4] and One-to-One [5] studies, study group women did see a smaller number of caregivers overall, and in The Scottish Antenatal Care Trial [7], the study group women saw significantly fewer caregivers antenatally than the control group. However, in the West Essex study [6], the study group women actually saw more midwives both antenatally and postnatally than women in control group II. All of the studies that present relevant data suggest that women, whether study group or control, are still seeing a large number of caregivers overall. In the One-to-One study [5], the target that low-risk study group women should be looked after by no more than six staff during pregnancy was met for only 44 per cent of women at QCCH and 48 per cent at Hammersmith Hospital.

EVIDENCE FROM THE FOUR MULTI-SCHEME DESCRIPTIVE STUDIES
The multi-scheme descriptive studies cannot give us comparative data, but an interesting point is raised in the Allen et al. (1997) study regarding the number of midwives seen antenatally. In all the schemes, most antenatal consultations were with the named midwife. In Deptford, nearly 75 per cent of the women had also been seen by another team midwife at some point in pregnancy, but this was because the Deptford team often had two midwives present, rather than because the named midwife was not giving continuity of care. In Ashford only 20 per cent had also been seen by another team midwife at some point in pregnancy and in Lewisham 23 per cent. Although such a high level of one-to-one care is in keeping with the schemes' aims, it does mean that in Ashford and Lewisham women were not getting to know other members of the team, so that their chances of knowing the midwife at the birth, if it were not their named midwife, was reduced. Thus, a trade-off may be needed.

Knowing the midwives who give postnatal care
EVIDENCE FROM THE SEVEN COMPARATIVE STUDIES
Another way in which continuity of carer may be assessed is whether the woman knows the midwives who care for her at home postnatally. This was assessed only in the One-to-One study [5] and in West Essex [6]. As we reported above, 71 per cent of the One-to-One women at QCCH had previously met all their postnatal caregivers, but only 7 per cent of the comparison group. In West Essex [6], 48 per cent of the study group had met all of these midwives before and 46 per cent had met some. In the three comparison groups 18 per cent, 57 per cent and 36 per cent had met all and 65 per cent, 39 per cent and 48 per cent had met some.

EVIDENCE FROM THE FOUR MULTI-SCHEME DESCRIPTIVE STUDIES
Of the multi-scheme descriptive studies, those by Garcia et al. (1996) and Allen et al. (1997) also addressed this question. In Garcia et al.'s study, one scheme provided almost complete continuity of postnatal midwifery care at home while in the other two, 50 per cent and 65 per cent of women had not met any of the midwives who visited them at home after the birth. In the Allen et al. (1997) study most postnatal consultations involved the named midwife – over 70 per cent in all three schemes.

In summary
Continuity of carer was most frequently assessed in the seven comparative schemes in terms of number of carers. Definitions differed between studies. In four of the comparative studies (Know-Your-Midwife [1], Glasgow MDU [4], One-to-One [5], The Scottish Antenatal Care Trial [7]) study group women saw fewer caregivers, during some specified period, than the comparison group, but no such advantage was

demonstrated in the Aberdeen Midwives Unit [3] and West Essex [6] studies. All of the studies that present relevant data suggest that women, whether study group or control, are still seeing a large number of caregivers overall. Continuity of carer into the postnatal period has received less attention. The limited available data indicate that it is often achieved by the new schemes.

Continuity of carer: Questions still to be answered

The evidence presented tells us that there are many definitions of continuity of carer. Some definitions are not considered by some evaluations and it is assumed that these were not outcomes of interest. In most cases women's views of whether a midwife is 'known' have not been considered.

We have not attempted in this section to address any of the following questions:

• what determines success or failure to achieve continuity of carer?

• what are the costs, either financially or to midwives, of providing continuity of carer?

• what does it mean to 'know' your midwife?

• is continuity of carer associated with better outcomes for women?

These questions have been partly addressed by the multi-scheme descriptive studies, and will all be discussed further in subsequent chapters.

CHAPTER TEN

Are New Ways of Organizing Services Associated with Different Clinical Outcomes?

Evidence from the seven comparative studies

Introduction

All seven comparative studies present data on clinical outcomes. Some also present process data such as the number of antenatal/postnatal consultations, and, where appropriate, the number of women transferred out of the scheme. In some of the studies the quantity of such data is overwhelmingly large, and it has been necessary to be selective. We are therefore giving priority to serious outcomes and those that may have implications for other aspects of the organization of services, such as resource use.

Data could, in principle, be presented about any part of the care cycle from booking to postnatal discharge to the health visitor. In practice, these data were presented for very few of the studies. The three that we have chosen to present are: mode of delivery, pain-relief in labour and perineal trauma. The reasons for choosing these three are that: six of the seven studies report data (the exception is The Scottish Antenatal Care Trial [7] which was not concerned with intrapartum care); all have cost implications and all have implications for women's satisfaction. Data are also presented on perinatal mortality, although not all seven studies present complete data.

A decision was made not to carry out a meta-analysis of these outcomes. As has been described, the schemes vary very widely in their context and design. Combining the results in a meta-analysis, although increasing the statistical power of the findings, could be seriously misleading. This is especially the case for the rarer, serious outcomes such as perinatal mortality.

Before looking at the comparative data, we need to remember that the five RCTs were all analysed by intention-to-treat, in other words the outcomes given were for the women randomized to the different groups irrespective of whether or not they were transferred. The numbers of women transferred were substantial in three of the studies, as shown in Table 10.1.

Table 10.1: Transfer data from the seven comparative studies

Know-Your-Midwife [1]	Development of problems needing obstetric input did not preclude women from having KYM midwives in labour. Numbers not given, but 25% of the KYM group were admitted to hospital antenatally (cf 31% of the control group – difference not significant).
Home-from-Home [2]	45% were transferred – 537 (23%) antenatally and 408 (18%) during 1st stage (and 4% in 2nd stage or subsequently). 1069 delivered by the midwife led team (46% of those so randomized). Most common reasons for antenatal transfer were hypertension, prolonged pregnancy and bleeding (40%).
Aberdeen Midwives Unit [3]	54% transferred – 727 (38%) antenatally and 303 (16%) intrapartum. 870 (46%) gave birth in the Midwives unit. The antenatal transfer group included 80 women who miscarried, moved or terminated the pregnancy. 155 women (8%) were transferred because of postmaturity – this was the most common reason for antenatal transfer, followed by hypertension and prolonged rupture of membranes. Primiparous women were more likely than multiparous to be transferred intrapartum (43% cf 8%).
Glasgow MDU [4]	66% transferred, but 33% were only temporary transfers. 33% permanently transferred, (29% clinical reasons, 4% non-clinical). 76% of the temporary transfers were in the intrapartum period mainly for induction or epidural.
One-to-One [5]	n/a
West Essex [6]	n/a
Scottish Antenatal Care Trial [7]	Up to 37 weeks, 17% of the study group had their style of care changed, cf 7% of the control group. Between 37 weeks and 24 hours before delivery, 21% and 18% respectively.

Mode of delivery in the seven comparative studies

The seven studies showed a very consistent pattern with regard to mode of delivery (Table 10.2). There was a very slight tendency for there to be more normal deliveries in the study group, but this never reached statistical significance. There was considerable variation between studies, the high rate of caesarean sections at Queen Charlotte's being particularly noticeable. However, it should be remembered that five of the studies covered only low risk women, while two (One-to-One [5] and West Essex [6]) covered all risks. The differences between One-to-One [5] and West Essex [6] may be partly because the One-to-One group was drawn from a particularly disadvantaged population. The difference in the proportion of unassisted vaginal deliveries between the Glasgow MDU [4] and Leicester Home-from-Home [2] studies (74% versus 84%) may similarly reflect the highly disadvantaged population served by the Glasgow MDU.

Table 10.2: Mode of delivery in the seven comparative studies

Know-Your-Midwife [1]	KYM group: 80% unassisted vaginal; 12% assisted; 8% caesarean section. Control group: 75% unassisted vaginal but difference not significant.
Home-from-Home [2]	Home-from-Home group: 84% unassisted vaginal; 1% vaginal breech; 8% assisted; 7% caesarean section cf control group: 82% unassisted vaginal; 1% vaginal breech; 10% assisted; 7% caesarean section. Difference not significant.
Aberdeen Midwives Unit [3]	Midwives unit: 78% unassisted vaginal; 1.3% vaginal breech; 12% assisted; 8% caesarean section cf control group: 75% unassisted vaginal; 1.3% vaginal breech; 13% assisted; 10% caesarean section. Difference not significant.
Glasgow MDU [4]	MDU group: 74% unassisted vaginal; 14% assisted; 13% caesarean section. No different from control group.
One-to-One [5]	One-to-One at QCCH (audit data): 67% unassisted vaginal; 14% assisted; 19% caesarean section cf comparison group: 63% unassisted vaginal; 19% assisted; 18% caesarean section. Difference not significant.
West Essex [6]	Study group: 74% unassisted vaginal; 11% assisted; 15% caesarean section. No different from comparison groups.
Scottish Antenatal Care Trial [7]	Study group: 79% unassisted; 0.4% vaginal breech; 12% instrumental; 9% caesarean section. No different from control group.

Pain-relief in labour in the seven comparative studies

Table 10.3 shows the findings relating to pain-relief in labour in the seven comparative studies. In four cases it is clear that study women were less likely to have an epidural than control women. In the case of the Glasgow MDU [4] there were no significant differences, and in West Essex [6] there was no difference between the study group and Control I which was the comparison group that delivered in the same hospital, although both were less likely to have an epidural than the other two comparison groups which delivered at a different hospital. There is considerable variation in the proportion of women having an epidural across the studies, the very high rates at Queen Charlotte's in the One-to-One study [5], even in the study group, being particularly noticeable. Between-hospital differences are generally higher than those between groups within studies. Epidurals were not available to women delivering in the Home-from-Home unit [2], so the percentage given represents women who, although randomized to Home-from-Home, delivered elsewhere.

Table 10.3: Pain-relief in labour in the seven comparative studies

Know-Your-Midwife [1]	KYM women were less likely to have an epidural (18% cf 28%) and more likely to have no pain relief or entonox only (51% cf 38%).
Home-from-Home [2]	Home-from-Home women were less likely to have an epidural (16% cf 20%), equally likely to have no pain relief (13% cf 12%) and more likely to use entonox only (32% cf 23%).
Aberdeen Midwives Unit [3]	Midwife unit women were less likely to have an epidural (15% cf 18%).
Glasgow MDU [4]	Equal numbers in each group had an epidural (33% cf 34%); used no pain relief (13% cf 12%). Slightly more of the MDU women used TENS, entonox or a bath (12% cf 9%).
One-to-One [5]	At QCCH, 59% of One-to-One women reported having epidurals cf 76% of comparison group. Equal numbers used 'natural methods' (19%). Audit figures were 58% and 70%, and for no pain relief were 10% and 5%.
West Essex [6]	Epidurals were used by 22% of the study group cf 20%, 36% and 37% of the comparison groups (differences primarily associated with different delivery hospitals).
Scottish Antenatal Care Trial [7]	data not given

Perineal trauma in the seven comparative studies

Table 10.4 shows the findings on perineal trauma in the seven comparative studies. No data were presented in the The Scottish Antenatal Care Trial [7]. In five of the remaining six studies there was a clear finding of fewer episiotomies in the study group, the exception being West Essex [6]. The findings are slightly less clear in terms of the proportion of women having an intact perineum. As one would expect, these between-group differences are generally smaller. There is a higher rate in four of the studies, and no difference in two. Note, again, the variation *between* studies, with an intact perineum rate for control women varying from 21 per cent to 36 per cent. This may well reflect differences in the populations such as the number of primiparous women in the sample, but may also reflect practice differences. The mismatch in episiotomy rates in the One-to-One study between women's accounts and the audit, is somewhat worrying. The rates reported by women in both groups are 50 per cent higher than those given by the audit.

67

Table 10.4: Perineal trauma in the seven comparative studies

Know-Your-Midwife [1]	Women in the KYM group less likely to have an episiotomy (34% cf 42%) but equally likely to have an intact perineum (24%).
Home-from-Home [2]	Women in the Home-from-Home group less likely to have an episiotomy (23% cf 31%) and more likely to have an intact perineum (33% cf 30%).
Aberdeen Midwives Unit [3]	Women in the midwife group were less likely to have an episiotomy (25% cf 29%) and more likely to have an intact perineum (24% cf 21%).
Glasgow MDU [4]	MDU women were less likely to have an episiotomy (28% cf 34%) and more likely to have an intact perineum (31% cf 24%).
One-to-One [5]	One-to-One women at QCCH were less likely to report having an episiotomy than comparison group (27% cf 41%)(p33). Audit data (p72) give figures of 19% and 30% with 34% and 26% intact.
West Essex [6]	22% of the study group had an episiotomy and 36% an intact perineum. This was no different from the comparison groups.
Scottish Antenatal Care Trial [7]	data not given.

Perinatal mortality in the seven comparative studies

The death of a baby is, fortunately, a rare event, and perinatal mortality should not be used as the principal outcome by which the schemes are judged. Nevertheless, we do need to be reassured that the schemes are safe. Table 10.5 shows perinatal mortality data from the seven studies. Not all have used the same definitions. Appropriate data are not available from the two schemes that were not evaluated by randomized trials, and we should, in any case, have considerable difficulties in interpreting them, given the pre-existing differences between the groups. In three of the five RCTs there was a higher proportion of deaths in the study group than in the control group; in the other two there were relatively more deaths in the control group. The studies present details of the deaths to demonstrate that they were unavoidable and not the result of substandard care. Numbers are necessarily very small. Across the five studies, the rate for the study groups is 51 deaths out 6,108 = 8.3 per thousand. For the control groups it is 32 deaths out of 4,110 = 7.8 per thousand.

We have not carried out a meta-analysis on these data for two reasons. Firstly, the context and design of the schemes are very different, and the results would be hard to interpret. Secondly, such a meta-analysis should, ideally, include all available RCTs.

This report has looked only at studies from the United Kingdom. A meta-analysis of international RCTs is in progress (Turnbull and Waldenstrom, personal communication).

Table 10.5: Perinatal mortality in the seven comparative studies

Know-Your-Midwife [1]	Still births + early neonatal deaths: 8/503 in the study group (15.9 per thousand); 4/498 in the control group (8.0 per thousand); 5/577 in the shared care group (8.7 per thousand).
Home-from-Home [2]	Neonatal deaths: 18/2304 in the study group (7.8 per thousand); 5/1206 in the control group (4.1 per thousand).
Aberdeen Midwives] Unit [3]	Still births + early neonatal deaths: 15/1819 in the study group (8.2 per thousand); 6/915 in the control group (6.6 per thousand).
Glasgow MDU [4]	Still births + neonatal deaths: 4/648 in the study group (6.2 per thousand); 9/651in the control group (13.8 per thousand).
One-to-One [5]	Not known: incomplete data from the audit due to removal of notes.
West Essex [6]	3 stillbirths in the study group (N=1520). Other data not given.
Scottish Antenatal Care Trial [7]	Still births + early neonatal deaths: 6/834 in the study group (7.2 per thousand); 8/840 in the control group (9.5 per thousand). Data are also given for fetal losses <24 weeks (9 cf 15) and terminations (3 cf 4).

Evidence from other studies

We should note here two other older studies: Klein et al. (1978) [8] and Chapman et al. (1986) [9]. Klein's study was a retrospective case-note comparison between shared consultant-led care and an integrated GP Unit. Although the study is presented as being about the place booked for delivery, it is actually much more than this because community midwives were delivering all aspects of care to women booked for the GPU, in other words the antenatal care received by the groups would have differed as well: 'In the GP Unit the personal community midwife is the key figure' and she delivered the baby. The analysis was restricted to low risk women and two groups of equivalent obstetric risk status were identified. Of the 5,005 births at the study unit in 1976, 1,436 met the criteria. Of these, 1,188 were booked for delivery in the consultant unit and 248 at the GP Unit. Characteristics of the two groups were similar. Analysis was by intention-to-treat, i.e. where the woman had been booked, irrespective of where she delivered. Significant differences were found in rates of obstetric intervention. Both multiparous and primiparous women were more likely to have induction, epidural and forceps if they were booked for consultant-led care and multiparas were also more likely to have an emergency caesarean section. Differences were particularly large for multiparous women. Most of the interventions in the GP Unit group were after transfer. GP Unit-booked women had higher rates of breastfeeding at discharge for both multiparas and primiparas. These are impressive results, even though this was not a randomized study. The differences reported are rather greater than in the seven comparative studies, none of which, for example, found any differences in breastfeeding initiation or maintenance.

Subsequent analysis of a subgroup of these women who were admitted because they were in spontaneous labour, or thought that they were, showed substantial differences between the groups in the management of early labour.

> 'Home visiting was a major part of the management of early labour in the GPU-booked women, 62% of the nulliparaous women were visited at least once by the community midwife... One-third of the multiparous women in the GPU-booked group were seen in early labour in the home and 22.2% of them in the GP surgery.' (Klein et al., 1983b, p. 126)

On admission, 22.2 per cent of the nulliparous women booked for shared care were found not to be in labour, compared with 6.4 per cent in the GPU-booked group ($p<0.05$).

The other study of relevance is that by Chapman et al. [9]. This was a randomized controlled trial comparing a birthroom (as in the Home-from-Home study) with a hospital labour ward. Like the One-to-One study [5], this study was carried out at Queen Charlotte's hospital in London. All women in the study were under the care of community midwives. The same group of midwives cared for women in either setting, as in the Aberdeen Midwives Unit study [3]. Women were multiparous with normal pregnancies and normal previous deliveries. Women were told that epidurals and electronic fetal monitoring would not be available. Of 253 eligible women, 148 (59%) agreed to take part and 86 (34%) refused because they wanted an epidural and a further 13 because they wanted monitoring. Note that this is a higher refusal rate than was reported in the core comparative studies, and is perhaps related to the pro-epidural culture at Queen Charlotte's hospital. Results showed that birthroom women were considerably more likely to use no analgesia (57% compared to 29%). There were similar rates of perineal injury but less suturing in the birthroom group. There were no differences in breastfeeding – an impressive 85 per cent in each group. Birthroom women were much more likely to say that they would like the same location for a future delivery. Unfortunately, the paper tells us little about ante- and postnatal care, so it is not clear whether these women were getting a start-to-finish service. Mean length of hospital postnatal stay was 3.5 days in both groups, so these were not DOMINO deliveries.

The study was not very large and probably suffers from some methodological bias[1], but this is unlikely to be large enough to radically affect the findings. Clearly these are

---

1. Three women were withdrawn from the birthroom group because they decided that they wanted an epidural. This introduces a bias because this would not have excluded them from the other group.

a selected group of women, but this study is still of considerable interest because women were randomized and all that differed between the groups was the planned location for delivery.[2] Not even the caregivers differed since the same community midwives cared for women in both settings.

In summary

The data from the comparative studies have been fairly consistent in indicating that the schemes were associated with lower use of epidurals, and often of other forms of pain relief, and with less perineal trauma. There were no significant differences by mode of delivery. Other labour outcomes were considered by the different studies, some of which were found to be different between study and control groups (e.g. induction) but these have not been presented here. There is the possibility that the new forms of care may be associated with a slightly higher rate of perinatal deaths, and we await the publication of a meta-analysis by other authors (Turnbull and Waldenstrom, personal communication).

Two additional studies were presented as an aid to interpreting the data from the core comparative studies. The first dates from the 1970s and compared care by community midwives and planned delivery in an integrated GP Unit with standard consultant-led shared-care. This showed greater between-group differences than were found in any of the core studies. The second (carried out in the early 1980s) was an RCT which bears a number of resemblances to some of the core comparative studies. The reason why it is of particular interest is that only the planned location of delivery differed between the groups, even the intrapartum caregivers were the same. Nevertheless, between group differences were found that are in line with those found in the core studies. This suggests that it is not necessarily the *organization* of midwifery services that is the relevant factor.

Outcomes: Questions still to be answered

We know relatively little about what aspects of care lead to differences in outcomes. The major difficulty in interpreting any of these studies (and this will apply to subsequent questions also) is that so many variables have been changed simultaneously. Thus, when we do find differences between new and old style care, we have no way of knowing which aspects of the care may be responsible. What we do know about the determinants of labour outcomes is that women do better when they are relaxed and when they have the presence of a supportive person (Hodnett, 1997). These may well be the key aspects of these schemes that influence outcomes. However, there are a large number of competing explanations. Let us take the example of episiotomies. The reduced rate for women in the study group was a consistent finding over a number of studies. Possible explanations are:

* midwives were less inclined to perform episiotomies because of the scheme ethos

---

2. It is for this reason that this study did not qualify as a 'core comparative study' i.e. it did not have the organization of midwifery services as the main independent variable.

- midwives were less inclined to perform episiotomies because the setting gave them confidence to deliver without

- midwives encouraged women to move around more and find comfortable positions (a finding in some of the studies), which reduced the need for episiotomies

- a more relaxed atmosphere made women less tense and thus reduced the need for episiotomy

- fewer women had epidurals. Epidurals are associated with instrumental deliveries which in turn require an episiotomy.

There are doubtless further possible explanations. The study by Chapman et al. [9] must make us cautious in assuming that any differences observed are related to the organization of midwifery services. However, even though that study had only one variable – whether the room was homely or clinical – and the same midwives worked in both settings, all the hypotheses just listed apply. It is perfectly plausible that the midwives were affected by the birth settings, and the expectations associated with them, and were therefore behaving differently in the two settings. Such an effect could be robust, i.e. the two environments would always affect midwives in that way, or it could be a Hawthorne effect, as discussed above, that is, a reflection of the novelty of the birthroom setting. Considerable experimental ingenuity would be needed to distinguish between these and competing explanations.

CHAPTER ELEVEN

What are Women's Views and Experiences of Alternative Ways of Organizing Midwifery Services?

Evidence from the seven comparative studies

Introduction

Table 11.1 shows the timing and method of data collection from women in the seven studies. It will be seen that only three of the studies (Know-Your-Midwife [1], Glasgow MDU [4] and One-to-One [5]) collected data antenatally.

As with the previous chapter, the very large quantity of data presented in each of the studies means that we have to be selective in what we present. The selection process can again be aided by looking at common data presented in all seven studies, but this is less satisfactory for this chapter, firstly because measures are idiosyncratic between studies and secondly because some interesting and important question have not always been asked. Given the aims of the schemes, we will focus on women's satisfaction, women's views of their caregivers and the relationship between continuity and satisfaction.

Table 11.1: Timing and method of data collection from women in the seven comparative studies

Know-Your-Midwife [1]	Questionnaires given at clinic at 37 weeks, and at 2 days given on the ward and by post 6 weeks after birth; General Health Questionnaire was sent with the 6 week questionnaire. Response rates: antenatal 97%, 2 days 99%, 6 weeks 89% (difference between study and control groups not significant).
Home-from-Home [2]	Postal questionnaires sent to women 6 weeks postnatally. 72% response rate (most data were to appear in a forthcoming paper).
Aberdeen Midwives Unit [3]	Questionnaire completed after discharge home; interviews with a random 400 women from the study population (N.B. most of these data are not yet published). Response rate not given.
Glasgow MDU [4]	Questionnaires to women at 34/35 weeks, 7 weeks and 7 months postnatally. Response rates: antenatal 85% of the study group, 78% of control group (significant difference); 7 weeks: 72% & 63% (significant difference); 7 months: 68% & 63%.

One-to-One [5]	Questionnaires at 35 weeks, and 2 weeks and 13 weeks postnatally (+ Interviews/focus groups with selected women). Response rates (QCCH): antenatal 69%, 2 weeks 59%, 13 weeks 61% (difference between study and comparison groups not significant). Significantly lower response from women booked at HH (54%, 38% and 40% for the One-to-One group).
West Essex [6]	Questionnaire 10 days after birth. Response rate 88%.
Scottish Antenatal Care Trial [7]	Postal questionnaires sent 6 weeks postnatally to 97% of women in the trial. 78% response rate: N=668 from study group and 667 from control group.

Women's satisfaction in the seven comparative studies

Table 11.2 shows the data reported in the seven studies on global measures of satisfaction. There is a fairly consistent finding that study group women reported higher levels of satisfaction, although there are exceptions to this. Unfortunately, the Aberdeen Midwives Unit [3] data were not published in time to be included in this report, and we will not be able to consider this study in any more detail in this chapter. In the other studies, women have generally been asked for their satisfaction with individual phases of the care process.

- Five of the six studies had a measure of overall satisfaction with antenatal care. In The Scottish Antenatal Care Trial [7] there was no significant difference between the groups in overall satisfaction with antenatal care, although the study group women were more likely to say that they enjoyed their care. In all of the other four studies, the study group were significantly more satisfied than the control group, but in West Essex [6] this finding only applied to one of the comparison groups. Control I, the group that was not receiving antenatal care within the study district was significantly less satisfied than the study group. However, Control II, the group which received all of their antenatal and postnatal community care from the study district's non-team community midwives, were more satisfied with their antenatal care than the study group. In the One-to-One study [5], there was no overall measure of satisfaction with antenatal care, but women were asked a number of questions, for example, about location of care, waiting times and the usefulness of antenatal care, all of which tended to show higher satisfaction by women in the One-to-One group.

- Satisfaction with intrapartum care was reported for four studies. The study group were more satisfied in the Home-from-Home [2], Glasgow MDU [4], and One-to-One [5] studies but not in West Essex [6].

- Satisfaction with postnatal hospital care was reported in three studies: study group women were more satisfied at the Glasgow MDU [4] but there were no differences for One-to-One [5] or West Essex [6]. In all three studies it was the aspect of care that women were least satisfied with.

- Four studies report on satisfaction with postnatal care at home: Know-Your-Midwife [1] and West Essex [6] found no difference between groups while the

Glasgow MDU [4] and One-to-One [5] found study women to be more satisfied. The failure to find a difference in the Know-Your-Midwife [1] study may be an artefact of the way that the question was asked (see Table 11.2).

Table 11.2: Women's satisfaction in the seven comparative studies

Know-Your-Midwife [1]	From 3 response options (satisfied/mainly satisfied/not satisfied) *antenatal care:* 95% of KYM women 'satisfied' cf 87% of control group (significant difference) *intrapartum care:* not reported (?not asked) *postnatal hospital care*: not reported (?not asked) *postnatal care at home (*2 responses: satisfied/not satisfied) 94% of KYM women satisfied cf 93% of control group (not significant).
Home-from-Home [2]	On a 5-point rating from 'very satisfied' to 'very dissatisfied', *antenatal care*: 52% of study group were very satisfied cf 44% of control group (significant difference) *intrapartum care*: 73% of study group were very satisfied cf 60% of control group (significant difference).
Aberdeen Midwives	78% of the study group women liked their overall care and management by staff 'in every way' cf 73% of control group (it is not stated whether this is a significant difference).
Glasgow MDU [4]	A satisfaction questionnaire was devised in which women had to indicate levels of agreement with statements such as 'I feel I get too little information' for each phase of care and overall. These produced 5-point or 3-point ratings which were then summed. Satisfaction was high for both groups but was significantly higher for study group women for each of antenatal, intrapartum, postnatal hospital, postnatal home and overall care. (Details of the satisfaction measure are given in Turnbull et al., 1996, pp. 214–5 and 216).
One-to-One [5]	From 3 response options (very satisfied/satisfied in some ways but not in others/very dissatisfied) *antenatal care:* no measure of overall satisfaction with antenatal care, although study group women tended to be more positive e.g. in finding it useful *intrapartum care:* 79% of One-to-One women at QCCH were very satisfied cf 71% of comparison group (this is a significant difference although it is not stated in the report) *postnatal hospital care:* 50% of One-to-One women at QCCH were very satisfied cf 54% of comparison group (this is not a significant difference although it is not stated in the report) *postnatal care at home (*scored as above but with the additional option of 'not very satisfied'). 85% of QCCH study women were very satisfied cf 74% of comparison group (this is a significant difference although it is not stated in the report). *Looking back at 13 weeks over all care:* 73% of the QCCH study group were very satisfied cf 45% of comparison group (this is a significant difference although it is not stated in the report).

West Essex [6]	From 3 response options (very satisfied/ satisfied in some ways but not in others/ very dissatisfied): *antenatal care*: 72% of study group very satisfied cf 54% for Control I, 80% for Control II & 67% for Control III (differences significant) *intrapartum care*: 75% of study group very satisfied. Same in all groups. *postnatal hospital care*: 65% of study group very satisfied. Same in all groups. *postnatal care at home:* 84% of study group very satisfied. Same in all groups.
Scottish Antenatal Care Trial [7]	From 3 response options (very satisfied/ sometimes satisfied/ very dissatisfied): *antenatal care:* 68% of study group very satisfied cf 65% of control group (not significantly different). Also no difference between the groups in questions concerning: the arrangement of antenatal visits; access to a hospital doctor; waiting times; information acquisition; access to antenatal classes; opportunity to visit the labour ward in pregnancy. Study group women were more likely to say that they enjoyed their care (70% cf 63%) *intrapartum & postnatal care:* not asked.

WHAT IS SATISFACTORY ABOUT CARE?

'Determining the level of satisfaction is not in itself sufficient without being able to identify the actual features of the service that women particularly liked or disliked. Many of these factors are important in addressing the question of replicability.' (Allen et al., 1997, p. 119)

As Allen et al. so rightly point out, global satisfaction measures, while indicative, are of limited value. We need to know what aspects of the service are important in bringing about the differences between control and study group women. Given the variety of the services that we are considering here, as well as the variety of ways in which they were evaluated, it will not be easy to answer this question from the available data, but we will attempt to do so in the following sections.

Women's perceptions of their caregivers in the seven comparative studies

In order to try and understand more about the determinants of satisfaction, we attempted to extract from each of the comparative studies women's perceptions of their caregivers (Table 11.3). For two of the studies this information was not given. In the other five, there was, of course, no standardization of questions so limited conclusions can be drawn. The absence of a piece of information for a given study almost certainly means that nobody thought to ask that question. It does not mean that that dimension was not important to women in that study. The picture that emerges across the studies is that women in the study groups were more likely to feel that they had a relationship with their carers, that they were listened to and cared about as individuals. Interestingly, in more than one of the studies, the midwife being 'friendly' is not something that distinguishes the groups.

Table 11.3: Women's perceptions of their caregivers in the seven comparative studies

Know-Your-Midwife [1]	*Antenatally:* More study group women than control group perceived the midwives as personally interested in them, unhurried and encouraging questions, and helpful for anxiety. No difference in perception that she was friendly or that she explained things clearly. *Intrapartum:* More study group women than control group perceived the midwives as caring and that staff explained what they were doing. *postnatal hospital:* no difference in perception of adequacy of help given but KYM women described staff as more caring. *postnatal home:* More study group women than control group said that they could discuss problems with the visiting midwife 'very easily' (cf 'quite easily').
Home-from-Home [2]	data not given
Aberdeen Midwives Unit [3]	data not given
Glasgow MDU [4]	For each of antenatal, intrapartum, postnatal hospital, postnatal home and overall care, study group women scored significantly higher for: being given choices; information transfer; the extent to which they felt able to make decisions about their care; individualized care (e.g. 'I feel that staff are interested in me and not just my pregnancy'). Also helpfulness/pleasantness/confidence in staff (but not significant intrapartum).
One-to-One [5]	*Antenatally:* study group more likely to feel that carers encouraged them to ask questions, explained things clearly, listened to them, knew and remembered them. Study group more likely to say knew main carer 'quite well' (58% cf 37%) or 'very well' (16% cf 4%). Equally likely to describe the relationship as 'friendly'. *Intrapartum:* in both groups most women felt that staff listened enough, explained enough, and were very kind and understanding. *postnatal hospital care:* study group women *less* likely to describe staff as 'almost always' friendly (69% cf 75%) and were more likely to feel neglected or overlooked (11% cf 8%) but these differences are not significant. *postnatal home care:* more study group women described the relationship as 'close' (19% cf 5%), similar numbers described it as 'friendly' (77% cf 74%). Only 11% of both study and comparison groups said that there were things that they wanted to discuss with the midwives but could not. 63% of study group women said that it was hard to say goodbye (at final discharge) cf 15% of comparison group.

West Essex [6]	*Antenatally:* 73% of the study group felt that they had formed a relationship with midwives cf 68%, 82% and 50% in the comparison groups. 21% of study group would have liked more opportunity to talk about what might happen in labour cf 27%, 13% and 29% of the comparison groups. *Intrapartum:* 71% of study group said staff 'always' took enough notice of their views during labour. Same for comparison group.
Scottish Antenatal Care Trial [7]	The study group were more likely to say that they got on 'very well' with their main caregiver: 71% cf 67%. There were also differences between the groups in their preferences for continuity of carer: 29% of the study group preferred to see the same person each time cf 18% of the control group.

What aspects of continuity are important to women?

An underlying assumption of many of the changes that have been made in maternity care is that 'continuity of care' is associated with better outcomes for women. However, as we have seen, there are many different aspects to continuity. What evidence do we have about which aspects are important to women?

Background

The past two decades have seen a number of studies of women's experiences of maternity services, most of which were descriptive surveys (e.g. O'Brien and Smith, 1981). These have been reviewed by others (e.g. Reid, 1994). There have also been more detailed sociological studies such as Graham (1980), Oakley (1980) and MacIntyre (1982). These earlier studies contributed to the move for change. There were consistent messages that women did not like fragmentation, inconsistency, long waiting times and being treated like a number. They wanted to be treated with some respect and dignity, they wanted their views taken note of and their questions answered and they did not want to be given conflicting information and advice. Improving continuity of carer was seen to be a way of overcoming these problems, not necessarily an end in itself.

So, 'continuity of *care*' refers to care that is not fragmented, where there is good communication within the system and consistent policies. Thus, on any given encounter with the maternity services, a woman can feel confident that her caregiver will know what has gone before, she will not have to repeat her history yet again, and decisions about her care will have been made as a result of policies which are shared by all her caregivers and to which all are willing to adhere, so she will not be given conflicting advice. Total continuity of *carer* i.e. care given by just one person, is often seen as one way of achieving this.

In practice, as we have seen, a single carer is rarely achievable and when people talk of 'increasing continuity of carer' they generally mean 'decreasing the number of caregivers' (see Chapter 9). We should also note that having a single caregiver throughout does not guarantee continuity of care if that person behaves in an inconsistent way.

Clearly, continuity of *care* and continuity of *carer* do not have to go together, and neither guarantees woman-centred care, which is a separate issue.

There is a very considerable difficulty in looking at these new schemes and trying to discover what it is in them that women find satisfactory. This is partly because the goal of continuity has generally been intertwined with a woman-centred philosophy. It is unlikely that continuity is valued as an end in itself, but rather as a means to some other desirable ends such as consistent care or having a trusting relationship with a caregiver.

As we observed in Chapter 9, 'continuity of carer' can be looked at within phases of care (antenatal, intrapartum, postnatal) and between phases: antenatal-to-postnatal, antenatal-to-intrapartum, intrapartum-to-postnatal, and across all phases (start-to-finish). The emphasis has been on antenatal-to-intrapartum continuity, i.e. being cared for in labour by a known caregiver, and it is a 'Changing Childbirth' target that at least 75 per cent of women should know the person who cares for them during labour. But is this the aspect of continuity that matters most to women?

Evidence from the seven comparative studies

Unfortunately, very few attempts are made in any of the seven comparative studies to make a direct link between satisfaction and components of continuity. The Know-Your-Midwife study [1] presents an appendix on determinants of satisfaction with birth, pooled across both study groups, but, although perceiving a midwife as caring is important, knowing her is, curiously, not mentioned.

The Scottish Antenatal Care Trial [7], which only concerned antenatal care, did not make a direct link but presented data on women's preferences for antenatal continuity of carer. Interestingly the study and control group differed more in answer to this question than to any other in the study. The options offered are shown in Table 11.4. Presumably, since this was a large RCT, these differences between the groups are a result of women's experiences in the study, rather than pre-existing. Since we have already seen that the study group had fewer antenatal carers and also that they were somewhat more likely to report that they got on 'very well' with their main caregiver,

Table 11.4: Preferred level of continuity of antenatal care in the
Scottish Antenatal Care Trial [7]

	Study group (N=665)		Control group (N=664)	
Didn't mind someone different each time	85	(13%)	123	(18%)
Small group of 3–4 people	85	(13%)	98	(15%)
One person but didn't mind someone different	301	(45%)	326	(49%)
Same person each time	194	(29%)	117	(18%)

fromTucker et al., 1996

this finding presumably indicates that, having experienced some continuity, this is what they would now prefer. However, despite this, the study group were no more satisfied with their antenatal care than the control group, perhaps because they did not get as much continuity as they would have liked.

The West Essex study [6] did attempt to link continuity and satisfaction. It was observed that the women most satisfied with their antenatal care were those in Control group II, who saw fewest midwives antenatally, were most likely to have a named midwife, felt best prepared, and were most likely to say that they had formed a relationship with a midwife. The irony is that this was the comparison group, who were having care from non-team community midwives. The same study also found that women who had seen more than two midwives antenatally (either in the study group or overall) were very significantly less likely to say that they had formed a relationship with them than those who had seen only one or two. We should also note that, although women in the study group were very much more likely to be delivered by a known midwife, their satisfaction with intrapartum care was no higher than women in the comparison groups.

The other study that comments directly on the relationship between continuity and satisfaction is that from the Glasgow MDU [4]. It will be recalled that the limited data presented concerning delivery by a known carer suggested that this was a relatively rare occurrence, although the scheme was successful in reducing the number of caregivers relative to the control group. On the other hand, of the seven comparative schemes, it was the only one to demonstrate consistently higher satisfaction in the study group across all the phases of care. The authors comment:

> 'Given that this programme of care still resulted in enhanced satisfaction and continuity of care and carer, it is suggested that it may not be necessary for the named midwife to go on call to deliver clients. Future research is necessary to determine to what extent it is important that women know the person who cares for them during delivery.' (Turnbull et al., 1995a p. 72)

We would strongly endorse that conclusion in the light of the evidence that we have reviewed from the other studies.

One of the analyses that is missing from all of these studies is within-group comparison of women who were cared for in labour by a known midwife with those who were not. Obviously there must be caveats to interpreting such a comparison since there may be reasons why a known carer was not achieved that are associated with systematic differences between the sub-groups, e.g. precipitate labour, transfer to consultant care. However, a carefully carried out retrospective analysis along lines similar to Klein et al.'s study [8] should be possible.

Since completing their main report, the research team responsible for the evaluation of the Glasgow MDU have, in fact, undertaken such an analysis (Shields et al., in press). The analysis was restricted to women who had all their care from MDU midwives and who had normal deliveries: 47 women cared for and delivered by their known midwife and 109 women cared for and delivered by an unknown associate midwife. No statistically significant differences were found between the groups in terms of socio-demographic variables or clinical outcomes. There were also no significant differences in satisfaction except for one item: women who had had an unknown carer in labour were *more* likely to say that they were treated as an individual during labour.

Evidence from the four multi-scheme descriptive studies

Two of the multi-scheme descriptive studies, Garcia et al. (1996) and Allen et al. (1997), investigated women's views of their care, and both studies represented a range of continuity of care.

In the study by Garcia et al. (1996), women were asked to rate various characteristics of care as very important, fairly important or not very important. Skilled staff, being given information and being treated kindly and respectfully were all rated as 'very important' by over 80 per cent of the women in all three services. Being convenient and letting the woman herself make the decisions were both rated as 'very important' by between two-thirds and three-quarters of the women. The characteristic rated as 'very important' by the smallest proportion of women (between a third and a half) was 'care from someone you know'. This would suggest that what is important to women are characteristics of individual encounters with caregivers. This is similar to the findings of Currell (1985) (see below and [10]). The chances of achieving the desired encounter may be increased by having a known caregiver, but that the caregiver should be known is not rated as important for its own sake. In other words, as we have suggested, having a known caregiver is a means to an end, rather than an end in itself.

In the Allen et al. (1997) study there was a very high level of satisfaction with antenatal care in all the schemes. Women in all the schemes were very positive about their midwife: they could talk to her, she explained things clearly and respected their wishes, as we have seen in the comparative studies. Women were asked what they liked best about their antenatal care. Unfortunately, it is not clear from the report whether this was an open-ended or closed question, nor how many answers could be coded per woman. The responses are shown in Table 11.5. Continuity is only picked out by around a quarter of the women in each scheme, although a higher proportion refer to a personal or individual approach. In Lewisham, the most popular feature appeared to be home visits.

Over half the women in the Allen et al. (1997) study were attended in labour by a named or known midwife. Those who had this experience were generally positive about it, but most of those who did not said that it did not matter – less than one in ten said that they were disappointed. This is consistent with other studies (e.g. Walker et al., 1995 [11]).

When asked to comment on their care overall, women said that their main sources of satisfaction were the high professional standards of the midwives and their friendliness. They also appreciated being treated like a human being. Continuity of carer was mentioned by less than 20 per cent. Curiously, it was mentioned least in the scheme which gave greatest continuity.

Table 11.5: What women liked best about their antenatal care in three schemes

scheme:	Lewisham	Ashford	Deptford
home visits	<50%		
one-to-one/continuity	25%	<50%	25%
friendliness	<33%	<25%	25%
trusting relationship with midwife			c.39%
personal/ individual approach	25%	between 25% and 33%	39%

constructed from data given in the text of Allen et al., 1997, (pp. 119–120), and probably incomplete (e.g. it is unlikely that no women in Ashford or Deptford mentioned home visits)

Evidence from other studies

Given the paucity of relevant evidence from the core studies, it seemed particularly important to consult a wider literature in order to tackle the question of what aspects of continuity are important to women.

One study of relevance was carried out by Currell (1985) [10] (reported in Currell, 1990). This was a comparative study in two areas of the south of England which looked at shared care, GP Unit care and home births. It was hypothesized that the organizational patterns of maternity care would be found along a continuum with continuity of care at one end and fragmented care at the other and that women who received the greatest degree of continuity would be the most satisfied and vice versa. This second hypothesis was not supported. Both praise and criticism of midwives and their care were found in all the patterns of care, and there were no significant differences between groups. However, the study did find that satisfaction (both for mothers and midwives) was associated with effective problem solving e.g. breastfeeding. She concluded, therefore, that improved satisfaction is to be found 'not by reorganising the areas in which midwives work, but by focusing on every encounter between mothers and midwives, wherever it takes place, and whether the mother and midwife have met before or not' (Currell, 1990, p. 33).

Garcia et al.'s (1996) finding that a known caregiver is not valued in isolation was also reported by Drew et al. (1989) [12]. In this study 183 women on a postnatal ward (and also midwives and doctors) rated each of 40 items on a 7-point scale from 'irrelevant' to 'essential' for a mother's satisfaction. Mean scores for each item were calculated and they were then rank ordered. The two most important items, after 'the baby being healthy', were 'the doctors talking to you in a way you can understand' and 'having all your questions answered by staff'. Being attended by the same midwife throughout pregnancy was ranked 21st.

A study by Lee (1994, 1995) [13] used a similar technique. The study was based on interviews with 12 midwives (half of those in four teams of six) and 32 women, some of whom had had care from the teams. The midwives worked a 24-hour on-call system, and carried bleeps. Women were asked to rank characteristics of an ideal system. Being able to reach the midwife by bleep was ranked top of the list, followed by knowing the labour midwife. However, when women were asked to rank the qualities that they wanted in a midwife, 'inspires confidence and trust' was top of the list, followed by 'safe and competent care'. 'Is known to you' came only half way down. A 'small majority' would prefer a good midwife that they had not previously met to one who was known but was neither very good nor very bad. Most women (81%) had previously met their labour midwife and they were significantly more satisfied than those who had not. Unfortunately, the reports give no details of the methods used to assess this.

The author discusses women's conflicting responses – the fact that they seemed to rate a known midwife in labour highly, and yet it came only half way down their list of qualities that they wanted in a midwife. Her explanation is that women want a known midwife in labour because they want the reassurance that they will have good quality care. This was also the conclusion reached in the One-to-One study [5]:

> 'Continuity of care is not an end in itself but it is something that women want because it helps to ensure that the sort of care that they value is in place.'
> (McCourt and Page, 1996, p. 88)

However Lee [13] argues that the assumption that the good quality care was a result of having a known midwife is not necessarily justified.

In a study by Green et al. (1988, 1998), many characteristics of the staff caring for women in labour were found to be related to subsequent satisfaction and emotional well-being. Having one caregiver throughout labour was very important, but having met that person before was *not* significantly related to any of the outcome measures. Despite this, analysis of sub-groups showed that, irrespective of whether it happened, *expecting* to be looked after during labour by a known midwife was associated with higher postnatal emotional well-being. The worst outcomes were for women who wanted this but did not expect it. Women who said that they 'didn't mind' had the best outcomes. These are surprising findings with far-reaching implications, which will clearly need to be replicated in other settings.

A study by Melia et al. (1991) assessed the feasibility and usefulness of consumer surveys for quality assurance and planning maternity services. Questionnaires were completed by 1,434 women in the South East Thames RHA, some antenatally and some postnatally. Part of their questionnaire covered opinions on continuity of midwifery care. Forty-six per cent of women thought it 'very important' (from four options) to have the same team antenatally and postnatally, and 40 per cent thought it 'very important' to know the delivering midwife. Women also favoured a home-like environment in the delivery suite, with 75 per cent attaching some importance to this.

Another study of relevance is the National Childbirth Trust (NCT) Choices project (Gready et al., 1995) [14]. The study included a survey of all women who gave birth within the North Essex Health Authority during a six week period in November-December 1994. Sixty-seven per cent of eligible women (N=797) completed a questionnaire. There were also seven focus groups with women with particular experiences or needs and a survey of user representatives on maternity committees in the district.

The project's aims were to find out:

- what women got from the maternity services and what they wanted

- how the services compared with the recommendations in 'Changing Childbirth'

- how aware the women were of research evidence

- how much parents and user representatives were consulted and involved in the planning and monitoring of services.

We will present only that evidence related to continuity and satisfaction.

A surprisingly high proportion of women (92%) said that in pregnancy they had had a doctor or midwife who remembered them and their progress from visit to visit. This did not vary according to where they had had most of their antenatal care. The small number who did not felt less well informed on some topics and less involved in decisions, but differences were not large.

Of the 743 women who went into labour, 31 per cent had met at least one of the midwives who looked after them in labour. This was generally higher in the GP Units, but also at Princess Alexandra Hospital, where they have team midwifery (66%). Fifty-four per cent had at least one midwife who was with them throughout their labour and delivery. Asked whether they would have liked to have got to know the doctor or midwife more before they gave birth, only 14 per cent said definitely, 33 per cent possibly and 53 per cent no. This did not differ between those who had and had not met them before or by unit. However, those who had met the midwife before were positive about it. Of the 772 women delivering in hospital, 57 per cent had not met any of the midwives who cared for them postnatally. This was significantly better at the GP Units and at Princess Alexandra Hospital where over half had met at least one. Women who had had a known midwife at any stage were more likely to say that it mattered than those who had not.

Fleissig and Kroll (1996) [15] published an account of the team midwifery scheme in South Camden which included a user survey. The scheme consisted of three community-based teams with a combined caseload of 1,000 women per annum. Midwives were generally organized in pairs with the aim that a woman would see either the named midwife or her partner. All women (high or low-risk) were allocated to a named midwife for booking after seeing the GP. During pregnancy women and their partners were invited to social meetings to get to know the team midwives.

Women were sent questionnaires six weeks postnatally. Three-quarters of eligible women responded. Seventy-seven per cent said they saw their named midwife regularly in pregnancy – 90 per cent said that their antenatal care was given by one or two people that they got to know. Fifty-three per cent were attended in labour by a midwife that they had met during pregnancy. Most women were happy with the way they were looked after intrapartum, for example 77 per cent said that staff always took enough notice of their views and wishes. However, having met the midwife before made no difference to these answers. Those who had had a known carer said it made them feel more at ease, but only 14 per cent of those who had not said that it mattered.

> 'Because I couldn't have asked for a more caring and professional person to deliver my baby. I felt I knew her for years, and amazingly became very close in only about seven hours. I trusted her completely.'

and

> 'I thought it would matter and was hoping for one of the midwives I had a very good relationship with. However it was completely fine and she made me feel very comfortable.' (Fleissig and Kroll, 1996, p. 14)

These echo the findings from a qualitative study by Murphy-Black (1993) [16] where women and midwives discussed their concepts of continuity of care. Most women in the study had not experienced care in labour by a known caregiver, but, as one woman said:

> 'After 5–10 minutes, it feels like they always knew you.' (Murphy-Black, 1993, p. 24)

A recent report published by the Audit Commission (1997) also contributes to this debate. This included a survey of a random sample of 3,570 women from eight maternity units, four months after birth. There was a 67 per cent response rate, with a total of 2,406 women. Nine hundred and eighty-three volunteered additional comments. We will only select here the findings relevant to our current discussion.

Women were asked about the importance of having the same staff throughout labour and about having met the staff before labour. Overall, having the same staff throughout labour was rated as more important, with 48 per cent saying it was 'very important' compared with 24 per cent who said that it was 'very important' to have met the staff before. Eighty-three per cent reported that having the same staff throughout was 'very' or 'fairly' important compared with 56 per cent who said that having met staff before was 'very' or 'fairly' important. As we have seen in other studies, women who had had a known carer in labour were considerably more likely to say that this was important than women who had not.

Paragraph 28 of the report states that:

> 'Continuity of care (which means that care is delivered in a consistent way, regardless of the professional providing it) is important to all women. Continuity of carer, on the other hand, means that care is provided by a small number of professionals or by professionals who women know. Moreover, it is important only to some women.'

Continuity: conclusions

There is relatively little information available about the aspects of continuity that women value. It appears to be the case that very few women value continuity of carer for its own sake, but it may be valued as a means to an end. This conclusion should not surprise us: naturally there are other requirements, such as competence, that one would expect to take priority.

Regarding the emphasis on a known intrapartum carer, the evidence from a variety of sources suggests that those who have this experience are positive about it, but that most of those who do not, do not see it as important. High levels of satisfaction can be achieved without this.

We should guard against the assumption that higher satisfaction is *directly* related to increased continuity. The Know-Your-Midwife [1] report (p. 248) states that 'women feel cherished and supported when they are able to get to know their caregivers'. While the evidence does support the idea that feeling cherished and supported is important to women, the conclusion that this automatically results from getting to know your caregivers is unsupported. It is not an inevitable effect if the caregivers do not behave in a caring way and, conversely, there are other ways of feeling cherished and supported.

Summary

From the comparative studies, there is a fairly consistent finding that study group women report higher levels of satisfaction, although there are exceptions to this. Five of the studies asked about antenatal care, and in four of the five the study group were more satisfied than the control group. Improved satisfaction with intrapartum care is more obvious for the hospital-based schemes. The picture that emerges across the studies is that women in the study groups were more likely to feel that they had a relationship with their carers, that they were listened to and cared about as individuals.

The evidence telling us what aspects of continuity are important to women is patchy, and, in particular, how important it is to a woman that she should be delivered by someone that she already knows. The studies examined give no basis for prioritizing this aspect of continuity over any other. On the present evidence, continuity within the intrapartum period would seem to be more important (Hodnett, 1997).

Women's views and experiences: Questions still to be answered

As with clinical outcomes, we know relatively little about what aspects of care lead to differences in women's satisfaction, although the task of finding out may be less daunting. There is a particular need to address questions about continuity, rather than making assumptions about its benefits. We need to know whether continuity of carer is just a means to ends that could be met in other ways, or whether there are, for example, benefits from developing a close relationship with one caregiver that could not be met in other ways. We also need to know whether continuity has to be 'start-to-finish' to be beneficial, and, if not, when it matters most, and to whom. Finally, we need to know whether the benefits of 'continuity' are, in effect, the benefits of 'woman centred care' or whether separate effects may be operating.

We have been obliged in this section to focus on 'satisfaction' as an outcome, but there are many other aspects of women's behaviour and feelings that might be considered. For example, do the schemes have any impact on postnatal depression or women's confidence in themselves as mothers? These are questions that were addressed by two of the schemes (Know-Your-Midwife [1] and One-to-One [5]). These studies found no differences, but further research is needed. Lower confidence in mothering and negative perceptions of the baby were found in Sikorski et al.'s (1996) RCT of reduced antenatal care [17], which should make us very cautious until we understand more about the determinants of these variables. A number of studies (e.g. Green et al., 1988, 1990; Hodnett and Simmons-Tropea, 1987) suggest that a key variable may be a woman's sense of control. This was also a significant finding in the Know-Your-Midwife study [1]. If this is the case, then it may be that giving women more control over the way in which their maternity care is organized will prove to be effective. An ongoing RCT in Bristol is comparing women who are able to negotiate their pattern of antenatal care with those who are not (see Appendix E), and should shed light on this question.

Other unanswered questions concern whether, from the woman's point of view, a named midwife is better than a pair or vice versa, as suggested by a woman in the Allen et al. (1997) study, or indeed whether the number of midwives matters at all compared with the quality of the care.

Finally we should consider the important question of whether leading women to expect more continuity will mean more disappointment if they do not get their named midwife in labour. The evidence from the Allen et al. (1997) study and from Green et al. (1988) suggest that it may not be a major problem, but further research is needed on this question.

CHAPTER TWELVE

What are the Views and Experiences of the Midwives Who Work in the Schemes?

Evidence from the seven comparative studies

Introduction

Table 12.1: Data gathering from scheme midwives in the seven comparative studies

Know-Your-Midwife [1]	Personal accounts written by the team midwives as an appendix to the report. Questionnaires sent by Head of Midwifery Services to all midwives, but only basic presentation of results (no comparisons).
Home-from-Home [2]	none
Aberdeen Midwives Unit [3]	All midwives in the study completed a form for each delivery that they carried out and rated their own satisfaction with it.
Glasgow MDU [4]	The 21 MDU midwives were compared with 64 other midwives in the hospital (who had been eligible for the MDU but who had continued with their usual pattern of work) using questionnaires sent both before and after implementation.
One-to-One [5]	Ethnographic study of the organizational change based on interviews, focus groups, participant observation and documentary analysis (this was ongoing and only a summary is presented in the report). Appendix details career moves of all midwives who ever worked in the scheme.
West Essex [6]	Unstructured interviews with team leaders/co-ordinators which led to the development of questionnaires that were sent to all community midwives working in teams and all hospital-based midwives.
Scottish Antenatal Care Trial [7]	The study included 'measures of staff satisfaction', but these have not yet been published.

As Table 12.1 shows, six studies collected data from scheme midwives, but the form that this took was very variable. Of these, The Scottish Antenatal Care Trial presented no data and Know-Your-Midwife [1] and One-to-One [5] presented no comparative data.

Comparative data from the seven comparative studies

The Aberdeen Midwives Unit study [3] was unusual because the same midwives worked in both settings, thus the comparison was not between two groups of midwives but the same individuals comparing two settings. This is a very valuable control against pre-existing differences between the groups – we must remember that even in the RCTs *midwives* have not been randomized, and the tendency is for scheme midwives, who are nearly always volunteers, to be younger and more enthusiastic. In the Aberdeen Midwives Unit [3] midwives worked wherever they were needed, but, in practice, this actually meant that higher grade midwives spent more time on the midwives' unit because of the extra responsibility involved. Midwives completed a form for each delivery that they carried out and rated their own satisfaction with it. A multiple regression analysis was then carried out. Many variables were found to predict midwives' satisfaction with a birth. The five most important were:

Positively associated:
• all labour management decisions were made entirely by the midwife at delivery and the woman
• the midwife at delivery was the primary caregiver.

Negatively associated:
• the number of other midwives involved
• medical staff did perineal repair
• complications during labour and delivery.

Neither the trial group allocation nor the area in which birth actually occurred independently predicted midwives' satisfaction. There were many positive comments concerning the satisfaction of being able to give continuity of care. Not being able to do this was more likely to be mentioned by the Labour Ward group (i.e. births that had been allocated to the Labour Ward). Comments to do with low self-esteem were also more common in the Labour Ward group. There were difficulties for some midwives in switching between the two settings. Thus, one midwife who felt that a doctor had queried her vaginal assessment commented:

> 'I'm finding it difficult to work in one area and then the other and know really how responsible to be/how much I can work on my own – personal confidence can be eroded'. (Hundley et al., 1995b, p. 170)

Comparative data also come from the Glasgow MDU [4] study where the 21 MDU midwives were compared with 64 other midwives in the hospital who had been eligible for the MDU but who had continued with their usual pattern of work. Questionnaires which focused on four sets of attitudes, professional satisfaction, professional support, professional development and client interaction, were sent both before and 15 months after implementation. The MDU midwives also received a questionnaire every three months to monitor the programme. All MDU midwives completed every questionnaire. For non-MDU midwives the response was 73 per cent at baseline and 80 per cent at 15 months. There were some demographic differences between the groups. MDU midwives were younger, less experienced and on substantially lower grades: 81 per cent E grade and 19 per cent G compared with 33 per cent E, 16 per cent F and 51 per cent G. Ninety per cent of MDU midwives described their functional area as Hospital, compared to 70 per cent of non-MDU midwives. The findings from the attitudinal data indicate that MDU midwives started with more negative attitudes – consistent with the fact that they had volunteered for a new style of working while the others had not – but that their attitudes had become steadily more positive. At the time of the 15 month assessment, non-MDU midwives attitudes were the same as baseline, while MDU midwives were now significantly more positive than non-MDU.

The final comparison comes from the West Essex [6] study. Questionnaires were sent to 92 midwives working either in community teams or in the hospital. The response rate was 95 per cent for community and 84 per cent for hospital midwives. Community midwives were younger and less likely to be married or to have children, and had fewer years of experience, although there were no differences in the number and types of qualifications held. Correspondingly, the hospital midwives tended to be on higher grades: 47 per cent G, 27 per cent F and 17 per cent E, compared with 28 per cent G, 34 per cent F and 38 per cent E in the community sample. There were differences between the two groups in their ratings of their job satisfaction, although these were not significant as analysed. Nonetheless, Table 12.2 shows that 70 per cent of the community teams expressed high job satisfaction compared with only 47 per cent of those who were hospital-based. Grouping together the two most satisfied reponses compared with the three least satisfied yields a 2x2 Chi-squared analysis significant at $p<0.05$. Community midwives were also more likely to feel that their skills were being fully used and that their job gave them the opportunity to develop their skills.

Table 12.2: Midwives' job satisfaction in West Essex [6]

	community teams (N=49)		hospital based (N=30)	
amount of job satisfaction reported	N	%	N	%
a great deal	15	31	3	10
quite a lot	19	39	11	37
a moderate amount	11	22	13	43
very little	3	6	3	10
none at all	1	2	0	0

constructed from data in Farquar et al., 1996 (pp. 24–25)

The Glasgow Midwifery Process Questionnaire (that used in the Glasgow MDU [4] evaluation) was also administered. The community team midwives were significantly more positive in three of the four areas. The only area where there was no difference was 'professional support' where both groups scored very negatively.

Midwives were asked a large range of other questions including their perceptions of their working relationships with other healthcare workers, which were not found to be significantly different between the groups. They were also asked to agree or disagree with statements about their work. Hospital midwives were significantly more likely to say that their 'skills and knowledge were not fully used' (67% compared to 12%), that they had 'strict guidelines about what I can and cannot do' (54% compared to 18%) and significantly less likely to say that they felt 'happy in the profession of midwifery' (50% compared to 68%). However, more community midwives found that their current post was more disruptive to their family and social life than previous posts (93% compared to 30%). Community midwives were more likely than hospital midwives to think that the quality of care had been affected by the scheme (84% compared to 41%). However, two thirds of these community midwives and eight of the nine hospital midwives thought that care had been *adversely* affected. This is a very important finding that we will return to below when we consider the descriptive data.

The midwives were asked to list up to three things that they liked most about their present post. Most frequently mentioned by the community teams were: using all of their skills (61%), the variety (35%), seeing women at all stages of care (25%) and autonomy/independence/responsibility (25%). Hospital midwives were most likely to mention: support from colleagues (44%), fitting in with their family life (32%), using their experience/skills (24%), and the pleasure of working with mothers and babies (24%).

Asked what they liked *least*, community midwives most frequently mentioned: long hours/on-call/unsociable hours (98%), caring for women from other teams (26%), poor relationship with women because the caseload is too big (18%) and lack of support within the team (14%). Hospital midwives most frequently mentioned: lack of staff (44%), lack of time (22%), low pay/grading (22%) and lack of continuity of care (15%).

These lists are of some interest, particularly those features that the community team midwives liked least which give an eloquent description of the practicalities of their jobs. Similarly, the most frequently mentioned 'dislike' by hospital midwives was lack of staff, which may be exacerbated by transferring posts to the community.

When asked whether they would like to go back to the old way of working, 73 per cent of community midwives said 'no' compared with 38 per cent of hospital midwives. Hospital midwives were much more likely to say 'don't know' (29% compared to 5%).

Descriptive data

Comparative data are of limited usefulness since the groups of midwives are in many ways not comparable. We will therefore continue this section on midwives views by looking at descriptive data, not only from the comparative and multi-scheme descriptive studies, but also from a number of other sources.

Evidence from the seven comparative studies

Descriptive data come from the Know-Your-Midwife [1], One-to-One [5] and West Essex [6] studies. The personal accounts in the Know-Your-Midwife study [1] are effusively positive, which is to be expected from midwives hand-picked for a high profile scheme. In the One-to-One study [5], only a brief summary of midwives' views is presented. The positive features mentioned are very similar to those that we have already seen above: autonomy and the satisfaction of giving continuity of care. None of the scheme midwives wanted to go back to the old way of working. However, the report does also summarize some of the difficulties that midwives say that they encountered. Many of these are seen as being interface problems with the rest of the service. Some of these are to do with the extra administrative work required of the scheme midwives; some to do with caring for women in two hospitals one and a half miles apart. Learning to work without regular shifts was clearly onerous for some midwives, especially in the early stages. This is, of course, a very important issue. The Appendix of the One-to-One report details career moves of all midwives who ever worked in the scheme, 32 over two and a half years, in other words, over half of the midwives left the scheme.

The West Essex study [6], in addition to the comparative data already presented, also presented descriptive data from the scheme midwives. This is particularly valuable because these are not, on the whole, midwives who started out with a strong commitment to working in this sort of way. They are, furthermore, delivering a service to a wide range of women of all levels of risk, and, as we saw above, both hospital and community midwives felt professionally unsupported. We also saw that many felt that the quality of care had deteriorated under the scheme. It was apparent that the midwives felt that the scheme was not working as intended. As one community midwife wrote:

> '... for some women the teams work well. I have had the opportunity to book a woman, see her at parentcraft etc., then have the pleasure of delivering her baby, however this is the minority of women. Most women meet between four and eight midwives antenatally and I don't think that you can say you know your midwife just because you met her once before! At least previously women knew the antenatal/postnatal community midwife – now it is pot luck? ...care in the hospital has really deteriorated due to lack of staff and poor motivation (for example, no promotion opportunities), and everyone is so tired!' (Farquhar et al., 1996, [6])

However, some midwives queried whether it was important to women to be delivered by a known midwife:

'When you are delivering a woman from another team, no-one has complained to me that I'm not from their team. I think knowing a midwife who delivers you is the icing on the cake. I mean you could know her and not like her!' (ibid)

The system of rostering community midwives on-call to the labour ward was clearly not ensuring that women were always delivered by a member of their team. It was also criticized by one midwife

'It is not fair for the midwife to put her life on hold while on-call, be not called out, and then to have to work extra hours in order to make up the hours.' (ibid)

Evidence from the four multi-scheme descriptive studies

The studies by Garcia et al. (1996) and Allen et al. (1997) both included the views of the midwives involved. Their findings were described earlier (Chapter 8, pp. 47, 52–53), and so will only be summarized here. Garcia et al.'s (1996) findings are very similar to those that we have just seen in West Essex [6]. There were similar demographic differences between team and non-team midwives. Team midwives were much more likely than non-team to say that they felt that they were using their midwifery skills to the full and to make positive comments about professional development, although disadvantages were also mentioned. They were more likely to describe their job as 'satisfying' or 'very satisfying' (60% compared to 39%). Team midwives were more likely to report an adverse effect of their job on the rest of their life, but the differences were not large.

The Allen et al. (1997) study included interviews with the midwives, including those who had left. The midwives had generally joined the scheme because of disaffection with their old way of working, wanting more autonomy and wanting to work with a team that had a shared philosophy. Thus they were on the whole rather more committed to their schemes than those in the last two studies that we have considered. The main points that emerged concerned group dynamics and the demanding nature of the job which in Ashford had led to changes to on-call arrangements: 'We were getting too tired. We were too ambitious. We took it literally – 24 hour cover'. There was a shift in emphasis over time from continuity of carer to continuity of care, although by some midwives more than others. Although job satisfaction was high, there were reservations in all the practices about the replicability of the scheme because they thought that other midwives would not wish to work this way. Relationships with hospital midwives were universally reported as a problem.

Evidence from other studies

A very important study of midwives experiences of different ways of working has recently been published by Sandall (1997) [18]. She interviewed midwives working in three different models of care:

- 'City' – independent group practice (7/7interviewed);

- 'Woodhurst' – traditional community midwifery (19/23 interviewed);

- 'Patchville' – community teams (six whole time equivalent in each of four teams – 22/28 interviewed including some who had recently left).

Three main themes emerged from the interviews: occupational autonomy, social support and developing meaningful relationships with women. The study was particularly concerned with 'burnout', which nine of the 48 midwives across the three schemes identified themselves as experiencing.

> 'Oh work… I can't be bothered with it really, and that's sad. You see, as a midwife, at a birth where you think "Oh just get on with it and have the baby. I want to go home, I've had enough". And I think that's why I'm taking a break. I'm getting to the point where I think I can't be bothered, and I felt I'd a lot to offer these women, it's robbed me of the absolute joy I had in that job beforehand. I don't think I'll ever go back to clinical work. I don't miss it one bit and that's made me very very bitter, that it's done that to me.' (Sandall, 1997[18], p. 107)

Another midwife in Patchville noted the devastating impact on staff:

> 'Sophie started and left after six months, she couldn't deal with on call. Sarah just got burnt out, she'd been in the job for quite a few years and was finding the on call such an intrusion on her life and she's gone in a different direction. Sally, same thing, she's been in the team for quite a long time now and she's fed up and getting burnt out, so she's going to do job share. Caroline, she'd been with us for quite a few years as well, was off sick for three months, burnt out or whatever. She's left now, handed in her notice; doesn't want to come back either.' (ibid, p. 107)

Midwives who lived near their work found it easier to balance or integrate home and work. All the midwives said that the amount of stress they felt was related to the degree of control they had over how they worked rather than to the actual workload itself. They felt that they had more control over a personal caseload than a shared team caseload.

> 'The only thing that you have to worry about is births. Everything else you can fit in absolutely to your own life…' (ibid, p. 108)

Providing continuity of care was a source of satisfaction to the midwives while inability to develop a relationship was a source of frustration and stress. Continuity occurred more for the group practice than for the patch team. The Woodhurst midwives did develop relationships, and with a bigger caseload, but did not attend births.

The independent midwives said that although they were on call a lot, they did not get night calls except for births because (a) women knew them and therefore treated them with consideration and (b) they anticipated problems and could spend more time with the women earlier to avert problems. In contrast Patchville midwives implied that women called for trivial things.

Organizational practices that fostered team building and collegial support suffered less burnout and less staff turnover. Midwives in all sites cited support from colleagues as one of the greatest stress reducers. Patchville midwives met each other less frequently and lacked team spirit. In all three settings the following factors were associated with burnout:

- lack of colleague support

- more fragmented client contact

- workload too high

- idealistic expectations

- lack of emotional or social support at home.

The opposite was high levels of personal accomplishment, which was associated with:

- being assertive in agreeing clear expectations of work and practice with colleagues, women and at home

- having collegial support at work and social and emotional support at home

- being able to establish meaningful relationships with women

- having clearly defined time off work and outside interests.

Sandall concludes that:

> 'The implications are that continuity of carer is as important to midwives as it is to women and that personal caseloads incorporating regular time off may be more sustainable in terms of less burnout and greater personal accomplishment than team caseload.' (ibid, p. 111)

Another recent study, however, would challenge the desirability of individual caseloads from the midwives' point of view. Pankhurst (1995) [19] reports on two midwifery group practices trying to institute caseload midwifery within one health Trust in south-east England. One was urban ('Redham') and one rural ('Greenfields'). Both used 'Bluebell' Hospital. The schemes covered high and low-risk mothers regardless of lead professional.

The Redham group was based on one GP practice, four miles from the hospital. The team consisted of four midwives (1 G grade, 2 F, 1 E) and they practised in pairs. One would be on call for 24 hours for the whole group. They were not responsible for postnatal beds but were supposed to be coming in to give antenatal and postnatal ward care to their women (who tended to go home as soon as possible). The Greenfields team was based at the Greenfields cottage hospital, 13 miles from Bluebell hospital. This had a two-bed postnatal ward, for which the team were responsible. Staffing consisted of three full-time and a varying number (one to three) of part-time midwives over the study period, due to staff turnover and sickness. Midwives worked a seven and a half hour day, including a lateshift if there was an evening parentcraft class. One would be on call for 24 hrs for the whole group. Initially, another midwife would be second on call as well, but this was changed after the first six months so that the second on call was for home births only. At the time of the study, the hospital was being renovated and 14 midwives were on maternity leave.

The evaluation of these schemes is of a different style from those that we saw for the comparative studies, being largely qualitative and based on repeated interviews throughout the study period with all stakeholders particularly the midwives. The study found that both schemes were encountering difficulties, but that these were more severe for the Greenfields team. Neither group found that caseloads worked, in practice they were delivering team midwifery.

> 'I suppose we're not actually working as caseload envisaged us, where you had your own specific women and you looked after them. If a lady goes into labour and she's "my" woman, and I'm on duty, I'll go in to Labour Ward during my shift – nine to five – if at five o'clock she's not doing anything, I would then go off-duty and the on-call person takes over from me, whereas if she was imminent, I would stay and look after her until she was done and dusted. But if I happen to be off-duty that day when she went into labour, they wouldn't call me to come and look after her – whoever is on-call would take her care. So in many ways it's more of a team than caseload. ...Caseload officially would be three women at term per month that you are responsible for, which gives you your thirty-six per annum, but we can't do it like that, ...the problem is [that] when they come up to delivery, you'd [have to] be on-call constantly, twenty-four hours a day, seven days a week, for your three women of that month and some might be late and some might be early. We don't want to be on-call constantly seven days a week.' (Pankhurst, 1995) [19])

The Redham group had a shared philosophy and a team identity and got on well together. One had previously been the community midwife associated with the GP practice at which they were based and was already known and trusted. Good relationships continued between the GP practice and the midwifery team. In contrast, the Greenfields midwives felt that they were on their own from the start. The planned induction session was cancelled because of heavy hospital workload, and they felt that they had had no guidance, for example, about the best way of organizing themselves. The team had an inexperienced team leader with no team management experience and the group did not have a shared ideal of what they were trying to achieve. Although they got on well initially, and communication was helped by weekly meetings, relationships became stressed by workload peaks when midwives started having to miss meetings and resented decisions taken in their absence. They also experienced problems of group dynamics; mixed relationships with GPs and problematic relationships with core midwifery staff at the hospital. They felt that there was no approachable group with whom they could discuss ongoing problems.

The Greenfields group, serving as they did a rural area, spent a considerable amount of time travelling, covering 400 to 500 miles per month. They found that they had to rely much more on core labour ward midwives than the Redham group partly because of longer transit times to the hospital. Some core midwives were seen as unsupportive and this was a particular problem for inexperienced midwives. Labour ward relationships were, in part, a function of pre-existing relationships. Group midwives who had themselves previously worked there and knew and got on with the core staff experienced fewer problems.

Some women felt neglected on the wards, feeling that core staff felt that they were not their responsibility. Some scheme midwives also felt that it was inefficient for them to deliver postnatal care to women at the hospital:

> 'It's better to have somebody who understands about postnatal wards, in general keeping an overview. It must be quite chaotic actually, hundreds of midwives all going in at nine o'clock one day, to all these postnatal women. That's a waste of resources because, two midwives going to see these twenty women. It is a better use of resources than thirty midwives getting in their cars, driving ten miles to see these women because they've wasted fifteen minutes in their cars, fifteen minutes back again so they've wasted half an hour of work.' (Pankhurst, 1995) [19])

We will conclude this review of 'other studies' by drawing on three that have already been discussed in Chapter 11 (women's views). Lee (1994) [13] interviewed 12 midwives who thought that their bleep system was good but reported an adverse effect on their social life of being on-call. Relationships with and support from colleagues was highly rated and all but one midwife expressed high job satisfaction. Two thirds thought that it was more important to get to know a woman well, even if they then did not deliver her, than to deliver a woman they had met but did not know well. They felt that feeling comfortable with a woman did not mean having to have met her before.

Currell (1985, 1990) [10] interviewed 95 midwives. She found that, as with mothers, midwives' satisfaction was related to successful problem solving and the giving of 'focused care'. She reported that midwives had difficulty reconciling the medical 'cure' aspects of maternity care with the less specific 'care' aspects of midwifery. This was most easily achieved in labour and least successful antenatally. She suggests that the concept of 'continuity of care' should be replaced with the concept of 'unity of care', with care centred on each woman rather than on the organization or the providers of the service.

In the South Camden study [15] (Fleissig and Kroll, 1996) questionnaires were completed by 25 of the 28 community midwives, including 13 of the 15 who had worked in the local community before the introduction of the scheme. Midwives felt that the quality of care that they were now delivering was worse than under the old DOMINO scheme but better in that they were now extending community midwifery to more women. They were concerned at their inability to visit women at home in early labour leading to women coming to hospital earlier. Some friction with hospital staff was reported, although 15 of the 25 felt supported by core staff. It was felt that the system had been introduced too quickly and that there were administrative problems. Their system was criticized as being too vulnerable to one midwife's absence (e.g. holidays and study days) and not having enough core (hospital) staff. F grade midwives thought that they should be on G grade. A change to two shifts was welcomed for reducing the amount of time on call. All the midwives liked working in pairs.

Many said that they got a lot of job satisfaction and all except four said that their present job was rewarding. However, 18 said it was stressful 'some of the time' and seven 'all of the time'. Twenty-one said that their personal lives were adversely affected by their work. When asked what work they wanted to be doing in a year's time, only half said 'the same as now'. Some felt that they should care only for low-risk women and that they were not able to give them a good enough service if had to look after high-risk women as well.

In summary

Comparative data from two of the seven comparative studies show that study group midwives were generally younger and on lower grades but were more satisfied with their jobs than those working in other settings. What these midwives seemed to appreciate was working autonomously and delivering continuity of care. In the Aberdeen Midwives Unit [3] study this was the major determinant of midwives satisfaction, rather than the setting in which they worked.

Descriptive data reinforce the earlier data in suggesting that midwives' satisfaction in the schemes comes primarily from using their skills, autonomy and developing a relationship with women. Nonetheless there is also a consistent message that the new style of working interferes with midwives' social and domestic lives and is stressful. The dynamics of the group within which they work is very important to the midwives and is potentially their main source of social support, but may also be an added source of stress. Midwives in most schemes were reporting tensions with hospital based core midwives. This is in part due to a reduction of staffing levels in the hospital in order to create the schemes. In two schemes community midwives felt that the quality of care that they were now delivering was worse than it had been previously.

Midwives' views: Questions still to be answered

Unfortunately, we have only limited descriptive data from the schemes which are less disruptive to midwives' lives such as the Glasgow MDU [4] or the Aberdeen Midwives unit [3]. It may be that these forms of care offer midwives the same advantages as the community based schemes without the same degree of disruption to their lives. This requires further investigation. The relative lack of comparative data make it difficult to know how atypical the scheme midwives really are and the extent to which other midwives share their values. This will be examined further in the following chapter. Nicky Leap (1994), a midwife in the South East London Midwifery Group Practice, invited comments from other midwives on caseload holding within the NHS, and received 100 replies, both from midwives with and without experience of caseload working. The report of their views, which were generally very positive, makes interesting reading, but needs to be repeated with a representative, rather than self-selected, sample.

CHAPTER THIRTEEN

What are the Views and Experiences of Other Healthcare Workers?

Evidence from the seven comparative studies

Data collection methods from staff other than scheme midwives in each of the seven comparative studies are summarized in Table 13.1.

Table 13.1: Data gathering from other staff in the seven comparative studies

Know-Your-Midwife [1]	Towards the end of the scheme, the Head of Midwifery Services at St George's sent a questionnaire to all staff working in the unit, whether or not they had worked directly with the scheme, but the report includes only basic presentation of results.
Home-from-Home [2]	none
Aberdeen Midwives Unit [3]	none
Glasgow MDU [4]	survey of all obstetricians involved
One-to-One [5]	Ethnographic study of the organizational change based on interviews, focus groups, participant observation and documentary analysis included staff other than the scheme's midwives (this was ongoing and only a summary is presented in the report).
West Essex [6]	Unstructured interviews with team leaders/co-ordinators which led to the development of questionnaires that were sent to all GPs and Health Visitors in West Essex as well as all hospital-based midwives and community midwives working in teams.
Scottish Antenatal Care Trial [7]	The study included 'measures of staff satisfaction', which may include staff other than the scheme midwives, but these have not yet been published.

Four of the comparative studies present the views of other healthcare workers. In the Know-Your-Midwife study [1] this is limited to presentation of frequencies from a questionnaire sent to a mixture of staff which invited a judgement of the satisfactoriness of KYM midwives' relationships with various other groups. Unfortunately, this tells us little about how doctors or other midwives, for example, felt that they themselves were affected. Happily this was done in the other three studies.

At the Glasgow MDU [4], a survey of obstetricians was carried out during the first ten months of implementation, before the results of the RCT were known (Cheyne et al., 1995). All obstetricians concerned with the care of low-risk women were included (11 consultants, four senior registrars and five registrars). The 35-item questionnaire was developed after interviews with the consultants and consisted of statements with a five-point response from strongly agree to strongly disagree. The statements were about midwife-led care generally and the Glasgow MDU in particular. Responses to the first section were fairly predictable – generally agreeing that midwives were competent to give care, but not wanting to be completely excluded and believing that women want a doctor's in\voyementi. Regarding the MDU implementation, half thought that it could have been managed better and concern was expressed about the exclusion of the GP. Only half said that they felt that they could trust the midwives' clinical judgment but none were dissatisfied with the standard of care. Over 60% were confident that MDU midwives would refer when necessary; 30% thought they over-referred; 45% thought that they referred for trivial things. Eighty per cent thought that they needed a lot of informal support from the obstetric team.

The One-to-One study [5] reports briefly on the views of other caregivers. Tensions with the hospital-based midwives were clearly a major issue, with the feeling that One-to-One was taking resources away from them and that the scheme midwives got in the way on the labour ward. There was a feeling that scheme midwives were privileged in only having to look after one woman in labour while hospital midwives had to care for several, and resentment at having to give in-patient care to scheme women, which was also mentioned in the Know-Your-Midwife study [1]. As we have seen earlier from the accounts of scheme midwives, and even of the women, these sorts of tensions were universal for the community-based schemes. The implementation of One-to-One displaced a number of community midwives from their jobs. This meant not only the loss of considerable local knowledge and contacts but resentment and a feeling of inadequate consultation. Medical staff expressed support for the scheme, but they were concerned about whether midwives would be able to work in this way. However, several were appreciative of the extra time that they now had to concentrate on high-risk women. They did, however, report tensions on the delivery suite and felt uncomfortable not knowing what was going on.

In West Essex [6], as we have already seen, hospital midwives felt under-resourced, and their suggestions for improvement included: employing more midwives, correcting the skill-mix and raising the profile of the hospital service in line with the community.

GPs views were also sought. They were in favour of community-based care, but were not convinced that the system was working. It was felt that the size of team was critical. A woman may meet seven midwives from her team in pregnancy and then not be delivered by any of them. Thus, continuity is reduced, and more caregivers meant more conflicting advice. Some GPs thought that 'team midwifery' meant the GP and midwife worked together as a team, or an interdisciplinary team. Some did not know that they had a link midwife. Only 40% had met all of their team. Over half said that they would prefer to go back to the old way of working because the communication between midwife and GP was better. Half the GPs thought that the service had deteriorated as a result of teams because of less continuity for women. Health visitors gave very similar responses to the GPs. They too would prefer the old system because of better communication between health visitors and midwives, and also felt that the new system was worse because of lack of continuity. Consultant obstetricians were interviewed and were positive about the way that their time was released for seeing high-risk women. However, they were concerned at the effect of this on Senior House Officers, particularly GP trainees, who were getting a very biased view of obstetrics through not seeing normal women.

Evidence from the four multi-scheme descriptive studies

The Allen et al. (1997) study reports on interviews with 38 GPs in the three sites. This was described in Chapter 8 (pp. 53–4) and so will only be summarized. In brief, GPs were concerned that they were being excluded. This was felt to be bad for the woman – the GP would not know what had been going on if a woman developed a problem – and bad for the GPs too in that they were losing their skills. Some thought that there should have been more GP input initially and more ongoing communication: '..a lot of goodwill on the part of the GPs has evaporated, possibly beyond repair'.

Evidence from other studies

The South Camden study [15] surveyed the views of GPs, consultant obstetricians and core midwives. These surveys are, unfortunately, not very illuminating. Six of the eight core labour ward midwives responded. As in West Essex [6], short staffing and uneven skill mix, especially at nights, were raised as problems. They also raised the question of where the community midwives should be when on-call. Some core staff felt that they should be on the labour ward so that they could give reciprocal help if 'their' women did not need them, and be readily available if they did. Evidently the community midwives' response to this was that they should be at home or in the community so that they could give community-based care as needed.

The study by Pankhurst [19] also sought the views of hospital midwives, throughout the study period. Initially, there was resentment by those midwives who saw themselves as excluded from the scheme.

> 'It is assumed that it will involve a lot of on call work and call out at night and, therefore, people who have families who are young and dependent upon them for care, such as midwives with school age children, feel very resentful that they can't even apply for these jobs. How can they afford the necessary child care to cover any eventuality out of 24 hours? So they feel that the whole scheme discriminates against them and they feel very very hurt and there have definitely been two midwives who have said to me they don't hold a grudge

against me personally, but they just think it's all right for me. I can apply. They can't. They feel the choice has been taken from them in this whole scheme which is about choice for women. And they feel very upset.'

and

'The hospital staff didn't think it was a good idea and I got the impression that they were hoping that it wouldn't work and they were being very negative, because they don't want to do this. This is what will happen. If it's proved to be a success, then they will be forced to do it so the aim is that they will all come out and they don't want to.' (Pankhurst, 1995, [19])

They also raised grading issues and felt that E grade midwives should not be given that much responsibility. If they are fit for it they should be upgraded, otherwise they should not be doing it. Six of the caseload midwives had been recruited from the hospital but had not been replaced when the scheme started.

In Redham one GP was very enthusiastic:

'We are extremely fortunate in this practice that the midwife who's been with us throughout is fantastic, and there's never been any question in our minds that she would do anything detrimental to the doctor/patient relationship... and I think that the midwives who have joined her are going to be equally as good.'

and this excellent relationship continued throughout. Other GPs were less happy, raising similar issues to those in the Allen et al. (1997) study: that the lack of GP involvement was detrimental to women and deskilled the GP.

In summary

A number of studies have sought the views of other healthcare workers. A common finding, as we saw earlier from the accounts of the scheme midwives, is of friction with the core hospital staff. The extent of this is likely to relate to many local details as well as to core staffing levels which are often felt to be inadequate. GPs are not, on the whole, antagonistic, but are concerned about their exclusion from normal antenatal care.

Other healthcare workers' views: Questions still to be answered

Changes in the organization of a midwifery service have ramifications for many other people. The most obvious, non-scheme midwives, GPs and obstetricians, have been considered in a number of the studies that we have reviewed. The extent of their disquiet, particularly the first two groups, argues for further consideration of their views. GP support is likely to be crucial for community-based schemes, and further study is needed of the conditions which help and hinder a smooth working relationship between GPs and midwives. Other groups' views have received less consideration, for example, health visitors. A particularly notable omission is information about the views of administrative support staff, who may be severely affected by changes of the sort that we have been considering. Such staff are in a position to make the running of any scheme either much easier or much more difficult. More should be known about their views.

Another group of people who may be affected are student midwives and doctors in training, particularly GP trainees. Some schemes (e.g. One-to-One [5]) have specifically integrated them, but in most studies they are not mentioned. While a midwifery service should not be organized primarily around their needs, we need to be aware of how their training may be affected.

CHAPTER FOURTEEN

What are the Costs?

Methodological issues

When resources for health care are finite, information about the process and outcomes of different patterns of care (including clinical and pyschosocial outcomes) needs to be supplemented by information from economic evaluations, if rational choices are to be made between alternative patterns of midwifery care. The aim of economic evaluations is clearly stated by Jefferson et al. (1996, p.12):

> 'Complete economic evaluations aim to clarify, quantify and value all the relevant options, and their inputs and consequences.'

However, practice is often tempered by pragmatism and evaluations tend to be somewhat less ambitious. Nevertheless a common process underlies the practice of all economic evaluations which attempt to:

*   identify inputs
*   measure these inputs against appropriate physical units
*   place a value upon each unit of input (Jefferson et al., 1996).

What types of economic evaluation are available?

A range of methods are discernible for quantifying and valuing inputs and consequences of health care and these are summarized in Box 5.

Box 5: Methods of economic evaluation
Cost-minimization analysis (CMA) – when the consequences of the intervention are the same, then only inputs are taken into consideration. The aim is to decide the cheapest way of achieving the same outcome.   **Cost-effectiveness analysis (CEA)** – when the consequences of different interventions may vary but can be measured in identical units, then inputs are costed. Competing interventions are compared in terms of cost per unit of consequence.   **Cost-utility analysis (CUA)** – when interventions which we compare produce different consequences in terms of both quantity and quality of life, we express them in utilities. These are measures which comprise both length of life and subjective levels of well-being (the best known utility measure is the quality-adjusted-life-years or QALYs). In this case, competing interventions are compared in terms of cost per unit of utility gained (for example, cost per QALY).

> **Cost-benefit analysis (CBA)** – when both the inputs and consequences of different interventions are expressed in monetary units so that they compare directly and across programmes even outside health care.
>
> *from Jefferson et al., 1996 (pp. 12–13)*

There is, however, some debate about the most appropriate method to be employed in assessing the costs of different patterns of midwifery-service organization. While Piercy and Downe (1995) point to the need to ensure the cost-effectiveness of interventions, and their long-term sustainability, Garcia et al. (1996) suggest that it is opportunity costs that are the most appropriate indicators for economic evaluation: opportunity costs focus attention upon the relative utility of one pattern of resource allocation against another possible (or actual) use of the same resources.

> 'The opportunity costs of using the resources in one way is the benefit foregone because they are denied for another use. If it can be shown that they would achieve greater benefit in that other use, then resources are being used inefficiently.' (Clark et al., 1991)

However, as Garcia et al. (1996) acknowledge, opportunity costs are notoriously difficult to measure. For maternity services, where evaluation is likely to emphasize the importance of psychosocial outcomes and measures of satisfaction, determination of opportunity costs becomes particularly problematic. As a proxy measure, evaluations of different patterns of midwifery care tend to focus upon financial costs. While, ideally, these should be definable, identifiable and capable of being costed for both tangible items (equipment, premises, drugs, ambulances, materials) and intangible items (time, knowledge, and know-how) (Jefferson et al., 1996), in practice, financial costs tend to be associated only with 'hard' or tangible items. Garcia et al. (1996) and Piercy and Downe (1995) suggest that, as a minimum, if financial costs are to provide useful insights they must be able to measure changes in the physical resources (staff, buildings, equipment) needed to operate the new care scheme and changes in the resources utilized.

The sensitivity of economic analyses, and therefore the extent to which these can give meaningful information for the evaluation of different patterns of service delivery, will be contingent upon the availability of data. Real or potential problems with routinely collected activity data have been highlighted, as have problems with, and inconsistencies in, the generation of costings. Greater sensitivity of costings may require routinely collected information to be supplemented with additional data collection.

Evidence from the multi-scheme descriptive studies

In this section of the report, analyses contained in the multi-scheme studies are reviewed before the seven comparative studies as they offer important pointers to the difficulties and pitfalls that researchers may encounter in undertaking economic evaluations. As Table 14.1 illustrates, three of the four multi-scheme descriptive studies include some discussion of costs. In the case of Wraight et al. (1993) this is not extensive for they are able to do little more than note that few schemes had formally evaluated the costs of team midwifery or were in a position to identify the costs associated with running a team scheme (Wraight et al., 1993, p. 67).

Table 14.1: Analysis of costs in the multi-scheme descriptive studies

	Costs analysis: Included	Costs analysis: Not included
Wraight et al., 1993	✓	
Stock & Wraight, 1993		✓
Garcia et al., 1996	✓	
Allen et al., 1997	✓	

Costing mechanisms: defining the service

A fundamental issue is raised by Allen et al. (1997). They highlight the difficulties inherent in identifying and measuring the parameters of particular schemes of midwifery care. Even within one Health Region (South East Thames Regional Health Authority) inconsistencies were revealed in the categories employed in defining services and costing for maternity care contracts.

Of the three midwifery group practice schemes that were subjected to evaluation:

• two schemes (Lewisham and JACANES) operated under contractual arrangements that did not show the midwifery group practice separately from the total service purchased

• the services of the self-employed midwives in the third scheme (Deptford) were purchased directly by two neighbouring purchasing commissions (Table 14.2).

Information about the three schemes was collected with some difficulty. In collating the information provided by both purchasers and providers, the report's authors note that information given was fragmentary, subject to different interpretation by purchaser and provider and, at times, considered to be of questionable reliability.

As Allen et al. (1997) point out, the cost bases of different schemes may be quite different and this, they argue, makes comparisons of costs between schemes inappropriate. However, Piercy (1995) notes that it is not only differences in provider – purchaser arrangements that render direct comparisons of local financial costs between schemes meaningless. The amount of 'hard cash' required locally will also vary according to the service configuration and local pay arrangements.

Table 14.2: Costing mechanisms: categories used in contracting for three midwifery group practice schemes

	Categories used for contracting purposes by relevant purchasers
Lewisham Maternity Focus	i. *Obstetric outpatients:* hospital out-patient/clinic based antenatal and postnatal attendances. ii. *Obstetric delivery:* everything that happened when a woman was in contact with the hospital on an inpatient basis: including antenatal, intrapartum and postnatal care. The purchasing authority purchased against deliveries, not finished consultant episodes (FCEs). It was estimated that one delivery on average was equivalent to 1.5 episodes of inpatient care per person. iii. *Community Midwifery:* included the total cost of the community service purchased by the purchasing authority: made up of direct costs with no hospital overheads included. This cost included the midwifery group practice midwives who transferred into the midwifery group practice and were not additional to the establishment.
JACANES midwifery group practice, Ashford	i. *Obstetric outpatients:* purchased on a hospital out-patient attendance basis, usually at consultants' clinics. ii. *Obstetric inpatients:* purchased on a Finished Consultant Episode (FCE) basis and not deliveries. FCE included deliveries and other in-patient stays involving the consultant. Therefore, FCEs did not equal the number of births. iii. *Community Midwifery:* some discrepancies as to the definitions used and the interpretations used between Trust and purchaser. Contract based on indicative contacts, domiciliary visits and sessions: initially based on what the midwives had recorded for the year before instigation of the scheme.
Deptford midwifery group practice	Contract for episodes of care: the period from initial booking up to and including the postnatal period (postnatal period referred to the period of time up to 28 days after birth).

(Constructed from data in Allen et al., 1997)

While direct replication of financial costs between localities is unlikely, the change in resource utilization produced by a new scheme of midwifery organization *may* be able to be reproduced under similar conditions elsewhere. Economic evaluations therefore need to focus upon resource utilization rather than local financial costs (Piercy 1995, p. 629).

Activity and resource data

Garcia et al. (1996) provide one example of how routinely collected health service data can be used to identify resource utilization. They describe the use of information derived from one hospital's Minimum Data Set (MDS). Each hospital must maintain a MDS in which basic hospital information is collected. This can be used to trace hospital activity and to outline associated resource use (Table 14.3).

Table 14.3: Examples of information derived from one hospital's Minimum Data Set: Method of delivery and length of stay (LOS)

Type of delivery	Number	% of total deliveries	Mean LOS (days)
Elective c/s	99	5.0	5.7
Emergency c/s	154	7.7	6.8
Forceps	43	2.2	3.3
Vacuum	42	2.1	3.0
Normal	1557	78.2	2.4
Other	96	4.8	4.2
Total	1991	100	3.0

(Source: Garcia et al., 1996 p. 21)

In Garcia et al.'s analysis, MDS information was used for the following:

- to calculate total number of bed days required for different patterns of delivery
- to calculate the number of beds, by using an appropriate bed-occupancy rate (Sorenson, 1996)
- to identify changes in hospital resources associated with changes in midwives' practices (particularly, admissions and length of stay).

As Garcia et al. (1996) point out, however, even accessing information can be problematic. For their evaluation of new midwifery practices, information was only forthcoming from one of the two hospitals that were participating in the economic evaluation. (Since this study, however, the introduction of healthcare resource groups has led to a substantial improvement in this situation in many areas.)

In addition to the difficulties with access, a number of limitations were associated with, or inherent in the information that was available from the MDS:

- problems with accuracy were encountered, including duplicate records and difficulties in separating antenatal, intrapartum and postnatal admissions.
- MDS data provide a broad picture of hospital care, but little information about process or intensity of care and nothing about community activity.
- little information may be available about outpatient attendances (e.g. antenatal clinic appointments).

Information about costs

Cost information for particular schemes may be derived from finance departments of provider units. The sensitivity of available information for assessing the costs associated with maternity care tends to be very limited as information is often not collected in a manner that enables individual procedures to be defined, quantified and costed. Collation tends to be at the level of speciality cost centres such as out-patients, ward costs and community midwifery costs. These are broken down into fixed, semi-fixed and variable costs.

'The breakdown of costs into fixed, semi-fixed and variable is crucial, as it is the only indicator of cost savings associated with marginal changes in activity. The reason for this is that only variable costs change directly with changes in activity. Semi-fixed costs change if the activity changes enough (by a significant amount, not usually marginal changes), whilst fixed costs do not vary at all within a given period, usually taken to be a year.'(Garcia et al., 1996, p. 22)

Breakdown of costs into cost types

Garcia et al. (1996) describe the information provided by one of the evaluation sites for the Changing Midwifery Care Report. Data were supplied for wards, delivery suite, outpatients and community (Table 14.4).

Table 14.4: Hospital costs: breakdown by type in one provider unit

	Fixed %	Semi-fixed %	Variable %
Inpatient	17.9	77.4	4.7
Outpatient	42.0	49.7	8.3
Community	24.9	73.5	1.6
Total	23.4	71.8	4.8

(Source: Garcia et al., 1996)

For all costs centres, variable costs account for a small percentage of total costs.

Garcia et al. clearly point out the implications of this break down:

'the proportion of variable costs to total costs is low, hence marginal changes, such as the closure of one or two beds in a ward will not release much in terms of costs or resources freed for other uses. Certainly, the released costs will be far lower than the average cost per case or bed day as identified from top-down costing alone. This must be borne in mind when considering transfers of resources from hospital to community settings.' (Garcia et al., 1966, p. 22)

Their analysis suggests that only substantial and sustained changes to the organization of midwifery services are likely to be reflected in significant changes in costs and that, conversely, many of the evaluations reviewed in this report are, at best, likely to demonstrate only very marginal changes in costs. Rolling out of pilot schemes to embrace a more substantial proportion of maternity care provision would enable an effect on semi-fixed costs to be demonstrated. But as the subsequent discussion of the comparative studies demonstrates, this opportunity is rarely available.

Summary of issues from multi-scheme descriptive studies

In 'Mapping Team Midwifery', Wraight et al. (1993) note that only seven (five per cent) of the 141 schemes that they identified had undertaken any form of economic analysis and in the broader literature, few evaluations report on costs.

From Allen et al. (1997) (adapted from text pp. 224–25)

- detailed comparisons between different schemes may not be appropriate when the cost bases are quite different
- midwifery services may be organized according to quite different definitions and pricing structures for an episode of care
- the apparent 'cost-effectiveness' of a service is partly dependent upon how overheads are apportioned. Cross-subsidisation and hidden overheads can influence the apparent cost-effectiveness of a scheme that is integral to the total obstetric and midwifery services provided by a Trust. This would not be the case with independent midwifery services which effectively operate as a business partnership and which would have to produce full income and expenditure accounts
- duplication of costs might occur where women cross boundaries. Duplication could also arise between providers of midwifery services and General Practice item of service payments for maternity care.

From Garcia et al. (1996) (p. 23):

- Minimum Data Sets can be useful as they provide basic information about hospital activity. However, in requesting information from this source, it is crucial for the researcher to specify exactly which data are required, and in what format they would like the data to be sent
- there can be differences or discrepancies between MDS and locally held information, e.g. delivery suite information. If discrepancies exist, they will need to be identified and followed up
- hospitals often collect substantially more data than would be held on a MDS particularly for pathology and other diagnostic procedures
- this information is potentially useful, and is often patient specific, even though its primary use is for contract and activity monitoring. The scope and quality of information available will vary between hospitals
- cost information is usually only available on a top-down basis. It should, however, be split into various cost centres, e.g. wards, theatre, and into broad resource categories, e.g. midwives, clinicians, overheads. It will also be disaggregated into fixed, semi-fixed and variable costs
- undertaking more detailed costing requires large amounts of additional data collection, either through casenote analysis or if the evaluation is prospective, through following women throughout their care and recording resource use. The area in which this type of exercise is likely to be of greatest value is in identifying and analysing midwives' workloads, ensuring that they are not being asked to work unreasonable hours and that community midwifery is adequately staffed. This is particularly important in caseload midwifery.
- using routinely available finance data to analyse small or specific changes is likely to be very insensitive. For example, in estimating trade-offs or changes in resource use patterns, average costs such as average cost per bed if bed

requirement falls will not be released. Only a proportion of average cost is released, usually variable costs and if the changes are sufficiently large, some part of semi-fixed costs. Fixed costs, by definition, are fixed and will not change in the short run. To identify which costs can be released, discussions with finance and managerial staff will be needed.

Evidence from the seven comparative studies

The majority of the comparative studies reviewed in the Results section of this report have undertaken some form of economic analysis, as indicated in Table 14.5.

Table 14.5: Analysis of costs in the seven comparative studies

	Costs analysis: Included	Costs analysis: Not included
Know-Your-Midwife (KYM) [1]	✓	
Home-from-Home [2]		✓
Aberdeen Midwives Unit [3]	✓	
Glasgow (MDU) [4]	✓	
One-to-One [5]	✓	
West Essex [6]		✓
Scottish Antenatal Care Trial [7]	✓ (Not yet reported)	

Information collected (Table 14.6)

Three of the four comparative studies undertaking economic analysis sought and received routinely collected data (Aberdeen Midwives Unit [3], Glasgow MDU [4], One-to-One [5]). The source of some information used in the evaluation of the Know-Your-Midwife study [1] is not specified. However, it is clear that all of the comparative studies undertook additional data collection. Casenote review was used by all. This is clearly a labour intensive method of data collection and some studies concentrated their data extraction on a sample of the total study population (Know-Your-Midwife [1] and One-to-One [5]).

Some of the studies also increased the sensitivity of their data collection by using other sources of information. Questionnaires to women (Aberdeen Midwives Unit [3] and Glasgow MDU [4]) and questionnaires or logs completed by midwives (Aberdeen Midwives Unit [3], Glasgow MDU [4], One-to-One [5]) provide potentially reliable sources of information about care received by women.

Activities/resources considered (Table 14.7)

The extent to which studies draw upon activity data to assess resource use varies considerably. The Know-Your-Midwife [1] evaluation is relatively restricted while, by contrast, the Glasgow MDU [4] and One-to One [5] use a broad range of activity measures. These include, for example, antenatal visits, day care attendances, admissions, instrumental and operative deliveries and use of epidurals. These are used to assess resource use in the study location. However, definitions are not always given and it is possible that what appears to be the same activity may have been subject to different interpretations in each of the study locations.

Table 14.6: Information collected in economic evaluations of comparative studies

Know-Your-Midwife [1]	• data from small sub-group of women due to deliver in September and October 1994 • case note review for e.g. audit of carers, number of epidurals • source of information re. some costings of antenatal admission per day and of equipment for accelerating labour not specified.
Aberdeen Midwives Unit [3]	• prospective data collection via: questionnaires to women: short questionnaire completed by midwife at delivery • medical records review • audit of theatre records • hospital statistics • Scottish Morbidity Register (SMR2) data from the Aberdeen Maternity and Neonatal Databank • administrative data on costs of different services and resources • ad-hoc questionnaire to collect information about length of time taken to suture the perineum • professional consultation to estimate amount of medical and paediatric time involved in assisted vaginal delivery and the amount of anaesthetic time used in setting up for an epidural (NB: cost of an epidural was calculated using setting up time only).
Glasgow MDU [4]	• case records review • resource management information from the hospital • self-report questionnaire from women • conjoint analysis questionnaire to 143 women from MDU group and 142 from shared care group.
One-to-One [5]	• computerized records of hospital activities to identify key areas of resource use (all women receiving 1:1 care during period 1/4/94 to 31/3/95) • casenote review: random sample of 200 women in each care group. Sampling proportionate to the number of women delivering in each group in the two hospital sites.

Table 14.7: Activities /resources considered in economic evaluations

Know-Your-Midwife [1]	• antenatal admissions: although the sub-sample showed greatly reduced admission rates, there was no statistically significant difference in admission rates between the KYM and 'control' group of women in the full study. • perceived costs of consultations with different personnel during antenatal period: assumes length of consultation with different personnel does not vary. Costing (using mid-point of salary scales) for consultations that KYM women could be assumed to have required as low-risk women outwith the KYM scheme. • epidurals: number of epidurals in KYM and control group. Information about number of top-ups not available. • acceleration of labour: equipment used for giving intravenous fluids; in addition, assumes increased use of continuous fetal monitoring and increased analgesia.
Aberdeen Midwives Unit [3]	Health care resources used largely within the hospital. Categories considered included: • staff costs: additional midwives and promotions for set-up of unit: for caesarean section (elective and emergency): for assisted vaginal delivery time: for epidural: for perineal suturing. • consumables: application of fetal scalp electrode: epidural: continuous and intermittent fetal heart monitoring: TENS: episiotomy: assisted vaginal delivery: caesarean section: general anaesthetic: administration of naloxone. • capital costs: conversion of unit (per woman, assuming Unit's life-span of 35 years): equipment and furniture • overheads: not specified Costs borne by families assumed by authors to be similar for the alternatives evaluated because they were situated on the same site.
Glasgow MDU [4]	• antenatal: antenatal visits, day-care attendances, admissions • intrapartum: inductions, spontaneous vertex deliveries, instrumental deliveries, caesarean sections, epidurals • postnatal: postnatal stay, postnatal visits, postnatal day-care, re-admissions. • infants: admissions to SCBU Main differences in resource use between groups were for antenatal visits, induction rates and postnatal day-care which were all lower for women receiving midwifery managed care. For base cost estimates, the median caseload of 29 clients per midwife per annum was assumed. Sensitivity analyses were carried out to assess costs associated with higher MDU caseloads (39 women per midwife). • women's resource use: out-of-pocket expenses (travel, lost earnings and childcare costs); disruption to normal activity (activities foregone, e.g. time taken off work, lost housework and lost leisure time).
One-to-One [5]	• resource use comparisons: including length of stay; method of delivery; ante, intrapartum and postnatal admissions; out-patient attendances; day cases; ward attendances; physiotherapy contacts; diagnostic and pathology tests; operative procedures; postnatal contacts; use of ultrasound; epidural • staff time; – total amount of contact time spent by 1:1 midwives with women in 1:1 cohort; mean duration of contacts for ante, intrapartum and postnatal care. – amount of care delivered by all health professionals to 1:1 women. • capital costs.

The Aberdeen Midwives Unit [3] focuses upon health care resource use which is broken down into staff costs, consumables, capital costs and overheads. The latter two elements are either not mentioned or receive limited attention in the other comparative studies.

Assessing costs (Table 14.8)

Again there is considerable variability in the translation of resource use into financial costs. A guestimate is offered in Know-Your-Midwife [1] in relation to some resources (staff time). In relation to others (the acceleration of labour) an attempt is made to extrapolate costs from financial information supplied by another hospital in another area of England. (We have already discussed the difficulties in translating costs from one location to another.)

While the Glasgow MDU [4] is unique in giving consideratrion to the costs incurred by women who use the service, all evaluations attempt to identify some elements of the financial costs incurred by the Health Service. However these are illustrated in different ways. The Glasgow MDU [4] provides an interesting breakdown of costs into antenatal, intrapartum and postnatal services, while the Aberdeen Midwives Unit [3] delivers comparisons of staff costs, the costs of consumables and capital costs. The focus of One-to-One costings are quite different. While careful attention is paid to resource use in One-to-One and traditional care groups, these are only translated into costs in relation to a number of 'roll-out' scenarios in which expansion of the pilot scheme is considered.

It is, however, worth noting that two schemes, the Aberdeen Midwives Unit [3] and One-to-One [5] have attempted to increase the usefulness to purchasers and providers of their analyses. Both seek to increase the robustness of the conclusions that they draw by reporting a series of sensitivity analyses which cost a number of alternative care scenarios. Depending on the assumptions underlying a particular set of costings, both studies are able to demonstrate the potential for cost savings and the potential for additional costs associated with the new pattern of midwifery organization.

What conclusions can be drawn from economic evaluations of the comparative studies?

Comparison of the characteristics of economic analyses undertaken within four of the seven comparative evaluations highlights the variability in approaches used. This is a fundamental problem which imposes serious limitations upon the extent to which conclusions can be drawn across studies. In the broader midwifery care literature there is evidence of even greater variability and projections about cost-benefit or cost-effectiveness that are difficult to sustain on the basis of data and analysis presented.

Comparing even relatively discrete elements of care in different midwifery services is no less problematic. The costing of epidurals, for example, is approached in completely different ways in the evaluation of Know-Your-Midwife [1], the Aberdeen Midwives Unit [3], the Glasgow MDU [4] and One-to-One [5].

Table 14.8: Assessing costs

Know-Your-Midwife [1]	• antenatal admissions: overall savings from the (non-significant) reduction in antenatal admissions is suggested by the authors for KYM scheme. • perceived costs of consultations with different personnel during antenatal period: suggests 10% higher costs for consultations in control group. Guestimate of 20-25% higher if other staff (e.g. receptionists, midwife chaperones etc.) were included in costings. • epidurals: suggests extra costs of 60% for control group. • difficulty in assessing actual cost of an epidural administered in NHS is noted. Billing information from a local Private hospital used as a proxy. • acceleration of labour: a suggested cost for equipment use only (cost supplied by another hospital in another area of England; it is not specified how this was derived) is used to calculate an overall saving for KYM based upon lower rate of acceleration among KYM women.
Aberdeen Midwives Unit [3]	• items of resource use in which there were statistically significant differences between the 2 groups were costed. • where no statistically significant difference was found, but there was assumed to be a significant effect on clinical practice and resource use, such differences were also costed. • where there was uncertainty about the cost or amount of variables used, sensitivity analysis was undertaken. • Staff costs: cost savings in staff time involved in interventions was small. Overall, introduction of the Midwives' Unit resulted in an extra cost of £44.69 per woman. • Consumables: cost savings attributable to the introduction of the Midwives' Unit of £3.25 per woman. • Capital costs: overall capital savings of £0.73 per woman • Overheads: assumed to be the same for each group.
Glasgow MDU [4]	1. *Costs to the NHS* • antenatal: costs higher for MDU than shared care; not statistically significant • intrapartum: costs higher for MDU than shared care; not statistically significant • postnatal: MDU care costs significantly higher than shared care costs. Adjusted estimates for a caseload of 39 women per midwife: • antenatal: costs significantly higher for shared care • intrapartum: costs higher for MDU than shared care; not statistically significant • postnatal: MDU care costs significantly higher than shared care costs. 2. *Costs to the women who use the service* • MDU women incurred more costs attending hospital clinics than the shared care group who tended to incur more costs attending community clinics. • Conjoint analysis used to estimate the relative utility received from different attributes of care provided.
One-to-One [5]	No costings are reported in the 'Report of the Evaluation of One to One Midwifery' (McCourt and Page, 1996) Costings for expansion scenarios included in Piercy et al (1996): Includes sensitivity analyses.

It is perhaps not surprising, therefore, that the conclusions that are drawn about the relative costs of midwifery services in the comparative studies are somewhat contradictory (Table 14.9). Know-Your-Midwife [1] suggests that care received by women in the Know-Your-Midwife group actually cost less to provide than normal care. As we have noted, the cost estimates are not robust and are offered for a relatively narrow range of activities and resources. This conclusion therefore needs to be read with some caution.

One-to-One [5] which was able to identify changes in semi-fixed as well as variable costs concludes that midwifery care may be cost neutral, while the Aberdeen Midwives Unit [3] suggests additional costs associated with midwife-led care. The Glasgow MDU [4] reaches a similar conclusion. MDU care is considered to be economically more efficient than shared care in the antenatal and intrapartum periods but to be associated with significantly higher costs in the postnatal period and overall.

These conclusions can be seen as reflecting economic characteristics of particular patterns of service within particular locations at particular points in time. Conclusions advanced on the basis of evidence in the broader literature may be even more problematic, for at their worst, economic evaluations are so limited in scope or their reporting is so superficial that no meaningful appraisal can be made.

Managers and planners will want to be able to assess the generalizability of changes in resource utilization implicated in any new scheme of midwifery care and their translation into financial costs. However, the schemes evaluated in the comparative studies were all functioning, to a greater or lesser extent as pilot projects. That is to say, they have been developed on top of existing services. Evaluation may not therefore demonstrate potential economies of scale. The One-to-One [5] analysis, for example, demonstrated a significant reduction in in-patient length of stay among the One-to-One population. This suggests the potential to release resources through a reduction in the number of, and a change in the configuration of, maternity beds. However, the work of Dowswell et al. (1997) would urge some caution in proceeding with a system of care that reduces length of stay (LOS). They suggest that:

> 'reductions in LOS may have negative outcomes in terms of maternal emotional well being, which in turn may have effects on infant wellbeing.' (Dowswell et al., 1997 p. 135)

Assessing the implications of rolling out an existing pilot (such that the pilot form of organization becomes the service norm) can be extremely difficult. Similarly, it is inherently difficult anticipating the transfer of any particular scheme from one time and place to another. In this respect, the One-to-One [5] points to some potentially interesting issues. Unlike the other comparative studies both One-to-One care and the comparison, 'traditional' care, were delivered in two hospital units. Ostensibly the same midwifery service was delivered in two environments. However, for some measures, the site was of greater significance than the care group. Mean number of postnatal visits, for example, differed significantly between hospitals but not between care groups. While a significant difference in the care group populations is reported (there being more 'non-whites' in the One-to-One care group) no significant difference between the hospitals was found (Piercy et al., 1996, p. 16). The casenotes analysed were hospital-based notes and the potential for some under-recording is therefore noted. However, there is no indication that any under-recording could be expected to vary systematically by hospital site.

Table 14.9: Conclusions advanced in economic analyses of comparative studies

Know-Your-Midwife [1]	Care costs no more than that provided in the normal way: care received by women in the KYM group actually cost less to provide than normal care.
Aberdeen Midwives Unit study [3]	Net increase of £40.71 per woman as a result of introducing the Midwives' Unit. The extra cost of the introduction of the Midwives' Unit = additional 10.5%: sensitivity analyses suggest a range from a saving of 2.5% per woman to an additional cost of 11% per woman. A number of limitations to the cost analysis are noted and the authors urge caution in their interpretation.
Glasgow MDU [4]	From an economic perspective MDU care is said to be more efficient than shared care in the antenatal and intrapartum periods. However, midwife managed care was associated with significantly higher costs in the postnatal period and overall. Conjoint analysis suggests that: • women would prefer to pay more for MDU care than shared care • women believed that hospitals should pay more to create a homely environment and to have fewer carers.
One-to-One [5]	'Under certain planning assumptions it is likely that the 1:1 scheme could be expanded without increasing midwifery costs to the Trust.' (Piercy et al., 1996, p. ii) 'A potential and workable solution and financial costs relating to the expansion of the scheme'... could lead to .... 'a potential cost saving of £259,470. However, additional travel costs under this scenario would be £131,100 and caseload midwives' enhancements of £2,500 per midwife (total £115,000) would mean that the financial implications of the scheme in terms of midwifery costs would be broadly neutral' (Piercy et al., 1996, pp. 59–60).

A significantly higher mean number of postnatal visits for the One-to-One women in the Queen Charlotte and Chelsea hospital has obvious resource implications (notwithstanding, of course, any potential relationship to quality of care and women's

117

satisfaction). We cannot know whether this difference between sites arose as the result of other differences in care group populations between the sites, or whether it is more readily explained in terms of 'history, local resources, priorities and cultures' (McCourt and Page, 1996, p. 5). Whatever the explanation, the study indicates the potential for population characteristics and/or service factors such as treatment protocols, to influence changes in resource utilization.

Of course, assessing the extent to which the results from any scheme can be generalized is far from simple. This is not a problem peculiar to evaluations of midwifery care but is an issue for all economic evaluations and Jefferson et al's (1996) discussion of sources of bias are particularly pertinent. These are summarized in Box 6 below.

Box 6: Bias in economic evaluation literature: a typology

- Studies which are carried out to justify a decision already taken may have a higher chance of publication if they confirm the validity of the decision, especially if this is in line with current scientific wisdom.

- Studies which are independent may not be published for reasons which are linked to the outcome of the study. The direction of this type of bias may be difficult to predict because it may be dependent on current scientific opinion or interest.

- Studies which have been commissioned to assist a specific decision-making process may not be published. This type of bias is potentially important as these studies may be well conducted and funded. Their omission in any review is likely to weaken the conclusions.

Source: Jefferson et al., 1996, p. 92

Summary

Only a proportion of overall service costs change directly with changes in activity (such as a new midwifery care scheme), variable costs in particular may constitute only a small percentage of the total costs in any provider unit. Thus, many evaluations concerning small scale (relative to the total midwifery service) or short term schemes are likely to demonstrate only very marginal changes in costs. Furthermore, it is not appropriate to assume that financial costs can be reproduced from one locale to another. Economic evaluations of new ways of organizing midwifery services therefore need to pay particular attention to identifying changes in resource utilization.

Routinely available data may provide very limited insight into the organization and process of midwifery care. In-patient data sets often constitute the only reliable, contemporary source of activity data which can be used to identify resource use. Out patient data (including hospital antenatal clinic data) is notoriously unreliable and community-based activity remains largely, if not entirely, invisible. If the utility of economic evaluations is to be enhanced, information about both activities and costs may need to be supplemented. Generally, there is a need to consider the potential for developing systems of data collection that enable the costing of specific packages of care. For particular evaluations, specific data collection tools may need to be designed and research teams undertaking evaluations may benefit from the expertise of health economists. There are, of course, already examples of such collaboration (these include, One-to-One [5], the Aberdeen Midwives Unit [3] and the Glasgow MDU [4]).

It is clear that there is a growing recognition of the importance of evaluating the cost implications of different patterns of service provision. Walsh, for example, acknowledges that economic evaluation has become a necessity for stake-holders and sponsors of projects:

> 'To exclude it is folly in an environment where cost-effectiveness and value for money are at a premium.' (Walsh, 1996, p. 600)

Nevertheless, Walsh also notes that, in the evaluation of the Wistow project at Leicester Royal Infirmary, an attempt to examine costs did not progress because of an absence of any proven mechanism to determine it. Clearly, uncertainty remains about how economic evaluation can be realized. Walsh illustrates the urgent need for informed, authoritative guidance about appropriate methodologies and effective tools for researchers evaluating different patterns of midwifery organization, which is only now beginning to be addressed. The techniques of economic evaluation are gradually becoming more accessible to health care workers (for example, Jefferson et al., 1996 and Drummond, 1994). The summary of key steps that are required to undertake an economic evaluation which concludes Piercy and Mugford's discussion (1997) begins to lay down guidelines for good practice for those involved in the evaluation of midwifery services. This will be an essential first step in the process of increasing the robustness of data and of conclusions that can be advanced on the basis of economic evaluations.

Costs: Questions still to be answered

Currently, our ability to trace activity and identify changes in resource utilization is frequently hampered by inaccurate or insensitive data. Ongoing review of Minimum Data Set requirements should improve the sensitivity of a core of routinely collected information in the medium to long term within the health and social care sector. In particular, we still know very little about the economic implications of a shift of midwifery services from the hospital into the community and the increasing emphasis placed on community-based service delivery makes better routine collection of community-based activity data imperative.

Considerable uncertainty remains about how to ask and how to answer appropriate questions about the costs and benefits of alternative ways of organizing midwifery services: which methods under which circumstances for which purpose? There is a continuing need for accessible and authoritative information and guidance.

Purchasers, planners and providers do not have available to them the evidence on which to base informed decisions about service delivery. We still cannot say for certain whether new ways of organising midwifery represent cheaper or more expensive service options. Until a new, pilot, way of organizing midwifery care becomes the service norm and is subjected to systematic evaluation, we will remain unable to adequately address the apparently simple question of 'What are the costs?'.

119

CHAPTER FIFTEEN

Discussion

Themes across schemes

We have now addressed the six questions listed in Chapter 6 (p. 18). Of course, these are not the only questions of relevance, but they were those that seemed most important and potentially answerable from published evaluations. Many other questions could, and should be asked. We will flag some of these in this chapter, but their coverage will necessarily be less intensive than in the preceding chapters.

One important area concerns why it is that some schemes are more successful than others. This topic was addressed by the seminal Wraight et al., 1993 'Mapping team midwifery' study, and the other studies that we have focused on reinforce their conclusions. We will discuss briefly some of the relevant issues.

Where has the impetus for change come from and how has it been carried forward?

For change to occur there must be an impetus. That may be external (such as Changing Childbirth) or it may come from within. If from within, it may be from those with the power to implement the change, or from the relatively powerless. If the latter, then, in order for change to occur, others will need to be persuaded. Although this is a slower process, it is one that is likely to mean fewer people feeling that unwanted change is being imposed upon them. It should be remembered that those who are powerless to *implement* change are not necessarily powerless to frustrate it. An important lesson that emerges from the schemes studied is therefore: take as long as is needed to ensure that everyone involved knows what is happening, has a voice, and, if possible, is positively committed to the scheme's success. This last requirement may be overambitious where medical colleagues are concerned. Some may feel very threatened. It is striking that in the Wraight et al. (1993) report so many senior midwives made the same comment along the lines of 'consult the doctors but don't be put off by them – it's a midwifery decision'. However, co-operation from doctors may make a considerable difference. In South Camden [15], for example, implementation was facilitated by the obstetric consultants agreeing to divide up their referrals on a geographical basis that coincided with the teams. In 'Redham' (Pankhurst, 1995 [19]), an enthusiastic and involved GP almost certainly helped the scheme's relative success.

Many of the innovative attempts that have been made to reorganize midwifery services have resulted from the dynamism of one individual. The effect of this should not be overlooked – charismatic leadership may well be a prerequisite for successful change.

Leadership and management issues should both be on the agenda for future research studies.

Who are the scheme midwives?

What are their qualifications? Where were they working before? How did they come to be in the scheme? A number of schemes have considered that the more responsible role demanded of the midwife calls for a higher grade mix than was previously needed. This has cost implications, but it also raises questions about the deployment of midwives who do not have the required level of experience. At the same time, it tends to be the younger, more recently qualified midwives who volunteer for these schemes. In the One-to-One scheme [5], for example, most applicants were currently working in the hospital rather than the community, were recently qualified and had no experience of working anywhere else.

Many schemes have, very reasonably, started in a small way, and in circumstances that are likely to lead to success. Thus, the 'Know-Your-Midwife' scheme [1] involved only four, highly committed and carefully selected midwives. This, of course, raises questions of generalizability to a situation where midwives may not have chosen the new way of working, and may even be antagonistic towards it. Where the midwives have come from also matters. Do they have pre-existing contacts with, for example, GPs and health visitors? Are they used to community working? Do they know the particular community in which they are now working? Do they know each other? These factors are all likely to be relevant to the scheme's success.

What type of area does the scheme cover?

Most of the schemes considered have been in major cities, but some (e.g. Pankhurst (1995) [19], West Essex [6]) have included rural areas. In rural schemes especially, travel time becomes an important consideration if home visits are involved. In Pankhurst's study [19], which included two teams, one much more rural than the other, the audit of midwives' time showed that the rural team were driving 400–500 miles per month, which means that they were spending around ten per cent of their time in their cars.

Another geographical issue that has arisen for most schemes is the situation for women who cross boundaries. The West Essex [6] study provides a good example of the practical issues that can arise, particularly because the maternity unit lies close to the county boundary. This means that many women for whom that unit is the nearest hospital do not actually live in the area. In the extreme ends of the District, exactly the same situation arises in reverse and West Essex women deliver in out-of-area hospitals. This is a very common problem, and has been the subject of a recent study by Wilson (1997) which examines the solutions found in four project sites around the country. Complexities of this sort were a major cause of one project's conclusion that intrapartum continuity of carer could not be achieved within the lifetime of the project (Walsh, 1995b).

Risk status

One important issue is whether the schemes are attempting to care for all women within a geographical area or only those defined as 'low-risk'. Only two of the core comparative studies (One-to-One [5] and West Essex [6]) concerned schemes that catered for 'all risks'. These were both start-to-finish schemes. Broadly speaking the community-based start-to-finish schemes are the most likely to cater for all risks, since they often started from a more woman-centred ideology which led them to feel that women should not be compartmentalized or penalised for having problems. The hospital-based schemes were more likely to adhere to a medical model of childbearing.

This raises questions about the concept of risk status and the accuracy with which 'high' and 'low' risk women can be identified. There has been much debate on this subject, irrespective of any reorganization of midwifery services. The specific issue that arises in the present context is that women who are initially identified as low-risk and are thus eligible for 'the scheme' may cease to meet its criteria and so have to be transferred to consultant-led hospital care. This is likely to happen at a stressful moment because it will be associated with the discovery of some way in which the pregnancy or labour is not progressing normally. The woman will have to cope not only with the obstetric problem and its possible implications, but will also lose the support of the carers with whom she has supposedly been establishing a relationship during pregnancy, just at the time when her need for familiar carers may be greatest. This is a common situation. The Home-from-Home [2] and Aberdeen Midwives Unit [3] RCTs both allocated twice as many women to the intervention group as to the control group precisely because of the expectation that a large proportion of the women would be transferred. It is a situation which arises more frequently for women having their first baby than those in subsequent pregnancies. We know very little about the effects on women of being transferred in this way. This is a surprising omission given its frequency (Kean et al., 1996 [20]). A recently published qualitative study interviewed 12 women who had all booked for delivery either at home or at a community GP unit, but who had had to be transferred to hospital at some stage (Creasey, 1997). The study offers some insights into women's ways of coping with such a change of plan, as well as ways in which staff can ameliorate the disappointment that women are likely to feel. In the cases discussed, however, women returned to the care of their community midwife and GP after delivery, and they were able to help talk through what had happened. It is less clear in some of the schemes that we have been considering whether there will be any continuity for women who are transferred from low-risk care. The subsequent care for women whose status changes is not well explained in the reports.

The balance between hospital and community

The schemes whose evaluations we have examined in this report were variable in the extent to which they had shifted towards a community-based service, with the greatest variation to be seen in antenatal care. There was a range from all antenatal care at the hospital (Know-Your-Midwife [1]) to all in the community (West Essex [6], Deptford (Allen et al., 1997)). In many of the schemes, women had little contact with the hospital antenatally unless there was a specific indication. Thus, the service had become more community-based than previously, and, for large-scale implementation, that generally meant changing the ratio of community-based to hospital-based midwives.

In West Essex this meant nearly doubling the proportion of community-based midwives from 31 per cent to 60 per cent, and consequently making a substantial reduction in the number based in the hospital.

The Glasgow MDU [4] offered women a choice of location of antenatal care between home, hospital and community clinic. Apparently, the majority of women chose hospital. Since the completion of the RCT, the unit now offers women choices of different packages of maternity care, and women apparently still favour antenatal care from MDU midwives at the hospital. This is a surprising finding, since other studies suggest that community-based antenatal care is popular with women. The Audit Commission Report (1997), for example, found that women having shared care found the community component more satisfactory than hospital visits. MDU midwives spent just 17 per cent of their time in the community compared with 48 per cent on the labour ward, 30 per cent on antenatal and postnatal wards and five per cent in the (hospital) antenatal clinic. It would have been valuable to have comparable figures for all the other schemes considered. Those few studies, such as Allen et al. (1997), which did examine in detail how and where midwives spent their time revealed substantial differences. More such studies are needed.

The tendency was for start-to-finish schemes to be more community-based and, conversely, for hospital-based schemes to be less likely to offer a start-to-finish service. Start-to-finish schemes/community-based schemes were also quite likely to offer additional innovations such as drop-in clinics and pre-conception clinics. Postnatally, there was also a tendency for women to leave hospital as soon as possible. However, none of these characteristics need to go hand-in-hand with a start-to-finish service and the moves towards a more community-based service and early transfer home are ones that are also happening elsewhere. This leads to difficulties in disentangling the different elements. The only scheme which offered a hospital-based start-to-finish service was the Glasgow MDU [4]. Interestingly, this was the least successful of the start-to-finish schemes at achieving a known midwife present at the birth, but this is more likely to relate to the fact that midwives were not on-call than to their being hospital-based.

Relationships between scheme and 'non-scheme' midwives
Have existing community midwives been displaced by the scheme and has this caused resentment (as in One-to-One [5])? What proportion of the district's midwives are involved in the scheme? Does the scheme consist of a highly committed and carefully selected sub-group, while other midwives continue to work as they always have (but possibly with depleted resources), or is the new way of working the norm? Is there a core staff for the hospital maternity-unit? If so, does it consist of the 'rejects' from the scheme, e.g. those who don't drive, who work part-time (as 40% of midwives do) or who are unable to take on on-call commitments? There is a clear sense of this in the West Essex [6] scheme. Has implementation of the scheme taken resources (human or otherwise) away from the maternity unit? All the community-based schemes – whether teams are the norm or the exception – report tensions between the two sets of midwives, underlining the importance of involving all stakeholders in the planning of schemes. 'Involvement in planning', however, may not be a sufficient solution if midwives are left with inadequate resources for carrying out their jobs.

What is the role of the scheme midwife within the hospital maternity unit?

Routine antenatal care appears to be relatively uncontentious as far as relationships between the scheme and the maternity unit are concerned, presumably because there is little contact. In West Essex [6] the protocol suggests that the woman's named midwife should accompany her for ultrasound scans and amniocentesis. However, audit showed that only 12 women (1%) had had their midwife with them for scans. These were probably cases where a problem was anticipated since four women had their midwife with them for two scans and two women for three.

When women are admitted to hospital antenatally, in-patient care is generally provided by the hospital midwives although the scheme midwife may visit. In some schemes, however, the provision of in-patient antenatal care by community scheme midwives has been attempted (West Essex [6], South Camden [15]), but abandoned as being impractical. Presumably, for low-risk schemes, antenatal hospital admission coincides with transfer from the scheme.

An issue also arose in some schemes (e.g. Know-Your-Midwife [1] and South Camden [15]) about the care of women in early labour. It was consistent with the philosophy of a number of the schemes to support women at home in early labour and then to accompany them to the hospital at a later point. This policy was found to be difficult to implement in some cases (in Know-Your-Midwife [1] it was forbidden), which led to scheme women going to hospital earlier, perhaps when they were not even in established labour, and spending more time on the labour ward, possibly creating more work for core staff. However, the study by Klein et al. [8] suggests that this may be a crucial aspect of the service. This is therefore another area where the benefits and disbenefits of different policies need further investigation.

In-patient postnatal care seems to be one of the most difficult areas. In some schemes (Glasgow MDU [4], South Camden [15], 'Greenfields' postnatal beds in the cottage hospital (Pankhurst (1995) [19]) all such care is the responsibility of the scheme midwives, which is rarely easy to fit in with the other demands on their time. More usually, a scheme midwife visits the postnatal ward once or twice a day, and at other times care is given by the hospital midwives. As we have seen, this has been the most contentious area with considerable resentment from hospital midwives. The women are often the victims of these tensions (e.g. Ashford (Allen et al., 1997), One-to-One [5], Pankhurst (1995) [19]). It is unfortunate that the evaluations tell us less about the relationships between scheme and non-scheme midwives in the hospital-based schemes (Home-from-Home [2] and Glasgow MDU [4]). However, one of the Glasgow MDU [4] publications (Turnbull et al., 1995c) does allude to difficulties similar to those reported in the other schemes, although postnatal care is not specifically mentioned. Possibly the problems would be averted by complete separation, but this is an area where further information is needed. Apart from being bad for the midwives, it is quite unacceptable for women to suffer as a result, and the causes and solutions of these difficulties require urgent investigation.

Workload

There are many issues to do with workload, such as who controls it and whether it is controllable. In Lewisham and Ashford (Allen et al., 1997), midwives found themselves with a much higher caseload than anticipated which stretched the system. This has also been a problem for a number of other schemes. The Wistow project in Leicester, for example, found that one of its teams was carrying a load of 77.5 deliveries per midwife per annum (Walsh, 1995b). In Deptford (Allen et al., 1997) there was the opposite problem – lack of referrals and funding insecurity exacerbated each other. In pilot projects it may well be that midwives' time is protected to ensure that they do not become overloaded, which may not give a realistic picture of how the scheme would work if 'rolled out' and also puts a heavier workload on non-scheme midwives.

The Allen et al. (1997) study also raised the question of how workload should be defined. This in turn leads into the question of how the scheme midwives spend their time. This has been examined in some detail in a small number of studies (Allen et al. (1997), Pankhurst (1995) [19]), but requires much more investigation for the community-based schemes. In the hospital-based schemes the question is more easily answered because midwives worked fixed hours. Thus, in the Glasgow MDU [4] we know that the midwives were spending nearly half their time on the labour ward and just 17 per cent in the community. The studies that have examined the way in which midwives' time is distributed have found considerable variation. In the Allen et al. (1997) study varying proportions of time were spent on 'direct care', as opposed to other activities such as travelling or administration. In Ashford (Allen et al., 1997) it was less than 50 per cent and intrapartum care only accounted for 11 per cent of time recorded. Administrative work was often carried out when off-duty.

On-call arrangements

Being 'on-call' can mean different things in different schemes. There are a number of parameters. The particular combinations are likely to be important determinants of the likelihood of a woman being delivered by a known midwife.

Length and timing of on-call: Ashford (Allen et al., 1997) cut down from 24 hour shifts to splitting the day in two. Other schemes had different arrangements and also varied by whether the on-call period came immediately before or after a nine-to-five working day. In some schemes midwives were on-call for their own women at all times and the on-call rotas only covered times outside nine-to-five weekdays. It is not clear what happened in these cases if a midwife was called while running a class or a clinic.

Who the midwife is on-call for: Midwives may be on-call primarily for their own (and perhaps their partner's) caseload – a relatively small number of women that they know – or for a much larger number (the team's caseload). Obviously, this parameter interacts with the amount of time on-call: much more for an individual caseload, but with a reduced likelihood of being called out on any given occasion. Midwives in both the Allen et al. (1997) study and Sandall's study [18] found team caseloads much more stressful. Midwives in the Pankhurst (1995) study [19], however, found that individual caseloads became team caseloads in practice, because of the way in which on-calls were organized. Some midwives are likely to find some arrangements more stressful than others. For example, time on-call is always associated with some uncertainty, and some people tolerate uncertainty better than others. What matters is almost certainly the extent to which the midwife feels in control.

This question also covers the case mix of the women. The caseload may be mainly women to whom the midwife is delivering a start-to-finish service and is therefore more likely to know well or there may be a substantial number of women who deliver elsewhere with whom she may have more superficial contact (e.g. Ashford (Allen et al., 1997)).

What the midwife is called for: Many calls will be from women going into labour, but women may call with all sorts of other problems. No data seem to have been reported on this. It is likely to vary with the ethos of the scheme and the extent to which women feel encouraged or discouraged to telephone. There are few data in most of the evaluations on frequency of call-out, still less on what the call is for. When called, does this always mean attending the woman or can advice be given by telephone? When attending a woman, does this generally mean that the midwife is now going to be up for the rest of the night, or might some contacts be fairly brief and let her go back to bed again? Occasional glimpses are to be had from individual midwives' sample diaries (Know-Your-Midwife [1], One-to-One [5]) but much more information is needed to understand what different on-call arrangements actually mean to midwives' lives.

What happens when the on-call midwife is already busy?: This is another aspect of on-call work where there are few data. The West Essex evaluation [6] approached it obliquely by asking midwives how often they were called for women from another team. This was a relatively frequent occurrence. In the Greenfields scheme, a second-on-call system was abandoned after audit showed that midwives worked more hours when off duty than when they were second on-call (Pankhurst (1995) [19], Appendix 1). In the same study, the Redham team midwives agreed on a six-hour time attendance if called to the labour ward at night or week-ends, after which they were relieved by a standby midwife who was otherwise off-duty. This system apparently operated very flexibly.

Payment: We quoted a West Essex [6] midwife's indignation at the lack of remuneration for time spent on-call when she was not called and the unfairness of then having to work extra hours to make up. None of the studies discuss the handling of this issue. For schemes like One-to-One [5] where midwives spent a great deal of their time on-call with a relatively low probability of being called it is a particular issue.

These parameters can be combined in many ways. For example in Sandall's study [18] both Patchville and Woodhurst midwives were on night call two to three times per week and every third weekend. Woodhurst midwives did not deliver women, so presumably being on-call had different implications. On the other hand, they had a much larger caseload. If they still attended women at home in early labour, even though that woman would then go to hospital to be delivered by a different midwife, one could see how their on-calls could be very onerous.

Clash between the aims of continuity for women and midwives having time off

'Woman-centred' services are the cornerstones of Changing Childbirth. If 'woman-centred' means centred around the childbearing woman's needs and wishes, then this goal flows from women's complaints that existing services denied them a voice, and were arranged around the needs of the medical profession rather than their own. However, the term 'woman-centred' is open to other interpretations, because being '*woman*-centred' implies contrast with a different focal point. The contrast is often thought of as being 'doctor-centred' but there are other contenders: midwives, for example, or men, or other women, or babies. The phrase 'woman-centred' then takes on rather a different interpretation according to the comparison group assumed. (Changing Childbirth always refers to 'the woman', rather than 'women' doubtless to underline its philosophy of individualized care).

There is an additional problem of what being 'woman-centred' actually means in terms of how far the service should swing in favour of the woman's needs and wishes rather than, say, those of the midwife. Is the suggestion that the woman's needs and wishes are absolute? Even at the expense of major disruption to midwives' family and social lives? Presumably that was not the intention, but where and how should the line be drawn? If the same midwife is always going to be available to a given woman then she has to be permanently on-call. Most midwives would not consider this a reasonable way to work. Even the One-to-One scheme [5], which is the scheme most committed to this as an ideal, has midwives working in pairs, and the pairs work within groups.

In fact, this great dilemma is something of a red herring, since there is little suggestion that women want or need a service which is so closely dedicated to their needs. A *personalized* service does not have to mean having your own personal midwife, just being treated like a person. As Murphy-Black said in 1992 [21]:

> 'There is still confusion between individualised care and continuity of care ...If midwives are to stop "failing to provide continuity of care"[1] then it is of vital importance to midwifery to increase its understanding of what continuity of care is, how it can be facilitated by midwives and what difference it makes to the outcomes of midwifery care.' (Murphy-Black, 1992 [21], p. 123)

In a subsequent publication (Murphy-Black, 1993 [16]), the same author also pointed to the potential conflict between continuity of care and professional autonomy

> 'In the days of the autocratic manager it was easy to have continuity of caring because the old-fashioned sister would only allow one way of doing things.' (Murphy-Black, 1993 [16], p. 22)

The conflict is not just with professional autonomy. If individualized care, rather than uniformity is being sought, then there is a potential clash here also. The solution must

---

1. A quote from the final chapter of *Effective Care in Pregnancy and Childbirth* (Chalmers et al., 1989).

lie in having policies about the way in which issues are handled, that is, common approaches, rather than inflexible edicts about what must be done.

Optimum number of carers

What is the optimum number of midwives that a woman should see? The West Essex [6] study suggests that women are much less likely to feel that they have formed a relationship if they see more than two midwives antenatally. Two midwives was also suggested by a woman in the Allen et al. (1997) study as being preferable to one. However, even this may be unrealistic. The Glasgow MDU [4] consciously rejected this as a goal.

The ideal size of team is a dilemma. The minimum workable number is likely to be four, but it depends what the team is trying to achieve. Know-Your-Midwife [1], for example, which worked with just four midwives, delivered all antenatal care at the hospital which is a more efficient use of time than visiting women's homes. This issue is also related to the distances that need to be covered. In rural areas a substantial proportion of midwives' time is likely to be spent travelling, thus effectively reducing the number of hours available for midwifery care and requiring either a bigger team or a smaller caseload. The studies were very varied in the total number of caregivers that a woman saw. This may be the result of differing definitions (e.g. whether student midwives are included), but it is likely that this is not the only difference, since there are also within-study differences (e.g. West Essex [6]). Further detailed study is needed of this issue, including an explanation of why any given encounter takes place and, for each newly encountered caregiver, why it has involved that person rather than one who is already known.

If more than one caregiver is to be involved, there are also questions about the balance between them. Is it better to know one midwife well and three superficially, or to know four on equal terms? This also leads onto the question of what it means to 'know' your midwife. In the Home-from-Home study [2], women only met the scheme midwives on three antenatal clinic visits – all the rest of their antenatal care was given as shared care. What did these women think of this arrangement? How did they rate the relationship with each of the midwives that they encountered? It seems quite likely that they will have regarded their community midwife as 'their' midwife, and not considered their relationship with the scheme midwives to be important at all. Unfortunately, we do not know. Yet, the study group women were significantly more satisfied with both their antenatal and intrapartum care than controls. What caused this increase in satisfaction? These gaps in our knowledge all argue for more independent, detailed, qualitative research.

Other issues

Our discussion so far has focused on the issues raised in the evaluations that we have examined. In this final discussion section we will raise some additional topics which have received less attention.

Women with special needs

Schemes catering specifically for women with special needs were outside the remit of this review. However, the question still remains of how such women should be catered for within the 'all-risks' schemes. The umbrella term 'special needs' covers such a wide range that it is not in fact very useful. Arguably every woman has special needs at some time or another. That is what is being recognized by the idea of 'woman-centred' care. Some needs, however, are perhaps more special than others. Within the context of this report, it may be useful to distinguish two groups: those whose 'special needs' are evident from the start and those who develop problems during pregnancy.

WOMEN WHO REQUIRE MORE RESOURCES

Some women require more resources than others. This may relate to high obstetric risk, but often the issues are social, for example women who do not understand or speak English, or those who are 'hard to reach' such as drug users or women who are homeless. A dilemma is then presented for the service in how it should use its resources. Midwives in Ashford (Allen et al., 1997) raised this as a general dilemma within the context of their own service: they had started out offering an 'all-risks' service, but were overwhelmed and obliged to establish a second team for high-risk women. The dilemma is likely to seem particularly difficult when the group requiring a larger share of resources is not viewed sympathetically by society.

WOMEN WHO DEVELOP PROBLEMS

The second 'special need' has been touched on in the discussion of women who are transferred from 'low-risk' care to 'high-risk' care. This is to do with women who become in need of specialist care during the course of their pregnancy. This issue arises frequently in the context of antenatal screening.

Antenatal screening, at least in the form of ultrasound scanning, is now virtually universal in the United Kingdom. One would not guess that from reading most of the studies reviewed in this report. It is clearly viewed as something additional, and yet over the past 15 years it has become an increasingly major part of (usually hospital-based) antenatal care, with the first sight of the baby on the ultrasound screen being a high spot for many parents. Explanation of the tests on offer and their implications now takes up a substantial proportion of the booking interview in many places. Even those schemes which have been more community-based and which have discouraged the use of technology still include ultrasound scanning. Yet it still receives hardly any mention in discussion of the organization of midwifery services.

The issue to be raised here concerns the care of women who have a positive result on a screening test. There is a danger that the attitude revealed by the marginalizing of testing in discussion of services extends to marginalizing the women with positive results. An ongoing multi-centre study in the South of England (Statham, personal communication) suggests that some women lose the support of 'their' midwife once a screening test has suggested a problem and they are referred for specialist advice. This may be primarily a problem of inter-professional communication, and that study will be investigating this issue. However, it should be recognized that these women do have a 'special need' and that need is probably for more support and more continuity than other women, not less.

The content of care

The studies were very variable in the extent to which they described the content of care. Most descriptions were inadequate to allow one to assess what the important differences were likely to be between the new scheme and whatever was 'standard care'. This was particularly true for postnatal care.

Outcomes

A notable feature of the studies examined was the range of outcomes that had and had not been taken into account. Process and outcome data were the most frequently reported, but there were still substantial differences between studies, and more information concerning process issues would almost always have been useful. We had made it a criterion for the core studies that the views of women should also have been included, but, although collected, this was not always published. Another important source of information is the views of those working in the scheme and those of other health professionals. These would seem to be essential to understanding how a scheme is working, but were not always sought. Costs and long-term outcomes have been particularly poorly covered. The question of how schemes should be evaluated is the subject of recently published book by Cambpell and Garcia (1997).

Including non-midwives

A topic not explored by any of the schemes was making use of services supplied by non-midwives, for example maternity aides, which can release more of the midwives' time for midwifery. This is the mainstay of the Dutch community-based midwifery service (van Teijlingen, 1990), particularly postnatally, but seems to have received little attention in the United Kingdom. Similarly, there is scope for exploring the use of a supportive lay companion in labour, which has been shown to be effective in a number of studies (Hodnett, 1997).

CHAPTER SIXTEEN

Conclusions

The purpose of this report is to provide evidence on the organization of midwifery services which will aid the decision-making of purchasers and providers. We have presented evidence from a range of schemes. A number of general points have emerged. The first four are rather obvious, but need to be reiterated.

There are many ways in which the organization of midwifery services may be varied

No two schemes are quite the same. There are major organizational parameters such as the location of care and whether an attempt is made to give a woman a known carer in labour. On top of these, however, there will be organizational details, such as the way in which on-call work is managed, which may make a substantial difference not only to the likelihood of the scheme achieving its goals, but also to whether it is workable from the point of view of individual midwives (and it may not be possible to achieve both). Even when two schemes may appear similar on paper, the personalities involved, the history behind the project, the nature of the population served, the size of the workload and many other features will vary, and these are likely to be major determinants of success or failure. Given the large number of parameters involved, we must be very careful in reaching conclusions about the causes of different outcomes.

It is difficult to draw conclusions when so many features of a service have been changed simultaneously

At present, there are substantial difficulties in interpreting the evaluations because many aspects of the service have been changed simultaneously. If women are found to be more satisfied, for example, it is difficult to know just which aspect of the service may be responsible. A number of core studies compared midwife managed intrapartum care with that provided in the same hospital by a consultant-led team. Often the area designated for midwife-led cases had homely surroundings designed to be less intimidating than standard hospital delivery rooms. We are then faced with the problem of knowing whether any differences found are the result of the location, the personnel or the content of care. One way to approach this is to make comparisons with schemes that have made some, but not all, of the same changes. It was in this context that we were able to draw on other studies, such as the study by Chapman et al. (1986) [9], which had manipulated only one element of the package (location), while attempting to keep the rest, including the personnel, constant. That this study still found significant

131

differences between the groups is an enormous help to us in interpreting these more ambitious schemes. More studies that take a more controlled empirical approach could help us in answering some of the other unresolved questions in this area.

What comes out of an evaluation is a function of what goes in

The studies revealed by our literature search were very varied in quality. Many had been carried out 'in-house', often by people who were not trained researchers. However, even within studies that are methodologically rigorous, the above truism applies. If certain questions were not asked, then their answers cannot be presented. Independent evaluations tend to paint a less rosy picture of the schemes that they are evaluating than those carried out 'in-house'. This is not to accuse 'in-house' evaluators of deliberate bias, but it is more difficult to be objective when you are closely involved. This applies also to research teams which are absorbed into the project team. Independent evaluators, as well as generally being trained researchers, have nothing at stake and are able to take a wider view. This is revealed at all stages of the evaluation process:

- designing the evaluation – many 'in-house' evaluations included no comparison groups (and hence were not included in our core comparative studies). Very few studies have looked at the views of midwives who have left a scheme.

- deciding what questions to ask and how to ask them – this is a critically important part of any evaluation. Questions must be designed to reveal the problems as well as the successes.

- deciding how to analyse/report the results (e.g. failure to report on how many women were attended in labour by a known caregiver).

In addition, an independent evaluation which is perceived by respondents as being independent is more likely to obtain frank opinions.

People work more happily in a system that they have chosen than in one that has been imposed upon them

In this context this applies primarily to midwives, but the lesson extends to the GPs, obstetricians and others whose co-operation is also desirable. Clear messages emerge from all of the studies that sought GPs views that they often felt that they had not been consulted about the scheme and that they were being marginalized. Midwives may be working in a scheme that they have devised and are running themselves, or the scheme may have been devised by midwifery management with more or less input from the midwives, or midwives could have had no say at all.

In 1986, in the conclusions of a report on the organization of obstetric medical staffing, Green et al. wrote:

'We are aware that many people would just like a one-word answer to the simple question "Does two-tier staffing work". We make no apology for not providing one; an issue as complex as this cannot be summed up with monosyllables. Firstly, we need to consider just what is meant in that question by the word "work". As we have seen there are a number of possibly conflicting goals that the service should meet: doctor training, healthy babies, satisfied customers and so on. We, therefore, need to consider separately the perspectives of the different people involved: consultants, junior doctors, midwives, women in labour, for it may be that the answers will differ.

Secondly, we must consider whether, even allowing for different perspectives, this is the right question to ask. It begs the question of whether 3-tier staffing "works": in some ways it clearly does not, hence the ongoing proposals for change' (Green et al., 1986, p. 8:1)

These authors concluded that most systems are workable if the people working within them want them to work, and, conversely, may be unworkable otherwise. Much the same is true in the present situation. A major issue is the extent to which any individual midwife is willing to allow her job to impinge on her social and domestic life. It may well be that the higher the midwife's job satisfaction, the more willing she will be for this to happen. We should be very careful not to conclude that this intrusion is a necessary component of job satisfaction. We are not aware of any study that has sought the views of midwives' partners and children.

Continuity of carer is at least as important for midwives as it is for women

Some consistent findings emerged from the results of our review. Women prefer a smaller number of caregivers but being delivered by a known midwife is, as one midwife said, 'the icing on the cake'. It seems to be more important to women that the midwife who delivers them is competent and caring than that they should have met her before. Midwives value autonomy, using their skills and forming relationships with women. As far as the limited evidence allows us to judge, these features are valued by non-scheme midwives as well as those working in the schemes.

For many years, a large proportion of midwives have worked in settings where they had no opportunity to follow women through and to form relationships with them. The exception, of course, were community midwives, particularly in the days when there was a much higher proportion of home births, and, more recently for DOMINO deliveries. It is a great pity that we do not have data from those systems of care that are equivalent to those collected in some of the evaluations that we have considered in this report. The findings would be of enormous interest. Both the West Essex [6] and South Camden [15] midwives, however, drew this comparison for themselves and concluded that their scheme was achieving less continuity. It is interesting in this context that the One-to-One scheme [5] drew surprisingly few volunteers from the ranks of community midwives. Rather it was, as in other schemes, the disaffected hospital midwives that were keen to join. The implication is that community midwives were happy as they were.

It would be useful to know more about the Glasgow MDU [4] in this respect. One of the scheme's aims had been to improve continuity of carer. This was achieved in the sense of women seeing fewer caregivers overall, but not in terms of knowing the midwife who delivered them. Despite this, the scheme midwives had high job satisfaction and the women were consistently more satisfied across all time periods. No other study achieved this. The evaluation concludes that having a known carer at the birth may not be as important as had been thought. Certainly, the evidence presented in this report would support that conclusion.

We must think carefully about what it is that women value that is associated with having a known carer at the birth. Lee [13] suggests that it is competence: that if women get to know a midwife they get to have faith in her competence (although presumably that is not inevitable). We would offer an additional possibility, suggested particularly by some of the accounts in the Allen et al. (1997) study. Here many midwives were taking great pains to be available to 'their women'. We suggest that what women value is the fact that midwives are putting themselves out. Hence, women say things like 'she was wonderful, she even came in to deliver me on her day off'. What is important about this is the 'caring' implied by coming in on your day off, which makes the woman feel special. By giving the impression that she 'cares' the midwife is saying that she values that woman as an individual and is not just treating her as another pregnant uterus. Clearly, this can be achieved by a midwife who has not met a woman before, and without major disruptions to her own personal life.

Currell (1990) [10] suggests that the key is 'focused care', that is care whose aim is known and which is valued. This is contrasted with diffuse care where the aim of care is not known and the care is not valued (Kratz, 1978). She argues that much antenatal care is diffuse, but that where there is a specific problem that is identified and solved then this results in satisfaction for both mother and midwife. This requires midwives to be sensitive to a woman's needs. This would seem to be another example of a situation in which the requisite behaviour may be more likely to occur when the midwife and woman are already known to each other, but for which this is not essential.

Walsh (1995a) concluded an article entitled 'Continuity of carer: miracle or mirage?' with the observation that:

> 'Maternal perceptions of improved quality of care may not necessarily correlate with improved continuity of carer. There is a need to explore women's perceptions of quality to discover the relative importance of continuity of carer to those perceptions.' (Walsh, 1995a, p. 338)

We would concur with that conclusion, but with the caveat that there may not be absolute answers to these questions. Assessment of 'what women want' is notoriously difficult because it is so context specific, and because of the effect that Porter and MacIntyre (1984) have termed 'what is must be best'. Routine questionnaires are unlikely to be able address the complex and sometimes contradictory values that women may hold. A more probing qualitative methodology is likely to be more successful.

Attendance in labour by a known midwife should not be the main determinant of a service

From the evidence reviewed in this report (particularly 'What aspects of continuity are important to women?', Chapter 11, pp. 78–86) we have concluded that women who have a known intrapartum carer are positive about it, but that most of those who do not, do not see it as important. High levels of satisfaction can be achieved without this. We would therefore argue that there is no justification for making attendance in labour by a known midwife the main determinant of the service. This is important because it is this requirement more than any other that impinges on midwives' lives.

Most of the schemes that we considered which aimed for a known carer in labour were start-to-finish schemes. Such schemes, by seeking to have all care from booking to discharge given by only one or a small group of carers, implicitly include the aim of attendance in labour by a known midwife, but do not necessarily prioritize it over other presumed benefits of continuity of carer. There may be other good reasons for choosing start-to-finish services even if they cannot be justified in terms of a known carer in labour. However, the aim of providing start-to-finish care does place a number of additional constraints on the organization of a midwifery service. Firstly, a scheme midwife has to work in all areas of care: antenatal, intrapartum and postnatal, not just, for example, in the antenatal clinic or the delivery suite as she is likely to have done in the past. This is welcomed by many midwives, but not all. Secondly, she has to work both in the hospital and in the community. Thirdly, she has to abandon the idea of working regular hours and be prepared for a fuzzier delineation between her work and leisure time. The studies which included the views of non-scheme midwives, and of midwives who had left schemes, made it clear that many midwives do not wish to work in this way. It was also evident that all the schemes had difficulty in attaining the targets of continuity that they had set themselves.

'Start-to-finish' schemes cannot be justified simply by provision of a known carer in labour, but it may be that there are other benefits that can only be given by a start-to-finish service that we do not currently know about. To discover what these are, for both midwives and women, we would need a large randomized controlled trial that compares a start-to-finish scheme with a non-start-to-finish scheme which is otherwise as similar as possible, particularly in having a woman-centred philosophy.

CHAPTER SEVENTEEN

Recommendations

Recommendations for future research

In general there is a need for more independent, focused, qualitative research. Randomized controlled trials are also needed to answer some questions. These approaches are not mutually exclusive.

Continuity of carer

There is a particular need to address questions about continuity, rather than making assumptions about its benefits. A number of authors (e.g. Currell, 1990 [10]; Murphy-Black, 1993 [16]; Lee 1994, 1995 [13]; Garcia et al., 1996) have provided a basis for 'unpacking' the concept of continuity of care, and this report has attempted to take these ideas further. This work now needs to be built on, particularly to answer questions such as:

- What does it mean to 'know' your midwife? How many midwives can be 'known'?

- What are the aspects of continuity that are and are not important to women? Does continuity need to be 'start-to-finish' to be beneficial, and, if not, when does it matters most, and to whom?

- Are the benefits of continuity essentially the benefits of woman centred care or may separate effects be operating?

- Do women who expect a particular form of care, e.g. a known midwife in labour, but do not get it, have more negative outcomes than women who have no such expectation?

Which aspects of a service matter?

We know relatively little about what aspects of a service lead to differences in either clinical or psychosocial outcomes. Controlled studies are needed that manipulate fewer variables at a time instead of changing the whole system at once.

Midwives' views

We need to know more about midwives' experiences of schemes which focus on continuity of care but not continuity of carer, such as the Glasgow MDU[4]. It may be that these forms of care can offer midwives the same advantages as start-to-finish schemes without the same degree of disruption to their lives.

We also need to know more about the views of midwives who are not involved in new forms of care, and what their ideal patterns of working might be.

Costs

One of the most pressing needs, from a purchaser's point of view, is to know what different forms of care cost. However, we are still unable to make definitive comment on the economic implications of new ways of organizing midwifery services. In particular, we know very little about the economic implications of a shift of midwifery services from the hospital into the community. For a new way of organizing midwifery services to be able to demonstrate its potential to affect costs it would need to become the service norm (rather than an addition to the existing service). Systematic evaluation of such a 'rolled out' pilot is necessary if we are to adequately address the question of cost.

We also need to increase awareness of the importance of economic analyses and to meet the evident need for authoritative guidance about their practice and process.

Recommendations for practice

Introduce changes slowly and involve all stakeholders

This was the advice given by Wraight et al. (1993), and is amply supported by the other studies that we have reviewed. In particular, the views of *all* local midwives should be considered, not just those who will be working in the scheme. Those who are powerless to implement change are not necessarily powerless to frustrate it. It is unacceptable that women's care should suffer as a result of tensions between different groups of midwives.

Evaluate new systems of care

It is essential that new systems of care should be evaluated. This is necessary both for the sake of those involved in a particular schemes and to ensure that we are not constantly reinventing the wheel. Evaluations must be scientifically rigorous and, ideally, carried out by independent researchers. *The Organization of Maternity Care – A Guide to Evaluation* (Campbell and Garcia, 1997) should provide much needed standards in this area.

Continue to strive for a less fragmented, woman-centred service

The evidence presented in this report suggests that:

- Women and midwives both appreciate a less fragmented service in which each is seen as a person.

- This does not have to mean that each woman receives all of her care from only one midwife.

- In particular the evidence does not suggest a need for the enormous efforts of service reorganization which are needed to ensure that a woman is cared for in labour by a midwife that she knows.

Continue to care

A common goal of service providers has been improving the quality of midwifery care. The provision of continuous care by a known midwife has come to be perceived as a desirable objective, a means to that end. However, it may be that the effort and resources required to reorganize midwifery services, to facilitate this objective, have clouded the ultimate goal. Providing continuous care by a known caregiver has come to be an end in itself, rather than a means to an end. The way in which midwives are organized within the health care service is less important to a woman than the quality of the interactions that she has with her caregivers. What probably matters most is that she should feel that they are competent and that they care – about her.

References

Allen, I., Dowling, B.S, Williams, S.A. (1997). *A Leading Role for Midwives? Evaluation of Midwifery Group Practice Development Projects*. Policy Studies Institute. Report No.832.

Audit Commission (1997). *First Class Delivery. Improving Maternity Services in England and Wales*. Audit Commission Publications.

Barnsley District General Hospital NHS Trust Obstetrics & Gynaecology CMT (1995). *An Evaluation of the Penistone Pilot Project in Team Midwifery*. (internal publication).

Campbell, R., Garcia, J. (1997). *The Organization of Maternity Care – A Guide to Evaluation*. Hale, Cheshire: Books for Midwives Press.

Chalmers, I., Enkin, M., Keirse, M.J.N.C. (1989). *Effective Care in Pregnancy and Childbirth*. Oxford: Oxford University Press.

Chapman, M.G., Jones, M., Springs, J.E., De Swiet, M., Chamberlain, G.V.P. (1986). 'The use of a birthroom: A randomised controlled trial comparing delivery with that in the labour ward'. *British Journal of Obstetrics and Gynaecology*, 93, pp. 182–187.

Cheyne, H., Turnbull, D., Lunan, C.B., Reid, M., Greer, I.A. (1995). 'Working alongside a midwife-led care unit: what do obstetricians think?'. *British Journal of Obstetrics & Gynaecology*, 102, pp. 485–487.

Clark, L., Mugford, M., Paterson, C. (1991). 'How does the mode of delivery affect the cost of maternity care?'. *British Journal of Obstetrics and Gynaecology*, 98, pp. 519–523.

Creasy, J. (1997). 'Women's experience of transfer from community-based to consultant-based maternity care'. *Midwifery*, 13, pp. 32–39.

Currell, R. (1990). 'The organisation of midwifery care'. In: Alexander, J., Levy, V., Roch, S. (Eds). *Midwifery Practice - Antenatal Care: A Research Based Approach*. London: Macmillan Press.

Currell, R.A. (1985). *Continuity and Fragmentation in Matenity Care*. Unpublished M.Phil dissertation, University of Exeter.

Department of Health (1993). *Changing Childbirth. Part 1. Report of the Expert Maternity Group*. London: HMSO.

Drew, N.D., Salmon, P., Webb, L. (1989). 'Mothers', midwives' and obstetricians' views on the features of obstetric care which influence satisfaction with childbirth'. *British Journal of Obstetrics and Gynaecology*, 96, pp. 1084–1088.

Drummond, M.F. (1994). *Economic Analysis Alongside Controlled Trials. An Introduction for Clinical Resesarchers*. London: Department of Health.

Farquhar, M., Camilleri-Ferrante, Todd C. (1996). *An Evaluation of Midwifery Teams in West Essex – Final report*. Public Health Resource Unit & Health Services Research Group, Institute of Public Health, University of Cambridge.

Fleissig, A., Kroll, D., McCarthy, M. (1996). 'Is community-led maternity care a feasible option for women assessed at low risk and those with complicated pregnancies? Results of a population based study in South Camden, London'. *Midwifery*, 12, pp. 191–197.

Fleissig, A., Kroll, D. (1996). *Evaluation of Community-led Maternity Care in South Camden, London*. London: University College.

Flint, C., Poulengeris, P. (1987). *The Know Your Midwife Report*. Privately published: 49, Peckarman's Wood, Sydenham Hill, London SE26 6RZ.

Garcia, J., Ness, M., MacKeith, N., Ashurst, H., Macfarlane, A., Mugford, M., Piercy, J., Renfrew, M.J., Ball, J., Campbell, R., Ullman, R. (1996). *Changing Midwifery Care – The Scope for Evaluation. Report of an NHSE-funded project Evaluation of New Midwifery Practices*. Oxford: National Perinatal Epidemiology Unit.

Grampian Area Maternity Services Committee (1989). *Grampian Integrated Antenatal Care Schedule*. Aberdeen: Grampian Health Board.

Gready, M., Newburn, M., Dodds, R., Gauge, S. (1995). *Choices – Childbirth Options Information and Care in Essex during Antenatal, Labour and Early Postnatal Period*. The National Childbirth Trust.

Graham, H. (1980). *Having a Baby*. Unpublished thesis, University of York.

Green, J., Kitzinger, J., Coupland, V. (1986). *The Division of Labour: Implications of Medical Staffing Structure for Midwives and Doctors on the Labour Ward*. Cambridge: Child Care and Development Group, University of Cambridge.

Green, J.M., Coupland, V.A., Kitzinger, J.V. (1988). *Great Expectations: A prospective study of women's expectations and experiences of childbirth*. Child Care and Development Group, Cambridge. (2nd edition 1998, Hale, Cheshire: Books for Midwives Press).

Green, J.M., Coupland, V.A., Kitzinger, J.V. (1990). 'Expectations, experiences and psychological outcomes of childbirth: a prospective study of 825 women'. *Birth*, 17, pp. 15–24.

Green, J.M. (1994). 'Women's experiences of prenatal screening and diagnosis'. In: Abramsky, L., Chapple, J. (Eds). *Prenatal Diagnosis: The Human Side*. pp. 37-53. London: Chapman and Hall.

Hall, M.H., Chng, P.K., MacGillivray, I. (1980). 'Is routine antenatal care worth while?'. *Lancet*, ii, pp. 78–80.

Hodnett, E.D. (1997). 'Support from caregivers during childbirth'. In: Neilson, J.P., Crowther, C.A., Hodnett, E.D., Hofmeyer, G.J., Keirse, M.J.N.C. (Eds). *Pregnancy and Childbirth Module of the Cochrane Database of Systematic Reviews*. Available in the Cochrane Library. The Cochrane Collaboration. Issue 1. Oxford: Update Software 1997. Updated quarterly.

Hodnett, E., Simmons-Tropea, D. (1987). 'The labor agentry scale: psychometric properties of an instrument measuring control during childbirth'. *Research in Nursing & Health*, 10, pp. 301–10.

House of Commons Health Committee (1992). *Inquiry into Maternity Services. Vol 1. (The Winterton Report)*. London: HMSO.

Hundley, V.A., Cruickshank, F.M., Lang, G.D., Glazener, C.M.A., Milne, J.M., Turner, M., Blyth, D., Mollison, J. (1994). 'Midwife managed delivery unit: a randomised controlled comparison with consultant led care'. *British Medical Journal*, 309, pp. 1400–04.

Hundley, V.A., Donaldson, C., Lang, G., Cruickshank, F., Glazener, C.M.A., Milne, J.M., Mollison, J. (1995a). 'Costs of intrapartum care in a midwife managed delivery unit and consultant led labour ward'. *Midwifery*, 11, pp. 103–109.

Hundley, V.A., Cruickshank, F., Milne, J., Glazener, C., Lang, G., Turner, M., Blyth, D., Mollison, J. (1995b). 'Satisfaction and continuity of care: Staff views of care in a midwife managed delivery unit'. *Midwifery*, 11, pp. 163–173.

Jefferson, T., Demicheli, V., Mugford, M. (1996). *Elementary Economic Evaluation in Health Care.* British Medical Journal Publishing Group

Kean, L.H., Liu, D.T.Y., Macquisten, S. (1996). 'Pregnancy care of the low risk woman: the community hospital interface'. *International Journal of Health Care Quality Assurance*, 9, pp. 39–44.

Klein, M., Lloyd, I., Redman, C., Bull, M., Turnbull, A.C.A. (1983a). 'Comparison of low risk pregnant women booked for delivery in two systems of care: shared-care (consultant) and integrated general practice unit. I. Obstetrical procedures and neonatal outcomes'. *British Journal of Obstetrics & Gynaecology*, 90, pp. 118–122.

Klein, M., Lloyd, I., Redman, C., Bull, M., Turnbull, A.C.A. (1983b). 'Comparison of low risk pregnant women booked for delivery in two systems of care: shared-care (consultant) and integrated general practice unit. II. Labour and delivery management and neonatal outcome'. *British Journal of Obstetrics & Gynaecology*, 90, pp. 123–128.

Kratz, C. (1978). *Care of the Long-term Sick in the Community.* Edinburgh: Churchill Livingstone.

Leap, N. (1994). 'Caseload practice within the NHS: Are midwives ready and interested?'. *Midwives Chronicle & Nursing Notes,* 107, pp. 130–135.

Lee, G. (1994). 'A reassuring familiar face?'. *Nursing Times,* 90(17), pp. 66–67.

Lee, G. (1995). '"Free speech": the named woman'. *Midwives*, 108(1288), p. 162.

MacIntyre, S. (1982). 'Communications between pregnant women and their medical and midwifery attendants'. *Midwives Chronicle*, 95(1138)387, p. 94.

MacVicar, J., Dobbie, G., Owen-Johnstone, L., Jagger, C., Hopkins, M., Kennedy, J. (1993). 'Simulated home delivery in hospital: a randomised controlled trial'. *British Journal of Obstetrics & Gynaecology*, 100(4), pp. 316–23.

McCourt, C., Page, L. (1996). *Report on the Evaluation of One-to-One Midwifery.* London: Thames Valley University.

Meinert, C. (1986). *Clinical Trials: Design, Conduct and Analysis.* Oxford: Oxford University Press.

Meldrum, P., Purton, P., Maclennan, B.B., Twaddle, S. (1994). 'Moving towards a common understanding in maternity services'. *Midwifery*, 10(3), pp. 165–70.

Melia, R.J., Morgan, M., Wolfe, C.D., Swan, A.V. (1991). 'Consumers' views of the maternity services: implications for change and quality assurance.' *Journal of Public Health Medicine*, 13(2), pp. 120–6.

Murphy-Black, T. (1992). 'Systems of midwifery care in use in Scotland'. *Midwifery*, 8, pp. 113–124.

Murphy-Black, T. (1993). *Identify the Key Features of Continuity of Care in Midwifery. Report prepared for the Scottish Office Home & Health Department.* Nursing Research Unit, University of Edinburgh.

Oakley, A. (1982). 'The origins of antenatal care'. In: Enkin, M., Chalmers, I. (Eds). *Effectiveness and Satisfaction in Antenatal Care.* London: Spastics International Medical Publications.

O'Brien, M., Smith, C. (1981). 'Women's views and experiences of ante-natal care'. *Managing the Practice*, 225, pp. 123–125.

Pankhurst, F. (1995). *Great Expectations – The impact of caseload midwifery on women, practitioners and practice. Part 1: The first nine months.* Centre for Nursing and Midwifery Research. University of Brighton.

Piercy, J. (1995). 'Change: at what cost?'. Editorial. *British Journal of Midwifery*, 3, p. 629.

Piercy, J., Downe, S. (1995). *Changing Childbirth – Assessing the Cost.* Changing Childbirth Update, Issue 2, pp. 10–11.

Piercy, J., Wilson, D., Chapman, P. (1996). *Evaluation of One-to-One Midwifery Practice. Final Report.* York Health Economics Consortium, The University of York.

Porter, M., Macintyre, S. (1984). 'What is, must be best: a research note on conservative or deferential responses to antenatal care provision'. *Social Science & Medicine,* 19(11), pp. 1197–200.

Reid, M. (1994). 'What are consumers' views of maternity care?' In: Chamberlain, G., Patel, N. (Eds). *The Future of the Maternity Services.* London: Royal College of Obstetricians & Gynaecologists' Press.

Sandall, J. (1997). 'Midwives' burnout and continuity of care'. *British Journal of Midwifery,* 5, pp. 106–111.

Shields, N., Holmes, A., Cheyne, H., McGinley, M., Young, D., Gilmour, W.H., Turnbull, D., Reid, M. 'Knowing your midwife during labour: clinical, psycho-social and economic implications'. *British Journal of Midwifery* (in press).

Sikorski, J., Wilson, J., Clement, S., Das, S., Smeeton, N. (1996). 'A randomized controlled trial comparing two schedules of antenatal care visits: the antenatal care project'. *British Medical Journal,* 312, pp. 546–553.

Simms, C., McHaffie, H., Renfrew, M.J., Ashurst, H. (Eds). (1994). *The Midwifery Research Database MIRIAD: A sourcebook of information about research in midwifery. Second Edition.* Hale, Cheshire: Books for Midwives Press.

Sorenson, J. (1996). 'Multi-phased bed modelling'. *Health Services Management Research,* 9, pp. 61–67.

Stock, J., Wraight, A. (1993). *Developing Continuity of Care in Maternity Services: The Implications for Midwives. A Report to the Royal College of Midwives.* Institute of Manpower Services, University of Sussex.

Tucker, J., Florey, C.D., Howie, P., McIlwaine, G., Hall, M. (1994). 'Is antenatal care apportioned according to obstetric risk? The Scottish antenatal care study'. *Journal of Public Health Medicine,* 16(1), pp. 60–70.

Tucker, J.S., Hall, M.H., Howie, P.W., Reid, M.E., Barbour, R.S., C du V Florey, McIlwaine, G.M. (1996). 'Should obstetricians see women with normal pregnancies? A multicentred randomised controlled trial of routine antenatal care by general practitioners and midwives compared with shared care led by obstetricians'. *British Medical Journal,* 312, pp. 554–559.

Turnbull, D., Holmes, A., Shields, N., Cheyne, H., Twaddle, S., Gilmour, W.H., McGinley, M., Reid, M., Johnstone, I., Geer, I., McIlwaine, G., Lunan, C.B. (1996). 'Randomised, controlled trial of efficacy of midwife-managed care'. *Lancet,* 348, pp. 213–18.

Turnbull, D., McGinley, M., Holmes, A., Cheyne, H., Shields, N., Twaddle, S., Young, D. (1995a). *The Establishment of a Midwifery Development Unit Based at Glasgow Royal Maternity Hospital.* Midwifery Development Unit, Glasgow Royal Maternity Hospital, Rottenrow, Glasgow

Turnbull, D., McGinley, M., Fyvie, H., Johnstone, I., Holmes, A., Sheilds, N., Cheyne, H., MacLennan, B. (1995b). 'The implementation and evaluation of a midwifery development unit'. *British Journal of Midwifery,* 3(9), pp. 465–468.

Turnbull, D., Reid, M., McGinley, M., Shields, N.R. (1995c). 'Changes in midwives attitudes to their professional role following implementation of the Midwifery Development Unit'. *Midwifery,* 11, pp. 110–119.

Van Teijlingen, E.R. (1990). 'The profession of maternity home care assistant and its significance for the Dutch midwifery profession'. *International Journal of Nursing Studies,* 27(4), pp. 355–66.

Walker, J.M., Hall, S., Thomas, M. (1995). 'The experience of labour: a perspective from those receiving care in a midwife-led unit'. *Midwifery*, 11, pp. 120–129.

Walsh, D. (1995a). 'Continuity of carer: miracle or mirage?'. *British Journal of Midwifery*, 3, pp. 336–338.

Walsh, D. (1995b). 'The Wistow project and intrapartum continuity of carer'. *British Journal of Midwifery*, 3, pp. 393–396.

Walsh, D. (1996). 'Evaluating new maternity services: some pointers and pitfalls'. *British Journal of Midwifery*, 4, pp. 598–600.

Wilson, A. (1997). *Achieving Continuity of Care across Health Service Boundaries; An Overview of Project Work at Four Centres*. Manchester Multidisciplinary Audit and Quality Group

Wraight, A., Ball, J., Secombe, I., Stock, J. (1993). *Mapping Team Midwifery*. Institute of Manpower Studies, University of Sussex

Wright, B. (1994). *Caseload Midwifery at Queen Mary's Sidcup NHS Trust – The Evaluation of a Pilot Scheme Established February 1993*. Queen Mary's Sidcup NHS Trust

Zelen, M. (1979). 'A new design for randomised clinical trials'. *New England Journal of Medicine*, 300, pp. 1242–1245.

APPENDIX A

Policy History

Introduction

To understand the current organization of midwifery services, it is necessary to reflect on some of the major reports that have been published in an attempt to influence organizational change. One of the challenges that has faced midwifery services is to encourage and develop a different approach in the organization of care. Achieving this requires a change in traditional thinking from both professionals and users of the service. In reply, the midwifery profession has become increasingly responsive to the needs of women and their families and has encouraged professionals to develop flexible, innovative ways of working based on research based evidence.

Over the last 100–150 years, the life expectancy of an individual has increased. This has been as a result of major breakthroughs in technology, improvements in sanitation and education and in the diagnosis and treatment of many communicable diseases such as polio, measles and cholera. However, health gain is not necessarily dependent on any one variable and it is often issues that are outside of purely medical input and treatment that have the greatest impact on health such as housing, environment, finance and poverty. It has been stated that in every country:

> 'the major determinants of health lie outside the health care system. Moreover, inequities in health are only likely to be radically reduced through actions involving such sectors as income distribution, housing, agriculture, education and environment.' (WHO 1986, cited in Abel-Smith, 1994)

In 1977, the World Health Organization (WHO) adopted a 'Health for All' policy and twelve targets were identified and agreed. Each country represented agrees its own targets and develops its own health plan and strategy. In line with the European strategy and the WHO strategy of 'Health for All by the Year 2000', the UK government in 1992 introduced the Health of the Nation document.

Summary of policy developments since 1955

The Guillebaud Committee in 1956 acknowledged that maternity services lacked co-ordination and that the provision of care was duplicated by a number of professionals (Guillebaud Committee, 1956). As a result of the Guillebaud findings, a review of maternity services was undertaken by the Cranbrook Committee (Ministry of Health, 1959). The report recommended that beds should be made available in a number of hospitals to cater for 70 per cent of all deliveries. This created a marked change in the organization of care considering that during the 1930s, 70 per cent of births took place at home. Midwives were then, and still are, the most senior professionals present at birth (NHSME, 1993) yet midwives had little involvement in policy decision making.

After the introduction of the National Health Service in 1948, maternity care was 'shared' between the hospitals, local authority health services and the GPs. A policy statement from the Royal Colleges of Obstetricians and Gynaecologists in 1944 (cited by Robinson, 1990) advocated that 70 per cent of deliveries should take place in hospital under the care of a consultant obstetrician.

> '... Midwives should not be regarded as competent to undertake unaided the antenatal care of the expectant mother, but should always work in collaboration with the general practitioner or the obstetrician. Midwives and health visitors would be taught the management of breastfeeding from the paediatrician, who would direct its detail in the maternity ward.' (Robinson, 1990, pp. 72–73)

Women began to 'book' directly with their GP rather than the midwife, and the GP invariably became the first point of contact for a woman's introduction into the maternity services. The increase in birth rate (30% after the war) and the number of women delivering in hospital placed pressure on limited beds. Women began to be discharged earlier from hospital often within 48 hours, to alleviate this organizational problem.

> 'Forty eight hour discharges from hospital had been introduced in some areas as a matter of expediency. It is important to note how changes in organisation can come as the result of response to a practical difficulty rather than as the result of a changed philosophical concept or carefully planned research.' (Currell, 1990)

The number of home deliveries began to decline and in 1970, the Peel Committee emphasized the importance of teamwork, with care provided by midwives, GPs and obstetricians working in teams. Continuity of care was also commented on frequently but was not necessarily seen as purely a continuous relationship between the women and one midwife or doctor. The report also stated:

> 'We think that sufficient facilities should be provided for 100% hospital delivery. The greater safety of hospital confinement for mother and child justifies this objective.' (DHSS, 1970)

During the 1970s, obstetric technology and interventions such as induction increased. These types of procedures and interventions became the norm for many women, frequently resulting in restriction of the woman's mobility during labour. This emphasized the medical approach to childbirth yet, for the majority of women, pregnancy is a normal physiological event and not an illness.

One hundred and fifty recommendations were made as a result of The Short Report, which was an extensive review of maternity services (Social Services, 1980) and reference was made yet again to continuity of care. The Maternity Services Advisory Committee (established as a result of the Peel Report) produced a three part report 'Maternity Care in Action' (1982; 1984; 1985) which also emphasized continuity, the provision of a flexible approach in the delivery of care and team work. The reports also highlighted the importance of identifying, recognizing and acknowledging the views of consumers of maternity services.

The 1970s and 80s saw an increase in the consumer society. Many women and midwives raised concern about the increase in the number of deliveries induced and the total dominance of the medical approach to childbirth. The views of the consumer became more important and vocal and The Maternity Services Liaison Committees (established in the mid 1980s) and the Community Health Councils (CHCs) became active routes through which women could voice their opinions on the provision of maternity services.

The Cumberledge Report on Community Nursing (Department of Health and Social Security, 1986) highlighted the role of the nurse within the community which included community midwives. It advocated that practitioners should be allowed to utilize their skills and knowledge to offer comprehensive care and choice to patients. This process would require improved communication between professionals and clarity of roles and responsibilities.

A number of other recent policy documents have emphasized teamworking and clarification of professional roles and responsibilities. For example, 'Promoting Better Health' (Department of Health and Social Security, 1987) also placed more of an emphasis on disease prevention and health promotion and in providing patients with more choice and information. These recommendations were further emphasized in 'Working for Patients and Caring for People' (Department of Health, 1989). Achieving the objectives outlined in these documents would require practitioners, including midwives, to utilize and develop their skills and knowledge to provide a holistic approach to the provision of care. A number of recommendations from previous maternity policy reports were also reiterated in The 'Patients Charter' (Department of Health, 1992a) namely: empowerment of people, acknowledgement of the 'needs and wants' of users, with the emphasis on choice, quality, improvements in service delivery, the setting of minimum standards and a cost effective service.

Team work was again emphasized in the Health of the Nation (Department of Health, 1992b) where the provision of an effective service to meet the identified targets would require co-operation between professionals and agencies. Implementing the recommendations and the Health of the Nation targets would require professionals to:

- enable people to make choices about their healthier lifestyles by providing health education programmes and accurate information in daily, routine contacts with clients
- make changes in service delivery ensuring that they are accessible, appropriate and responsive to peoples' needs
- improve safety at home, work and on the road (Targeting Practice: The Contribution of Nurses, Midwives and Health Visitors, Department of Health, 1993a).

The two most influential policy documents in relation to maternity services in the last six years have been the Winterton Report (House of Commons, 1992) and Changing Childbirth (Department of Health, 1993b).

The House of Commons Health Select Committee chaired by Sir Nicholas Winterton in 1992 was established to investigate the maternity care provided for women. Evidence was obtained from a number of key professionals and groups. Ninety recommendations were made as a result of its findings. The following are some of the key elements identified within the report:

- continuity of care
- choice of care and place of birth
- the involvement of women in the decision making process about their own care
- that care for a woman experiencing a normal pregnancy should be provided by a midwife.

The committee also concluded that the policy of encouraging all women to give birth in hospital could not be justified on the grounds of safety.

In response, the government established an expert committee – the 'Expert Maternity Group' – chaired by Baroness Cumberlege. The remit of the group was to review the current policy on maternity care provided for women and make recommendations for change. The report ('Changing Childbirth') stated that women should be actively involved in the planning and delivery of maternity care and a flexible service should be provided to meet their needs. The provision of appropriate and unbiased information based on research based evidence was emphasized. This process would allow and encourage women to make informed choices in relation to their care.

The report also acknowledged that the current pattern and provision of maternity care was more appropriate for women experiencing ill-health than a normal physiological process such as pregnancy.

The publication of the 'Changing Childbirth' document was seen as a 'tool for change'. It identified ten indicators of success that should be achieved within five years:

1. all women should be entitled to carry their own notes
2. every woman should know one midwife who ensures continuity of her midwifery care
3. at least 30% of women should have the midwife as the lead professional
4. every woman should know the lead professional who has a key role in the planning and provision of her care
5. at least 75% of women should know the person who cares for them during their delivery
6. midwives should have direct access to some beds in all maternity units
7. at least 30% of women delivered in a maternity unit should be admitted under the management of a midwife
8. the total number of antenatal visits for women with uncomplicated pregnancies should have been reviewed in the light of available evidence and the RCOG guidelines
9. all front-line ambulances should have a paramedic able to support the midwife who needs to transfer a woman to hospital in an emergency and
10. all women should have access to information about the services available in their locality (Department of Health, 1993b, p. 70)

Amongst the Expert Maternity Group's recommendations were that:

- services should recognize the special characteristics of the local population
- they should be attractive and accessible, especially to those least inclined to use them
- a woman should be able to choose whether her first contact is with the GP or midwife
- each women should have a named midwife
- antenatal care should be community based
- throughout her pregnancy, and most particularly during labour, the woman should be cared for by people who are familiar to her
- the part which the midwife plays in maternity care should make full use of her/his skills and knowledge, and reflect the full role for which s/he has trained.

The document was seen by both professionals and users of maternity services as a positive step in implementing and enabling change, within the traditional pattern and organization of maternity care. The concept that care should become 'woman centred' is the underlying principle of the report and multidisciplinary team working is also emphasized.

Changing Childbirth was considered to be a 'manifesto for change' for purchasers and providers of maternity care who were encouraged to review their current organization of maternity services (Department of Health, 1993b, p. 71). For these changes to be effective, commissioners and providers of services would need to work together and draw on research based evidence to support, monitor and justify any changes.

Many of the points highlighted in both the Winterton report and 'Changing Childbirth' are reflected in the five objectives outlined in the government White Paper 'The National Health Service – A Service with Ambitions' (Department of Health, 1996). The objectives are; to have a well-informed public; a seamless service, working across boundaries; knowledge-based decision making; a highly trained workforce; and a responsive service, sensitive to differing needs. The recommendations in the maternity services reports are in line with the government's approach to a Primary Care-led NHS.

A shift from secondary to primary care is the recommended 'new path' for the NHS with the emphasis on health gain and the delivery of effective health care and the building of alliances: '…decisions about purchasing and provision of health are taken as close to the patient as possible' (Department of Health, 1993c). The proposal also emphasizes the role that consumers of the service can play in identifying their own health needs. The provision of health care will be dependent on accessing and utilizing research-based evidence and will require appropriate changes in clinical and organizational practice. A co-ordinated approach is essential and will require increased communication between health and social care sectors; the involvement of users of the service is crucial.

References

Abel-Smith, B. (1994). *Introduction to Health Policy, Planning and Financing*. London: Longman Group Ltd.

Currell, R. (1990). 'The organisation of midwifery care'. In: Alexander, J., Levy, V., Roch, S. (Eds). *Midwifery Practice – Antenatal Care: A Research Based Approach*. London: Macmillan Press.

Department of Health and Social Security (1970). *Domiciliary Midwifery and Maternity Bed Needs* (Peel Report). London: HMSO.

Department of Health and Social Security (1986). *Neighbourhood Nursing: A Focus of Care* (Cumberledge Report). London: HMSO.

Department of Health and Social Security (1987). *Promoting Better Health*. London: HMSO.

Department of Health (1989). *Working for Patients*. London: HMSO.

Department of Health (1992a). *The Patients Charter*. London: HMSO.

Department of Health (1992b). *The Health of the Nation. A Strategy for Health in England*. London: HMSO.

Department of Health (1993a). *Targeting Practice: The Contribution of Nurses, Midwives and Health Visitors*. London: HMSO.

Department of Health (1993b). *Changing childbirth. Part 1. Report of the Expert Maternity Group*. London: HMSO.

Department of Health (1993c). *A Primary Care-led NHS*. Executive Letter (79) 94.

Department of Health (1996). *The National Health Service – A Service with Ambitions*. London: Stationery Office Ltd.

Guillebaud Committee (1956). *Report of the Committee of Enquiry Into the Cost of the National Health Service*. London: HMSO.

House of Commons Social Services Committee (1980). *Perinatal & Neonatal Mortality. Session 1979–80. 2nd report. Vol 1. (The Short Report)*. London: HMSO.

House of Commons Health Committee (1992). *Inquiry into Maternity Services. Vol 1 (The Winterton Report)*. London: HMSO.

Maternity Services Advisory Committee (1982). *Maternity Care in Action, part I*. London: HMSO.

Maternity Services Advisory Committee (1984). *Maternity Care in Action, part II*. London: HMSO.

Maternity Services Advisory Committee (1985). *Maternity Care in Action, part III*. London: HMSO.

Ministry of Health (1959). *Report of the Maternity Services Committee* (Cranbrook Committee). London: HMSO.

Robinson, S. (1990). 'Maintaining the independence of midwives'. In: Garcia, J., Kilpatrick, R., Richards, M. (Eds). *The Politics of Maternity Care*. Oxford: Clarendon Press.

APPENDIX B

Details of Search Strategy

Sources searched

Literature searches were undertaken using existing literature from completed studies as well as on-line searches using:

- CCPC (The Cochrane Collaboration Pregnancy and Childbirth Database);

- HELMIS (The Health Service Management Information Service Database);

- MIRIAD (The Midwifery Research Database);

- MEDLINE (US National Library of Medicine Database);

- CRIBB (Current Research in Britain);

- EMBASE (Excerpta Medica Online);

- MIDIRS (Midwives Information and Resource Service);

- CINHAL (The Cumulative Index of Nursing Research and Allied Literature);

- BIDS (Bath University Interactive Data Services) and

the manual searching of a number of health service and nursing journals.

The process of manual searching was to ensure that recent articles not yet entered on electronic databases and future research were not overlooked.

Terms used for computer-based searches

```
#
exp maternal health services/
exp pregnancy/
exp health services/
2 and 3
nurse midwives/
((maternity or midwifery or childbirth) adj service$).tw.
maternity provision.tw.
```

(organisation or provision or administration or management or assessment).tw.
cost-benefit analysis/
health expenditures/
exp delivery of health care/
exp quality of health care/
*midwifery/
1 or 4 or 5 or 6 or 7 or 13
8 or 9 or 10 or 11 or 12
14 and 15
limit 16 to English language
limit 17 to (consensus development conference or consensus development conference,
nih or guideline or historical article or meta analysis or multicenter study or practice
guideline or randomized controlled trial or review or review literature or review of
reported cases or review, academic or review, multicase)
united states/
canada/
19 or 20
18 not 21

Flint and Poulengeris (1987)

Scheme	Authors of evaluation and date	Organization of midwifery service	Aim of scheme and pattern of care provided	No. of midwives involved in the scheme	Midwives' grades	No. of women cared for per annum
'Know-Your-Midwife Team' (KYM) St. George's Hospital London April 1983 – August 1985	Flint, C., Poulengeris, P. 1987 The 'Know -Your-Midwife' report (KYM). Supported by the South West Thames Regional Health Authority & The Wellington Foundation	One team of midwives offered nearly all antenatal, intrapartum and postnatal care to women booking for hospital – only antenatal care: randomized to scheme at booking. (The rest of the midwives continued to provide pre-existing pattern of care). *KYM rota system:* Team midwives worked hours organized to	*Aims:* to address the following hypotheses • that it is possible for a small team of midwives to provide continuity of care throughout the childbearing process for a group of maternity patients. • that mothers will experience greater emotional satisfaction if they get to know their midwives than if they are looked after conventionally. • that low-risk women have no worse obstetric outcomes when looked after almost exclusively by midwives than women cared for in a conventional way. • that care reorganized to provide continuity costs no more than the provision of conventional care.	The KYM Team consisted of 4 hospital-based midwives	The current grading structure was not in place at the time of this study	Approx. 250 women per annum

Scheme	Authors of evaluation and date	Organization of midwifery service	Aim of scheme and pattern of care provided	No. of midwives involved in the scheme	Midwives' grades	No. of women cared for per annum
		new model: KYM midwives worked approx. 7.45–4pm. One midwife always on-call for a 24 hour period approx. twice per week). One midwife from 1–9pm once per week to cover evening antenatal clinic. Approx. 37½ hours/week, 150 hours/4 weeks; flexible.	**Pattern of care** • most antenatal care provided by KYM midwives (women saw registrar/consultant at booking and 36 weeks) on-call midwife contacted by bleep by/for labouring woman. Early assessment in the home discontinued during scheme: intrapartum care provided in hospital then woman accompanied to postnatal ward by KYM midwife. • KYM midwife provided postnatal care in hospital postnatal ward each morning and then each evening; care outside of these visits provided by ward midwives. • After discharge, community postnatal visits undertaken by KYM midwives for women who 'lived within a reasonable distance of the hospital'.			

Flint and Poulengeris (1987)

Scheme	Authors of evaluation and date	Aim of the study	Methods and outcomes	No. of midwives involved	No. of women involved
Evaluation of 'Know-Your-Midwife' KYM Scheme St. George's Hospital London April 1983 – August 1985	Flint, C., Poulengeris, P. 1987 The 'Know -Your- Midwife' report (KYM). Supported by the South West Thames Regional Health Authority & The Wellington Foundation	To reduce fragmentation of care	Researcher appointed for evaluation; working alongside member of KYM team. *Methods* RCT involving women with low obstetric risk (according to agreed protocol) who booked for hospital-only antenatal care. *Data collection via:* • audit of case notes • women's self-administered questionnaires; ante & postnatal • clinical audit • costs audit *Outcomes* • survey of patient satisfaction • obstetric outcomes • no. of caregivers • costs (estimate via comparison between KYM and 'other' women for: antenatal admissions; epidurals; perceived costs of consultations with different personnel during antenatal period).	4 hospital based midwives in KYM team.	1001 pregnant women were involved in the RCT between April 1983 and August 1985. 503 were cared for by the KYM team and 498 received pre-existing, 'conventional' pattern of care. *Characteristics of the women:* The 2 randomized groups were similar with respect to: parity, age, social class, employment status, education. There were significantly fewer Asian women in the KYM group (9.5% compared with 18.2% in the 'traditional care' group).

Results: Know-Your-Midwife Team: a randomized controlled comparison with a 'conventional' pattern of care

Methodological issues:
- Consent was requested from women after randomization.
- Intrapartum care by KYM midwives had to be suspended for a period during the study.

Comparative findings include:
Number of caregivers, length of labour, use of analgesia, type of delivery, satisfaction, obstetric outcomes, costs.

Number of caregivers:
- Women in the KYM group saw fewer care givers antenatally.
- 48 out of 52 (92%) women in a sub-group (September and October 1994) of women enrolled into KYM care were cared for during labour by someone they had already seen in the antenatal period: compared with 9 out of 49 (18%) women in a sub-group receiving shared care.

Length of labour:
Women in the KYM group had longer first stages.

Analgesia:
Both groups were satisfied with their pain relief: women in the KYM group received less analgesia.

Type of delivery:
Higher number of women in the KYM group had a normal delivery.

Satisfaction:
- Women in the KYM group were able to discuss their anxieties, were satisfied with their antenatal care, felt well-prepared for labour and felt able to choose a comfortable position for labour.
- Six weeks postnatally, KYM women felt that labour was a 'wonderful and enjoyable experience' and that they had felt in control. They 'found it easier' being a mother than women in the control group.

Obstetric outcomes:

	KYM	Control
Pregnancy 37–41 weeks	89.8%	89.6%
Spontaneous onset of labour	71.8%	62%
Accelerated labour	17.2%	24.9%
Induced labour	11.0%	13.1%
ARM	53.1%	59.5%
Mean length of 1st stage (primiparous women)	9.5 hours	7.75 hours
No analgesia or entonox	52.4%	38.1%
Normal delivery (primiparous women)	69.7%	61.8%
Instrumental delivery (primiparous women)	19.3%	28.0%
Caesarean section (primiparous women)	10.9%	10.2%
Episiotomy (primiparous women)	46.5%	62.3%
APGAR score @ 1 min: 8 and above	80.9%	80.5%
APGAR score @ 5 min: 8 and above	96.4%	98.7%
Admissions to special care baby unit	4.8%	4.5%

Costs:
- Antenatal admission rate lower in the KYM group.
- KYM women spent a total of 920 days on an antenatal ward compared with 1075 in the control group.
- Estimated saving of £24,800 on antenatal admission in KYM group.
- Women in KYM group had fewer epidurals during labour.
- 80 women in KYM group had their labours accelerated compared with 114 in the control group.

Estimated costs: £19,360 for KYM group and £31,460 for control group over 2 year period. Equates to a cost saving of £12,100 in 500 women.

MacVicar et al. (1993)

Scheme	Authors of evaluation and date	Organization of midwifery service	Aim of scheme and pattern of care provided	No. of midwives involved in the scheme	Midwives' grades	No. of women cared for per annum
Midwife-led antenatal care with simulated 'Home-from-Home' (HFH) delivery in hospital (Leicester Royal Infirmary)	MacVicar, J., Dobbie, G., Owen - Johnstone, L., Jagger, C., Hopkins, M., Kennedy, J., 1993. *British Journal of Obstetrics & Gynaecology*, 1993;100(4): 316–23.	• one group of designated, hospital-based scheme midwives. • HFH midwives not normally involved with none-scheme women. • HFH midwives ran 3 x hospital antenatal clinics per week. • intrapartum care provided in 1 of 3 HFH rooms adjacent to the delivery suite. • all scheme midwives were volunteers.	*Aim* To provide midwife-led antenatal care and delivery, the latter to take place in hospital rooms organized to simulate home confinement. **Pattern of care** *Antenatal care* • scheme midwives provide antenatal care in hospital clinic at 26, 36 & 41 weeks; remainder of antenatal care from GPs and community midwives. • mandatory referral to consultant at 41 weeks antenatally. *Intrapartum care* • women encouraged to ambulate and could adopt any position. Women wishing for epidural analgesia transferred to the consultant-led labour ward.	10 designated midwives	2 x sisters + 8 x staff midwives	2,304 women randomized to HFH care over 16 month period *Characteristics of women in the scheme:* Not described.

Scheme	Authors of evaluation and date	Organization of midwifery service	Aim of scheme and pattern of care provided	No. of midwives involved in the scheme	Midwives' grades	No. of women cared for per annum
			• if problems developed, midwives could contact Registrar directly; Registrar made decision about whether to transfer a woman from HFH. • suturing normally undertaken by midwives. • rooms were each 'like a normal bedroom': carpeted, had patterned wallpaper, matching curtains. The beds (one a double) were made of pine. • all equipment was kept hidden behind curtains and out of view of the woman.			

MacVicar et al. (1993)

Scheme	Authors of evaluation and date	Aim of the study	Methods and outcomes	No. of midwives involved	No. of women involved
Evaluation of antenatal care with simulated 'Home-from-Home' (HFH) delivery in hospital (Leicester Royal Infirmary) Evaluation: Women booking between 1st Mar. 1989 – 6th Jul. 1990	MacVicar, J., Dobbie, G., Owen - Johnstone, L., Jagger, C., Hopkins, M., Kennedy, J. 1993 *British Journal of Obstetrics & Gynaecology* 1993;100(4): 316–23.	To compare the outcome of two methods of maternity care during the antenatal period and at delivery. One was to be midwife-led for both antenatal and delivery, the latter taking place in rooms organized to simulate home confinement. The other was consultant-led with the mothers labouring in the delivery suite rooms with resuscitation equipment in	Evaluation carried out by a research team of obstetricians and midwives with a medical statistician and a research assistant appointed for the trial. *Methods* RCT of women booking at Leicester Royal Infirmary Maternity Hospital • eligibility was decided after randomization. • post-randomization consent was sought from women allocated to the HFH scheme. They were also given information about what care would be provided under the HFH scheme. Randomization was to 2 groups: 1. women to receive midwifery-led antenatal care for hospital clinic visits (remainder of antenatal care from GPs and community midwives);	10 HFH midwives *Other staff* Number of midwives providing care on the consultant-led labour ward not specified. Number of other staff on labour ward not specified.	• 7906 women attended the antenatal clinic for booking. • 3510 (44%) were considered suitable for randomization. 1. 2,304 (66%) women randomized to HFH group • 189 (8%) women refused. • 537 (23%) transferred to consultant-led care antenatally. • 408 (18%) transferred to consultant-led care in the first stage of labour and 4% in the 2nd and 3rd stage of labour or after delivery. • 1069 (46%) delivered by midwifery-led team

Scheme	Authors of evaluation and date	Aim of the study	Methods and outcomes	No. of midwives involved	No. of women involved
		evidence and a conventional delivery bed.	simulated 'Home from Home' (HFH) delivery in hospital. 2.women to receive consultant-led shared antenatal care (shared between hospital, GP and community midwives); delivery in consultant-led labour ward. Women were randomized at a ratio of 2 (HFH): 1 (consultant-led care). Control group women were not identified to carers. *Exclusion criteria* • women defined as being at high risk. *Data collection via:* • women's postnatal questionnaire. • data sheets completed after delivery. *Outcomes* • maternal and fetal morbidity and mortality. • women's satisfaction with care.		2. 1,206 (34%) women randomized to consultant-led care group. The 2 groups were similar with respect to age, height and parity. The control group (delivering in consultant-led labour ward) had significantly more mothers who smoked.

Results: Simulated home delivery in hospital: a randomized controlled comparison with consultant-led care in Leicester

Methodological issues
Analysis was by intention to treat.

Transfers from HFH to consultant-led care
Antenatal transfers:
- Hypertension was the commonest reason for transfer followed by prolonged pregnancy and vaginal bleeding (together these accounted for 40% of all antenatal transfers).

Intrapartum transfers:
- The commonest reason was the presence of meconium stained liquor.

Variables	n	% Transfers
Hypertension	94	17
Post 41 wks	64	12
Vaginal bleeding	62	12
Breech	45	8
Suspected small for dates	34	6
Moved from the area	23	4
TOP/abortion	18	3
No reason given	17	3
Suspected fetal abnormality	17	3
Preterm labour/premature rupture of the membranes	13	2
Other	152	28
TOTAL	**539**	**100**

- No reason was given to explain the transfer of 17 women. This was mainly because the woman had been referred to consultant care by the GP or community midwife or because she had been admitted before 37 weeks gestation. Women tended to be retained for specialist delivery by default.

Maternal outcomes: Antenatal and labour
Ultrasound: 99% of both groups had at least one scan, usually at 10–12 weeks.

Antenatal admissions and procedures:
- No difference between the two groups in terms of either number of admissions or length of stay.
- Number of CTGs was significantly lower in the HFH group; 45% compared with 53%.

Variables	HFH		Control		P values
	n	**%**	**n**	**%**	
Onset of labour					< 0.0001
Spontaneous	1690	73	776	64	
Induced	218	9	131	11	
Augmented	270	12	192	16	
Intrapartum bleeding	38	2	13	1	0.21
Meconium staining	322	15	166	15	0.82
CTG	1074	50	982	89	< 0.0001
Fetal heart rate irregularity	480	22	336	31	< 0.0001
Duration of					
1st stage (median)		385 min		355 min	< 0.0001
2nd stage (median)		22 min		23 min	
Delay in 1st stage	267	12	132	12	0.82
Delay in 2nd stage	177	8	99	9	
Analgesia (excluding c/s)					< 0.0001
None	270	13	127	12	
Entonox	654	32	240	23	
Pethidine or meptazinol only	812	39	477	45	
Epidural	326	16	208	20	
Mode of delivery					0.286
Spont. vaginal delivery	1847	84	931	82	
Forceps/ventouse	187	8	114	10	
Vaginal breech	32	1	11	1	
Caesarean	144	7	78	7	
State of perineum (excluding c/s)					< 0.0001
Intact	669	33	308	30	
Episiotomy	475	23	326	31	
Vaginal/perineal tears**	914	45	417	40	
Paediatrician required	509	23	287	25	
Primary PPH over 500 mls	118	6	63	6	0.77
Manual removal of placenta	44	2	16	1	0.21
Secondary PPH	29	1	9	1	0.18
Blood transfusion	26	1	17	2	0.43

(** includes 15 3rd degree tears in HFH group and 6 in the control group)

Fetal outcomes:
- Similar outcomes between the two groups with respect to premature deliveries, light for dates, median Apgar scores, need for paediatrician at delivery.
- No statistically significant difference in the number of babies discharged alive and well in each group.
- There was a higher number of stillbirths and neonatal deaths in the HFH group (13 compared to 5) but this did not reach statistical significance.

(NB: The Report notes that the hospital and district perinatal mortality review groups did not identify any avoidable factors in the majority of cases and suggested that transfer to specialist care had been made at an appropriate time. Possible avoidable factors were identified in two cases of stillbirth in the HFH group).

Patient satisfaction:
- 3510 women were eligible to be sent the questionnaire six weeks postnatally (women who had a termination of pregnancy, a stillbirth or a neonatal death were excluded).
- 72% response rate (2489 women).
- 73% (1663) response rate in the HFH group.
- 69% (826) in the consultant-led care, control group.

Satisfaction was ranked on a scale: a) very satisfied b) fairly satisfied c) neither satisfied or dissatisfied d) fairly dissatisfied e) very dissatisfied.

The majority of women from both groups were either fairly satisfied or very satisfied with their care.

Overall, women in the HFH group showed significantly higher levels of satisfaction with their care during delivery and the antenatal period than women in the control group.

Satisfaction with antenatal care:

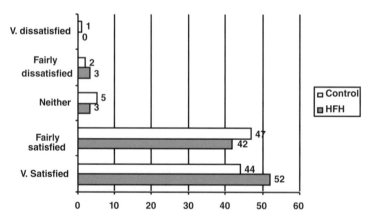

Satisfaction with hospital care:

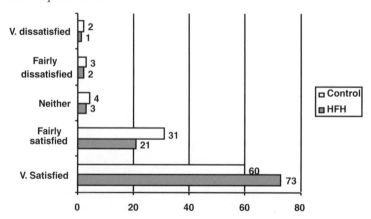

Conclusions:

- Just under 50% of all women referred for hospital booking were considered to be suitable for HFH care.
- More than half of these either refused the scheme or required transfer to specialist care at some stage.
- HFH midwives are reported as having improved job satisfaction despite the additional workload. No data or analysis is presented to illustrate this assertion.
- It is suggested that 25% of women initially referred to hospital booking clinic can achieve delivery without the assistance of doctors and without needing CTG monitoring or epidural analgesia.

Hundley et al. (1994, 1995)

Scheme	Authors of evaluation and date	Organization of midwifery service	Aim of scheme and pattern of care provided	No. of midwives involved in the scheme	Midwives' grades	No. of women cared for per annum
Intrapartum care in a midwife-managed delivery unit (Aberdeen) Unit established in April 1990	Hundley, V., Cruickshank, F.M., Milne, J.M., Glazener, C., Lang, G.D., Turner, M., Blyth, D., Mollison, J., Donaldson, C. *British Medical Journal* 1994; 309: 1400-4. *Midwifery* 1995a; 11: 103-109. *Midwifery* 1995b; 11: 163-173.	• midwife unit staffed and run by hospital midwives who work throughout the delivery suite (providing both midwife-led and consultant-led care). • midwife unit comprised of 5 midwife managed delivery rooms. • unit situated 20 yards from consultant unit.	*Aim* To provide midwife-led intrapartum care in a midwife-led unit for low risk women randomized to the scheme. **Pattern of care** • intrapartum care aimed for minimal intervention and encouraged active labour. • no medical input. • epidurals available on midwife-led unit. • care provided in homely environment. • all women received identical patterns of antenatal care.	Not known: data is provided for each woman involved in the evaluation of the scheme. No. of questionnaires (one per woman) does not therefore equal no. of midwives.	Grades E, F & G were employed. No. of staff in each grade is not reported although grade of midwife carer for each woman is reported. Midwives caring for women in the 'unit' were more likely to be of a higher grade, to have more qualifications and to have more experience than those working on the consultant-led labour ward.	1990 women booking over a period of 14 months were randomized to the midwife-led unit. Characteristics of women in scheme: women living in Grampian area who were suitable for booking in GP Units.

Hundley et al. (1994, 1995)

Scheme	Authors of evaluation and date	Aim of the study	Methods and outcomes	No. of midwives involved	No. of women involved
Midwife managed delivery unit: a randomized controlled comparison with consultant-led care (Aberdeen) Unit established in April 1990. Evaluation: women booking between October 1991 and December 1992.	Hundley, V., Cruickshank, F.M., Milne, J.M., Glazener, C., Lang, G.D., Turner, M., Blyth, D., Mollison, J., Donaldson, C. *British Medical Journal* 1994; 309: 1400-4. *Midwifery* 1995a; 11: 103-109. *Midwifery* 1995; 11: 163-173.	To examine whether intrapartum care and delivery of low-risk women in a midwife managed delivery unit differs from that in a consultant-led labour ward.	Evaluation carried out by a research team of midwifery and obstetric researchers, and researchers from the University of Aberdeen. *Methods* RCT of women identified as at low-risk at Aberdeen Maternity Hospital. Randomization to 2 groups: 1. women to receive intrapartum care in midwife managed delivery rooms. 2. women to receive intrapartum care in consultant-led labour ward. Women who agreed to participate were randomized in a ratio of 2 (midwife-led care): 1 (consultant-led care) because of the expected transfer of women with complications from the midwives' unit to the labour ward.	Not specified: 2734 midwife carer episodes are reported (1819 in midwives' unit, 915 in labour ward).	• 3451 women eligible: eligibility determined from GPs' booking letter. • 2844 women agreed to participate and were randomized into study groups. 1. 1990 women randomized to midwives' unit. • 727 (38%) transferred to consultant-led care antenatally (includes 80 (4%) lost to follow up). • 303 (16%) transferred to consultant-led care in intrapartum. • 870 (46%) delivered in midwives' unit. 2. 944 women randomized to consultant-led care.

Scheme	Authors of evaluation and date	Aim of the study	Methods and outcomes	No. of midwives involved	No. of women involved
			Exclusion criteria • low risk women opting for DOMINO delivery. *Data collection via:* • staff questionnaire. • women's questionnaire. • interviews with random sample from study population (n=400). • case note review. • Scottish Morbidity Register forms (SMR2). • Aberdeen maternal and neonatal data bank. *Outcomes* • maternal and perinatal morbidity. • womens' expectations, experiences and satisfaction with care. • midwives' roles, experiences and satisfaction. • costs of care.		The 2 groups were similar with respect to age, height, parity, social class and education of woman and partner.

Results: Midwife managed delivery unit: a randomized controlled comparison with consultant-led care

Methodological issues

The randomization ratio of 2 (midwife-led care): 1 (consultant-led care) ensured that the space in the midwives' unit was fully utilized.

The data from all women was analysed by intention to treat.

Maternal and perinatal morbidity:

Antepartum transfers:

Of the 199 women randomized to the midwives unit, 727 transferred antenatally (this number includes 80 women lost to follow up).

Of the 80 women who booked for midwife-led care who were lost to follow-up:

*   35 miscarried.
*   11 had a termination of pregnancy.
*   34 moved out of the district.

Reasons for antenatal transfers to consultant-led care are summarized in terms of 16 categories:

Of the 647 women who were transferred from midwife-led care antenatally, the largest categories were:

*   21% (n=155) transfers for induction of labour because of postmaturity.
*   12.8% (n = 93) pregnancy induced hypertension.
*   9.5% (n= 69) prolonged rupture of membranes.

These three categories together accounted for 44% of antenatal transfers.

Intrapartum transfers:

Primigravid women (255/596, 43%) were significantly more likely to be transferred to consultant-led care during labour than were multigravid women (48/577, 8%).

The most common reasons for transfer were:

*   Suspected fetal distress (40% of all intrapartum transfers).
*   Transfers because of delay in the 1st stage: similar % among primigravid women (25% n = 64) and multigravid women (23% n = 11).
*   Primigravid women were significantly more likely to be transferred because of delay in the 2nd stage (13%; n = 32) than were multigravid women (2%; n = 1).

Fetal monitoring:

Women in the midwives' unit were significantly less likely to receive continuous fetal heart rate monitoring. Fetal monitoring was mainly intermittent by Pinard or hand held Doppler method.

The authors suggest that the higher incidence of continuous fetal monitoring in the labour ward group may explain the more frequent observation of fetal distress. The use of fetal scalp electrodes was also higher in the labour ward group.

Analgesia:

	Midwives unit n = 1819 (%)	Labour ward n = 915 (%)
None	32 (1.9)	14 (1.8)
Natural methods	901 (53.8)	355 (45.0)
Entonox	1408 (84.1)	657 (83.3)
TENS	578 (34.5)	216 (27.4)
Pethidine or diamorphine	1063 (63.5)	498 (63.1)
Epidural/spinal	246 (14.7)	140 (17.7)

Mobility:

	Midwives unit n = 1819 (%)	Labour ward n = 915 (%)
Able to move most of the time	1030 (63.5)	388 (51.6)
Unable to move	592 (36.5)	364 (48.4)

Restricted mobility was usually because the woman was attached to a drip, a monitor or was having epidural analgesia.

Mode of delivery and condition of perineum:

	Midwives unit n = 1819 (%)	Labour ward n = 915 (%)
Spontaneous vaginal	1422 (78.2)	689 (75.3)
Vaginal breech	23 (1.3)	12 (1.3)
Forceps/ventouse	221 (12.2)	122 (13.3)
Emergency CS	126 (6.9)	73 (8.0)
Elective CS	27 (1.5)	19 (2.1)
Intact perineum	394 (23.7)	171 (20.9)
Episiotomy	420 (25.2)	238 (29.1)
Tear	850 (51.1)	410 (50.1)
3rd degree tear	15 (0.8)	3 (0.3)

Episiotomy:
The only outcome of labour that was statistically different was a lower episiotomy rate among women allocated to the midwife-led care unit. The higher incidence of episiotomies in the labour ward group may be related to the higher incidence of instrumental deliveries in this group of women.

Stillbirths and neonatal deaths:
The midwives' group had a higher percentage of neonatal deaths but the percentage of stillbirths was higher in the labour ward group.

Due to the small numbers the differences did not reach statistical significance.

Apgar scores:
Scores at 1 and 5 minutes and cord pH were the same in both groups. Babies born to women in the midwives' group were more likely to receive resuscitation, the authors state that this was accounted for by an increased administration of nalaxone.

A similar number of babies from each group were admitted to the neonatal unit.

Discussion and conclusion:

Clinical implications:
- Midwife managed intrapartum care results in more mobility and fewer epidural anaesthetics and episiotomies with no increase in neonatal morbidity.
- Half of the women who are identified as low-risk at booking, using existing criteria, will become high-risk during pregnancy or labour.
- The high rate of intrapartum transfer to consultant led care in primigravid women should be noted by those deciding on criteria for delivery in stand alone units.

The study concludes that midwife managed care is as safe as the standard consultant-led care, and that the lower rate of intervention among women allocated to the midwife unit indicates that this is the more effective option for women at low-risk. The authors do, however, highlight that the 'unpredictability' and high transfer rate for women previously determined as low-risk, demonstrates that antenatal criteria are unable to determine who will remain at low-risk throughout pregnancy.

Women's' expectations, experiences and satisfaction with care:
Not yet reported.

Midwives' roles, experiences and satisfaction:
Staff questionnaire was concerned with:
- Qualifications and experience.
- Continuity of care: length of time the midwife provided care prior to delivery, number of midwives involved in the woman's care and continuity after delivery.
- Procedures and interventions.
- Labour management and complications.
- The midwife's overall impression of the experience.

Multiple linear regression was used to identify which variables were important in predicting staff satisfaction using all variables from the staff questionnaires: additional data were included from the women's questionnaire and casenote review.

Continuity of carer
- In both groups the midwife was most likely to be the primary care giver. This was significantly more likely in the midwives' unit.
- Student midwives were significantly more likely to be primary care givers in the midwives' unit than in the labour ward.
- Medical students were significantly more likely to be primary care givers in the labour ward than in the midwives' unit.
- There was no difference between groups in the number of midwives responsible for the woman in labour, nor in the length of time the midwife had cared for the woman prior to delivery.
- In the midwives' unit, the midwife at delivery was significantly more likely to have carried out all vaginal examinations on a woman during labour (28%) than the midwife at delivery on the labour ward (24%). In both groups, remaining vaginal examinations were usually carried out by another midwife.

Continuity of carer after delivery
- Women allocated to the midwives' unit group were significantly more likely to be sutured by the midwife who was at the delivery than women on the labour ward.
- There were significant differences in the proportion of midwives who continued to provide care until the woman was transferred to the postnatal ward: 49% in the midwives' unit, 44% in the labour ward group. Shift changes accounted for 75% of all these occurrences.

Midwives' satisfaction
- Statistically different levels of satisfaction were reported between midwives in the two groups, with midwives on the midwives' unit being more satisfied.

Variable	Midwives' Unit (Max. n=1759)		Labour ward (Max. n=858)		Statistical test & degrees of freedom		Significance level
	n	%	n	%	x^2	df	
Primary care givers:							
midwife at delivery	1606	(91)	761	(89)	4.54	1	< 0.05
midwife (other)	752	(43)	361	(42)	0.11	1	0.7
student midwife	861	(49)	298	(35)	47.23	1	< 0.001
medical student	90	(5)	87	(10)	23.08	1	< 0.001
Who made labour management decisions?					21.53	5	< 0.001
midwife at delivery only	51	(3)	32	(4)			
midwife at delivery & woman	560	(34)	204	(25)			
midwife, other midwives & woman	334	(20)	159	(20)			

Variable	Midwives' Unit (Max. n=1759)		Labour ward (Max. n=858)		Statistical test & degrees of freedom		Significance level
	n	%	n	%	x^2	df	
med. staff, midwives & woman	641	(39)	369	(45)			
med. staff & midwives only	42	(2)	21	(3)			
med. staff only	32	(2)	21	(3)			
Perineal suturing by:							
midwife at delivery	590	(53)	267	(47)	6.03	1	< 0.05
midwife (other)	211	(19)	108	(19)	0.00	1	1.0
student midwife	44	(4)	14	(2.5)	2.57	1	0.1
Doctor	305	(28)	188	(33)	5.51	1	< 0.05
Care handed over after delivery:							
immediately	183	(11)	105	(12.5)	1.78	1	0.2
before woman transferred	661	(38)	350	(41.5)	2.36	1	0.1
at postnatal ward	846	(49)	373	(44)	4.92	1	< 0.05

The most important factor predicting midwife satisfaction was found to be the responsibility of the midwife for all management decisions in labour.

Factors affecting midwives' satisfaction in order of importance:
- Midwife was responsible for all management decisions in labour.
- Number of midwives involved in the woman's care (higher number, lower level of satisfaction).
- Medical staff carried out perineal repair (reduced midwife satisfaction).
- Midwife at delivery was primary care giver.
- Complications occurred during labour or delivery (reduced midwife satisfaction).
- Woman able, if she wanted, to move around and change position in labour.
- All vaginal examinations carried out by midwife at delivery.
- Women who did not answer the question: 'After delivery were you taken to the operating theatre' (reduced midwife satisfaction).
- Woman's satisfaction.
- Total time midwife looked after the woman prior to delivery.
- Midwives for whom the following question was not applicable: 'Please state why care was handed over prior to the woman being transferred to the postnatal ward'.
- The sex of the baby was a girl.
- No student midwives in delivery room at any time during labour or delivery.
- Woman had episiotomy (reduced midwife satisfaction).
- Baby required resuscitation (reduced midwife satisfaction).
- Midwife was a sister – grade G (reduced midwife satisfaction).

Although a difference existed in satisfaction scores between the groups, neither the group nor the area in which the woman actually delivered were predictors of midwife satisfaction. Midwives in the midwives' unit were more likely to mention atmosphere and surroundings as pleasing aspects of care but no measure for this variable was included.

Costs of care:
Cost estimates based on health care resource use, largely within the hospital. These included: staff costs, consumables, capital costs, overheads.

Consumables
The introduction of the midwives' unit resulted in a cost saving of £3.25 per woman in terms of consumables used.

Staff costs
- Estimate of increased staff costs associated with the midwives' unit: extra 3 x F grade posts + 7 promotions from E to F grade.
- Increase in salary costs of £46.63 per woman (significantly more women in the midwives unit group were looked after by an F grade than in the labour ward group).
- Overall staff costs attributable to the introduction of the midwife unit = + £44.69 per woman.

Capital costs
- Conversion costs (£82,461).
- Estimated 'life' of 35 years: cost per woman = £3.82.
- A net saving of £4.55 on furniture and equipment resulted from the establishment of the midwives unit.
- Overall capital cost saving attributable to the introduction of the midwives' unit = £0.75 per woman.

Baseline extra cost per woman
Net increase of £40.71 per woman as a result of the introduction of the midwives' unit.

Depending on the care provided, the grades of staff employed and the outcomes, this cost could vary from a saving of £9.74 per woman to an additional cost of £44.23 per. woman.

Postnatal costs
Although not central to the study, postnatal costs attributable to different patterns of intrapartum care are estimated. This estimate is based solely on length of stay and average cost per day in the maternity hospital.

- Additional cost to the labour ward group of £13.54 per woman, attributable to longer lengths of postnatal stay following assisted and operative deliveries.

The authors note a number of limitations inherent in the cost analyses and urge caution in their interpretation. Further research is called for.

Turnbull et al. (1995)

Scheme	Authors of evaluation and date	Organization of midwifery service	Aim of scheme and pattern of care provided	No. of midwives involved in the scheme	Midwives' grades	No. of women cared for per annum
Midwifery Development Unit – Glasgow (MDU). Glasgow Maternity Hospital Scheme in operation from January 1993	Turnbull, D., McGinley, M., Holmes, A., Cheyne, H., Shields, N., Twaddle, S., Young, D. 1995. The full report of the study is an internal publication from the Glasgow Royal Maternity Hospital, Rottenrow, Glasgow entitled: The establishment of a midwifery development unit based at Glasgow Royal Maternity Hospital.	• provision of midwife-led care for eligible women living in prescribed catchment area. • each midwife worked as 'primary midwife'; lead care-provider for women in her case load (midwives *did not* work in teams). • each midwife had an 'associate' midwife. • initially each midwife was expected to have a caseload of 35 women,	*Aims* • to introduce total midwifery care for normal, healthy women. • to encourage participating midwives to utilize their skills to the full. • to develop audit and educational tools for use by the midwifery profession. • to monitor and evaluate the unit. **Pattern of care** 'Women could expect to be cared for by a named midwife and up to three associate midwives, from booking through to transfer to the Health Visitor postnatally'. *Antenatal care* • every woman given an information pack about the MDU.	Management team (Head of midwifery services and 2 senior clinical midwifes) + 20 full time midwives.	4 G grades 16 F grades (up-graded from E's in recognition of the responsibility of case load holding).	Out of 1586 eligible women, 1299 consented to be included in the study. 648 received MDU care. *Characteristics* of the women involved in the study: Relatively disadvantaged community living in an area of high density housing. 50% of the Health Board's

Scheme	Authors of evaluation and date	Organization of midwifery service	Aim of scheme and pattern of care provided	No. of midwives involved in the scheme	Midwives' grades	No. of women cared for per annum
	Midwifery Development Unit. Findings are also reported in: *British Journal of Midwifery* 1995b; 3(9): 465–468. *Midwifery* 1995c; 11: 110–119.	the mean was 29, but ranged from 19-39 women per. midwife. • midwives invited to volunteer for scheme. *Rota system:* • fortnightly self rostering system developed. • midwives rotated through all clinical areas. • there was no 'on-call' rota.	• bookings done by midwife: women not seen by medical staff. • each MDU midwife recruits own case-load at the named consultant clinic. • programme of antenatal care based on 8 visits: care provided in hospital or home or community clinics. • clinical input provided by GP where this is requested by woman or GP. • women referred to consultant only for deviation from normality. • lead midwife & her associate midwife alternate at antenatal clinic. • lead midwife writes to GP at booking, at 26 weeks and on discharge. • women hold own notes + care plans. • women given the choice of whether or not to have a scan.			population live in the most deprived areas (compared with only 10% for the rest of Scotland). *Exclusion criteria:* women were not eligible for MDU care if they: • were late bookers (after 16 weeks). • were aged < 16 years and > 40 years. • were < 152 cm in height. • fulfilled clinical exclusion criteria e.g. diabetes, previous caesarean section.

Scheme	Authors of evaluation and date	Organization of midwifery service	Aim of scheme and pattern of care provided	No. of midwives involved in the scheme	Midwives' grades	No. of women cared for per annum
			Intrapartum care • every midwife spent approx. 50% of on-duty rota based in labour ward for clients admitted in labour. • women page MDU co-ordinator directly. Women go directly to one of the 3 'homely' MDU birth rooms in labour ward. • in the absence of a named midwife, women received care from MDU midwife rostered to labour ward at the time. *Postnatal care* • 'where there is no deviation from the normal', care planned and delivered by named midwives and associate midwives: aim was for the majority of planned care episodes to be provided by named midwife. • designated 8-bedded MDU postnatal ward. • after discharge, visits carried out in women's homes. No. of visits tailored to women's needs. • during final care episode, midwife and woman evaluate care plan and undertake debriefing.			

Turnbull et al. (1995)

Scheme	Authors of evaluation and date	Aim of the study	Methods and outcomes	No. of midwives involved	No. of women involved
Midwifery Development Unit (MDU) Glasgow Maternity Hospital Scheme in operation from Jan 1993 Recruitment to RCT from Jan 1993 to Feb. 1994.	Turnbull, D., McGinley, M., Holmes, A,, Cheyne, H., Shields, N., Twaddle, S., Young ,D. 1995. The full report of the study is an internal publication from the Glasgow Royal Maternity Hospital, Rottenrow, Glasgow entitled: The establishment of a midwifery development unit based at Glasgow	To compare midwifery managed care at the MDU and shared care (care divided between obstetricians, midwives and GPs).	Evaluation by a multidisciplinary research team in collaboration with the midwifery team and project steering group. *Methods* RCT: randomization of women who lived in the North East of the city (Glasgow) who booked within 16 weeks of conception between Jan '93 and Feb. '94, at a non-specialist hospital based consultant clinic, who were experiencing a normal healthy pregnancy. Comparison between women receiving MDU care and women receiving shared care. *Data collection via:* • retrospective case record review. • three questionnaires for women: 1 x antenatal and 2 x postnatal.	20 midwives providing MDU care. *Other staff:* • 64 non-MDU midwives. • 20 members of the obstetric team.	Out of 1586 eligible women, 1299 consented to be included in the study. 648 women allocated to the MDU and 651 to shared care. Of the 287 eligible women who did not consent, 71% declined because they wished to receive the existing style of care. • MDU and shared care groups similar in terms of age, smoker-status, marital status, parity • some disparities re. affluence of neighbour-hood between groups: not noted as significant.

Scheme	Authors of evaluation and date	Aim of the study	Methods and outcomes	No. of midwives involved	No. of women involved
	Royal Maternity Hospital. Midwifery Development Unit. Findings are also reported in: *British Journal of Midwifery* 1995b; 3(9): 465-468. *Midwifery* 1995c; 11: 110-119.		• interviews with women. • observation. • questionnaire surveys of midwives. *Outcomes: associated with RCT* • clinical. • economic: including cost effectiveness of midwife managed care compared to shared care. • audit of service (including continuity of care). • perceptions (including satisfaction) of women and midwives. *Other outcomes:* • survey of obstetricians' and midwives' attitudes. • development of audit and educational tools. • case study of management of change. • audit of 'choices for care' following completion of RCT.		A further 309 women were recruited to the post RCT audit of 'choices for care'.

Results: Midwifery development Unit: a randomized controlled comparison with shared care

Implementation process:
- Funded by the Scottish Office Home and Health Department for three years.
- Funding obtained primarily for the creation of a research team to evaluate the unit rather than the purchasing of additional midwifery staff.

- **Key stakeholders** were identified and targeted prior to the application for funding; 'any person or group or organisation that can place a claim on an organization's attention, resources or output, or is affected by that output' (Freeman, 1984, *Strategic Management: A Stakeholder Approach*. Boston: Pitman Press).
- Liaison with local medical council: every GP in catchment area was also written to.

- **Selection of midwives;** workshops organized for midwives.
- Midwives working full time, who had completed at least one year's post-registration rotation in all midwifery care areas were invited to volunteer for the scheme.
- 21 midwives appointed (one left before the scheme began): eight from labour ward: two from community posts: one from outpatients' clinic: nine from postnatal wards: one from women's reproductive health unit.
- All MDU midwives completed a personal inventory of skills: inventory comprised of 50 skills considered by senior midwives as necessary for providing total care. Each midwife was responsible for arranging an update where required.
- Multidisciplinary workshops were conducted where core care issues were overviewed.
- **Rotation system:** rotation of MDU midwives around clinical areas during the fortnightly rosta included: 3 x 8 hr shifts in the antenatal/postnatal wards; 3 x 12 hr shifts in labour ward; 2 x 5 hr shifts in community; 1 x 4 hr shift in antenatal clinic; 1 x 4½ hr shift to cover community and outpatients' departments.
- An initial six months was spent testing the new roster before implementation of the care programme.

- **Service specifications** were developed using Quality Assurance Model of Midwifery (QAMID) with consumer participation.

Clinical outcomes:
Antenatal
- Women in the MDU group received one fewer visit than women in the shared care group.
- The groups received similar number of attendances for daycare assessment.
- There was no difference between groups, in the number of tests or treatments carried out as in-patients or outpatients.

Intrapartum

	MDU	Shared care
labour induced	24%	33%
augmentation during labour	43%	40%
intact perineum	31%	24%
1st or 2nd degree tear	42%	42%
episiotomy	28%	34%
epidural	32.7%	34.1%
continuous fetal heart monitoring	79%	87%
mean length of labour in 1st stage	6hrs	6hrs
mean length of labour in 2nd stage	1 hr	1 hr
mean length of labour in 3rd stage	0.5hrs	0.6hrs
manual removal of placenta	4%	4%
mean gestation	39wks	39wks
born between 25 & 36 wks gestation	5%	7%
born at 42+ wks gestation	2%	2%
spontaneous vertex delivery	73.5%	73.7%
caesarean section	12.9%	11.9%
apgar score of 8-10 @ 1min	78%	76%
apgar score of 8-10 @ 5min	98%	97%
birth wts between 5th & 95th centile range	88%	89%
major fetal abnormalities	3	3
neonatal death	3	5

(Panel review concluded that none of the deaths were attributable to sub-standard care or management in either group).

Transfer from midwife managed care
- 34% were not transferred.
- 33% were temporarily transferred when intervention was required, or requested by a woman.
  - of the temporary transfers: 76% occurred during the intrapartum period. Main reasons for this were: priming and induction (30%); epidural (21%); deviation from normal in the mother (19%).
  - 24% of temporary transfers occurred antenatally, the majority for deviations from normal.
- 33% of MDU women were permanently transferred (29% for clinical reasons, 4% for non-clinical reasons).

Postnatal
- Mean length of stay was three days in each group.
- Both groups received a mean of five community postnatal visits.
- 4% of women in both groups were readmitted.

Satisfaction with care
Response rates from women's questionnaires:

	MDU	Shared care
Antenatal	85%	78%
Labour & postnatal	72%	63%
7mths postnatal	68%	63%

- Satisfaction scores for all women were in the positive range.
- Overall, general satisfaction scores were higher in the MDU group for each period of care.
- Satisfaction scores for 'information transfer' were higher in the MDU group for each period of care.
- Women in the MDU group were more highly satisfied with their 'social support' than women in the shared care group: the largest differences occurred in the antenatal period and for hospital based postnatal care.

Choices:
- This refers to women's attitudes about the amount, control and encouragement they experienced in making decisions about their care. Women in the MDU group scored higher for all stages of care.

Interpersonal relationships with staff:
This considered whether staff were perceived as helpful, pleasant and instilling confidence.
- There were higher scores from the MDU group of women for each of the time periods.

Continuity of care and carer:
Assessed by:
- Retrospective review of records of 180 MDU women and 180 shared care women who entered the trial three months after it commenced.
- Women's recollections of care providers; assessed in seven months postnatal questionnaire.
- Women in the MDU group saw an average of 10 care providers, the shared care group saw 17.
- 93% of women in the MDU group said they had seen 'just the right amount' of carers compared to 66% in the shared care group.
- 14% of women randomised to receive MDU care who had a spontaneous vertex delivery were delivered by the named midwife.
- Of the women who were delivered by the MDU midwives and who had a spontaneous vertex delivery, 18% were delivered by their named midwife.

Economic outcomes
Costs were apportioned through a detailed review of case records: each element of care was costed. Costs associated with admission to SCBU were not counted in postnatal care. A median case load of 29 women per midwife was assumed. Analysis was performed on the basis of intention to treat.

Resources
The major differences in resource use between the two groups were in antenatal visits, induction and postnatal daycare, with lower rates in the MDU group.

Costs
- No significant difference between cost of MDU and shared care in antenatal and intrapartum periods.
- The MDU group was associated with significantly higher costs in the postnatal period and overall.
- Estimates of costs incurred by women indicate that MDU women incurred more costs attending hospital clinics than the shared care group who tended to incur more costs attending community clinics.

143 women from the MDU group and 142 from the shared care group were asked to complete a *conjoint analysis questionnaire* to assess the relative utility of different attributes of care provided.

Results indicated that women would prefer to pay more for MDU care than shared care and that they felt that the hospital should pay more to create a homely environment and to have fewer carers.

MDU Service Audit:
Data collected through retrospective analysis of case records and questionnaires distributed to a sample of MDU women.
- 161 antenatal women (response rate 87%).
- 120 postnatal women (response rate 69%).
- 54% of MDU women were cared for by up to four midwives (the service specification).
- 46% were cared for by five or more midwives.
- 91% could correctly name their named midwife.
- 76% reported being given 'all' or 'most' of the information they wanted.
- 24% were given 'some' of the information they wanted.

Midwives' attitudes
The attitudes of 21 MDU midwives were compared with the attitudes of 64 hospital midwives.

Questionnaires were distributed prior to implementation of the unit and 15 months after implementation.

- MDU midwives achieved overall positive changes in attitudes to personal satisfaction, professional support, interaction with clients, and professional development.
- Positive changes were greater for MDU midwives than for the comparison group of midwives.

Obstetricians' attitudes

- 11 consultants: four senior registrars: five registrars: 100% response rate to questionnaire.
- 85% felt that there was a 'need for change'.
- 70% felt that midwives can provide the care that low-risk women want: they also believe that women prefer to have a doctor involved in their care.
- 65% believed that all women should see their consultant at least once.
- Only half the obstetricians felt they could trust the clinical judgement of the MDU midwives.
- Some concerns were expressed about impact of this type of service on GPs, SHOs and referral patterns and communication between midwife and obstetricians.

Audit of 'Choices for Care'

Following completion of the RCT:

- Questionnaire distributed to a sample of 203 women after the hospital booking visit (sample selection unclear). Response rate 84%.
- 50% of the women chose community-based shared care.
- 36% chose named-midwife care.
- 10% chose hospital-based shared care.
- 4% chose DOMINO.
- Less than 1% chose home birth.

The GP's role

- A survey of GPs' attitudes and experiences was not undertaken, however, of the 2128 women who were excluded at the outset from the study, 7% were excluded because the GP did not wish the women to be included. In the majority of cases, no clinical reason was given.
- Of the women permanently transferred from MDU care during the study, 7% were transferred at the GP's request; no clinical reasons were given.
- After completion of the RCT, when midwife managed care was offered as one option for care, GPs expressed an objection in 11% of cases when women were potentially eligible.

McCourt and Page (1996)

Scheme	Authors of evaluation and date	Organization of midwifery service	Aim of scheme and pattern of care provided	No. of midwives involved in the scheme	Midwives' grades	No. of women cared for per annum
One-to-One Midwifery Practice From Nov. 1993	McCourt, C., Page, L. (eds) 1996 Report on the evaluation of one-to-one midwifery. Thames Valley University, London.	• 3 group practices of midwives providing integrated hospital and community care for women residing in 2 geographical areas in London. • 1:1 care provided through partnerships: 'functional units' of 2 midwives which are organized into the 3 group practices.	*Aim* • to provide a named midwife for each woman who would care for her throughout pregnancy, birth and the postnatal period. • to promote excellence in midwifery practice, enabling midwives to use all their skills within their caseload and to develop them. • to implement an academic environment within which midwives work, utilizing a system of peer review and support and feedback through audit of practice. *Organizational targets*: • 95% of women to be attended by a midwife they know and have formed a relationship with for labour and delivery. • low risk women to be directly cared for by no	20 midwives in the 3 group practices.	Of the original 20 midwives, 11 were G grades and 9 were F grades. 'Partnership' consisted of one F grade and one G grade midwife.	Approx. 800 women per annum, (approx.15% of the maternity service). Each midwife carried a caseload of 40 women.

Scheme	Authors of evaluation and date	Organization of midwifery service	Aim of scheme and pattern of care provided	No. of midwives involved in the scheme	Midwives' grades	No. of women cared for per annum
		• the group practice provides support to the partnership during busy times including holidays. • each individual midwife in the scheme carries a caseload. • initial recruitment of 20 midwives already employed in the Trust, via 'careful selection'. • some existing community midwives had to be moved from 'their patch' to make room for 1-1.	more than 6 professionals in the course of their pregnancy. • over 75% of women to be cared for by their named midwife in labour. • 75% of total antenatal visits to take place in the community. • 50% of women to have midwife-led care throughout. • 75% of postnatal care to be by the named midwife. • no more than 5. professionals for midwife-led care in the postnatal period. **Pattern of care** Scheme midwives based at home (though with office at QCCH). Midwives carry mobile phones and the numbers of the named midwife and her partner are given to the women.			

Scheme	Authors of evaluation and date	Organization of midwifery service	Aim of scheme and pattern of care provided	No. of midwives involved in the scheme	Midwives' grades	No. of women cared for per annum
			Antenatal care • women are usually referred to the 1-1 scheme by their GP. • booking midwife usually allocated as named midwife for woman: booking normally takes place at the woman's home. • at the booking visit, the woman can choose the lead professional (GP, midwife or consultant) depending on preferences and medical need. • women can choose to book for home or either of the two units (QCCH or Hammersmith Hospital HH). *low-risk women* • care usually provided by midwife: affiliated obstetrician also allocated • hospital visits at 12 weeks (HH) or 15 weeks (QCCH) + at 19-21 weeks for scans + 41 weeks to review management if necessary.			

Scheme	Authors of evaluation and date	Organization of midwifery service	Aim of scheme and pattern of care provided	No. of midwives involved in the scheme	Midwives' grades	No. of women cared for per annum
			remainder of antenatal care usually via home visits; women may have GP care or hospital care if they wish. *high-risk care* • care led by consultant in hospital: named midwife provides 'care and support'. *Intrapartum care* • named midwife or partner on-call for labour: often home visits in early labour. *Postnatal care* • following birth, postnatal care led by named midwife/partner (usually only one postnatal visit per day on the postnatal ward from the named midwife). Transfer home within 24 hours if no complications. • postnatal care provided up to 28 days if required. *Cross-border issues* Women planning to give birth outside of the Trust were not included in the scheme.			

McCourt and Page (1996)

Scheme	Authors of evaluation and date	Aim of the study	Methods and outcomes	No. of midwives involved	No. of women involved
Evaluation of One-to-One Midwifery From Nov. 1993	McCourt, C., Page, L. (eds) 1996 Report on the evaluation of one-to-one midwifery. Thames Valley University, London. Piercy J Wilson, D & Chapman P (1996). One-to One-Midwifery Practice. Final Report. York Health Economics Consortium. University of York.	To evaluate : 1. impact on the staff and service overall of 1:1 scheme. • how do the different groups of staff respond? • how does the service handle such a change? 2. impact on women and families of 1:1. • experiences of mothers. 3. clinical outcomes. • safety of care compared with traditional system.	Evaluated by a research team that included independent researchers. *Methods* Ethnographic study of organizational change. • interviews. • focus GPs. • participant observation. • documentary analysis. Comparative study between two organizational areas. • W3 & W12: 1:1 care. • W4 & W6: traditional (usually shared) care. Areas matched 'to be as similar as possible'. Involved all women living in these localities who were due to give birth in the Trusts between 15 August 1994 and 14 August 1995. Excludes: women moving into/ out of area: births before 28 weeks.	32 midwives in 20 One-to-One posts over the period of the evaluation.	Total sample of: 1403 women. • 728 receiving One-to-One midwife care and • 675 in comparison area receiving pre-existing pattern of 'traditional' care. Most statistical analyses of results were conducted for the two units separately due to differences in the numbers of women delivering at each unit. *Characteristics of* women in the scheme: significant class and ethnic differences between 1:1 and comparison group at QCCH. The differences

Scheme	Authors of evaluation and date	Aim of the study	Methods and outcomes	No. of midwives involved	No. of women involved
		• impact on intervention rates of 1:1 scheme. 4. economic assessment. • implications for resource use and sustainability, and affordability.	Separate analyses were often carried out for the two hospitals (QCCH & HH); the numbers of women giving birth at each unit differed, due to the size of the units and difference across the groups in proximity to them (in particular, only small number of women receiving the 'traditional care' service were booking with HH). *Data collection* via: Survey of women's experiences. • questionnaires. • interviews. • focus groups. Clinical audit. • selected parts of *Midwifery Monitor.* • Lilford's 101 measures. • obstetrical interventions and outcomes. • continuity of carer audit.		were greater when the 1:1 women using HH were compared with those at QCCH. 1:1 group and women using HH reported as representing a more disadvantaged population reflecting characteristics of the local neighbourhoods which the hospitals serve. 'As a more deprived and ethnically mixed group based on epidemiological evidence about patterns of health, they would be expected to have a greater health problems and need for health care.' (McCourt and Page, p. 26).

Scheme	Authors of evaluation and date	Aim of the study	Methods and outcomes	No. of midwives involved	No. of women involved
			Economic evaluation. • hospital activity data. • audit of casenotes (on random sample of women in the 1:1 and traditional cohorts). • log of care provided. *Outcomes* • case study. • women's views. • clinical audit. • quality of care audit. • audit of antenatal, intrapartum and postnatal contacts with midwives. • workload analysis • costs audit.		

Results: One-to-One Midwifery care: a comparative study with traditional (usually shared) care

Methodological issues
All instruments were piloted prior to the study.

Quality control mechanisms
- A range of methods were used – triangulation – accuracy checks were conducted within each strand of the study.
- Notes were double checked (1:20).
- Interviews, if taped, were also checked for accuracy.
- Random checks of data from questionnaires were also made for accuracy.

Ethical issues
- Confidentiality was maintained for staff by coding of questionnaires.
- Women were asked to return the blank questionnaires if they did not want to be involved.
- Women who experienced pregnancy loss or bereavement were not sent questionnaires but offered a personal interview.

Analysis of information
SPSS was used: Mann Whitney or chi squared were used as appropriate.

Summary of the report
The main foci of care were considered to be choice, continuity and control.

Outcomes
- Midwives liked working under the One-to-One system and did not want to go back to the traditional pattern of care provision.
- Women gave very positive feedback on the care provided.

- Increased demand from women in both groups in relation to continuity of care and carer.
- Women were quite positive about the maternity services they received but these views were not uniformly positive.

Antenatal care
- Women in the One-to-One scheme received an average of 13 antenatal contacts.
- Women found community based antenatal care the preferred option.
  – visits were more convenient, informative and the care more personal.
- One-to-One women had a significantly lower mean number of doctor appointments in the hospital antenatal clinic ($p<0.05$).

Mean number of hospital outpatient attendances in each care group

	Attendances	Mean Number
One-to-One	691	0.90
'Traditional'	9151	3.07

- Women in the One-to-One group were happy with the quality of information and opportunities for discussion from midwives but dissatisfied with contacts with doctors.
- Women who received conventional care were critical of communication and information provided by hospital midwives and doctors.
- On the whole, women prefer having care provided by midwives but value access to GPs and others as required.
- Home visiting was a particularly beneficial aspect of One-to-One care.
- Women said that knowing the midwife helped to increase confidence and women wanted the same care in subsequent pregnancies.
- Women in both groups wanted more information, especially during the early stages of pregnancy, and information on support groups and classes.

Antenatal admissions by hospital and care group (LOS: length of stay)

	One-to-One			'Traditional'		
	No.	Rate	LOS	No.	Rate	LOS
HH	91	0.30	1.48	229	0.36	1.93
QCCH	81	0.17	1.19	573	0.24	1.39
Total	172	0.22	1.34	802	0.27	1.531

Labour
- Women prefer to be cared for in labour by midwives they know but some women also value the care from midwives they do not know.
- Shift changes were not appreciated and women would like to see the midwife who delivered them during the postnatal period.
- The majority of women in the One-to-One group had constant attendance during labour compared to just over half in the traditional group.
- Women value the supportive presence of a midwife they trust and have confidence in during labour.
- Women in both groups were critical of the role of some doctors in labour and how obstetric interventions were handled.
- Women from the One-to-One group experienced no problems in accessing delivery beds, unlike women from the traditional group.

Rate of interventions
- No significant increase in the number of normal deliveries.
- Use of epidurals reduced.
- Some women had no pain relief at all.
- Reduction in episiotomies without an increase in tears.
- Women in the One-to-One group were less likely to receive continuous fetal monitoring.

Postnatal care
- Postnatal care was characterized by the lowest levels of satisfaction, particularly in the first few days after delivery.
- All women felt that they received very little support on the postnatal wards for breastfeeding and routine care for the babies. Some of their personal needs were also ignored e.g. toileting, pain relief. Night staff appeared to receive the most criticism.

- Clinical standards of care were similar overall.
- Clinical audit indicated a need for improvements in record keeping in both systems of care.

Postnatal care at home
- Satisfaction with postnatal care at home was high but some women felt the visits were too brief to be adequate in the first few days.
- Women from both groups felt that postnatal visiting at home was stopped too soon or too suddenly.

Postnatal care in hospital
- Women in the One-to-One group were less well catered for on the postnatal wards. Some said that they actually experienced discrimination from ward staff who expected their own midwife to come in and provide care.

Neonatal outcomes
- No significant indications of poorer outcomes for babies born in One-to-One care group.

Organizational targets
- *Target* 1: 95% of women to be attended by a midwife they know and have formed a relationship with for labour and delivery: *achieved* 82% of 1:1 women at QCCH and 88% at HH.
- *Target* 2: over 75% of women to be cared for by their named midwife in labour: *achieved* 66% at QCCH & 77% at HH.
- *Target* 3: low risk women to be cared for by no more than 6 professionals in the course of their pregnancy: *achieved* 44% at QCCH & 48% at HH.
- *Target* 4: 75% of antenatal visits to be in the community: *achieved* over 50%.
- *Target* 5: 50% of women to have midwife-led care throughout: *achieved* 73.8% at QCCH & 76.4% at HH.

Analysis of midwifery workloads
40 women per midwife deemed to be a realistic number.

Economic analysis of hospital activity
- It is suggested that the scheme does not appear to increase midwifery costs.

The future
- Extension of the service to other districts within the area is encouraged, enabling the development of four group practices.
- It is acknowledged that involvement of staff is crucial at each stage and recruitment of midwives should be a gradual process. The service needs to be integrated into the rest of the midwifery service and the role of the hospital midwives needs to be explored.
- Discussion around the reprovision of maternity services on one site may lead to a reduction in organizational difficulties arising through the need to work across two hospital sites.

- Midwife led labour and delivery areas should be created at the existing Queen Charlottes' and the new Queen Charlottes'.
- Midwives should be supported by appropriate administrative staff.
- The caseload of 40 should remain.
- The service requires continuous monitoring and evaluation; any new options or changes to the service need to be piloted.

Replication of One-to-One midwifery by other Trusts and/or Health Authorities is urged to ensure that it fits with local needs, resources and services.

Farquhar et al. (1996)

Scheme	Authors of evaluation and date	Organization of midwifery service	Aim of scheme and pattern of care provided	No. of midwives involved in the scheme	Midwives' grades	No. of women cared for p.a
Community midwifery teams in West Essex. Pilot scheme 1992. Full scheme in operation since April 1994.	Farquhar, M., Camilleri-Ferrante, C., Todd, C. 1996 An evaluation of midwifery teams in West Essex – Final report. Public Health Resource Unit & Health Services Research Group, Institute of Public Health.	• 7 midwifery teams covering the whole of West Essex. • majority of midwives (60%) community based. • 40% of midwives form 'core' of hospital-based staff providing care in hospital. • midwives opted to join either a community team or hospital-based core staff.	*Aims* • to provide 24 hour midwifery care with each woman having a named midwife. • for each woman to have continuity of care (continuity seen in terms of the team rather than an individual midwife). • for each woman (high and low-risk) to be delivered by a member of the team whenever possible. • for parent education and relaxation classes to be available to all who request them. • to fully utilize the skills of the midwives. • to provide opportunities for further development.	Since 1994: • 7-8 midwives in each team (7 w.t.e.) • 55 community based midwives and • 36 core staff (midwives) based in hospital also 2 ENs and 4 nursery nurses. Other staff • 124 GPs. • 42 health visitors.	*Team midwives* Teams consist of E, F and G grades: team coordinator = G grade. An E grade development post exists in the community for newly qualified midwives to consolidate their skills.	Approx. 2,400 women/ annum (excluding cross-border).

Scheme	Authors of evaluation and date	Organization of midwifery service	Aim of scheme and pattern of care provided	No. of midwives involved in the scheme	Midwives' grades	No. of women cared for per annum
		• community teams carry caseloads relating to a group of GP practices and/or geographical area. • caseload per team theoretically no more than 350 per annum.	**Pattern of care** *Antenatal care* • women booked by team midwife in home or health centre: booking midwife becomes 'named midwife'. • antenatal visits shared GP+ team midwives – usually in GP clinics. • teams provide parent education + relaxation. • hospital antenatal visit for scan (etc) at 18 weeks + 41 weeks if necessary/desired. • team midwife accompanies woman for termination for fetal abnormality: also (if requested) for scans and amniocentesis. • hospital based antenatal care with core midwives available for high-risk women and may be chosen by low-risk women. • in-patient antenatal care provided by core midwives.		*Core midwives* G grade midwives = 'Clinical Specialists' based on delivery suite or wards: lower grades based on wards (with some rotation).	

197

Scheme	Authors of evaluation and date	Organization of midwifery service	Aim of scheme and pattern of care provided	No. of midwives involved in the scheme	Midwives' grades	No. of women cared for per annum
			Intrapartum care • rostered 'on-call' team midwife provides care for team bookings + transfers mother + baby to postnatal ward. • core midwives provide intra-partum care when >1 team-booked woman in labour + cross-border women. *Postnatal care* • in-patient postnatal care provided by core staff. • team midwives provide postnatal care in community (negotiated between woman and midwife). • postnatal care for women with babies in special care baby unit provided by core staff in hospital. *Cross-border issues* Approx 20% of deliveries represent cross border flow: 3 midwives providing community care in areas of substantial cross-border flow not included in team scheme. Also, a substantial number of women receive antenatal + postnatal care from a team but deliver elsewhere.			

APPENDIX C6B

Farquhar et al. (1996)

Scheme	Authors of evaluation and date	Aim of the study	Methods and outcomes	No. of midwives involved	No. of women involved
Evaluation of community midwifery teams in West Essex Pilot scheme 1992 Full scheme in operation since April 1994	Farquhar, M., Camilleri-Ferrante, C., Todd, C. 1996 An evaluation of midwifery teams in West Essex – Final report. Public Health Resource Unit & Health Services Research Group, Institute of Public Health	1. to describe the West Essex community based midwifery teams (case study). 2. to assess the satisfaction levels of those working in teams (community midwives) and those working with teams (GPs, health visitors, hospital midwives, managers, obstetricians) and to identify constraints.	Independent evaluation *Methods* • descriptive case study, plus comparison between study group: women receiving all antenatal, intrapartum and postnatal care from West Essex teams and three comparison groups 1. antenatal and postnatal care provided outside of area but delivering in study-linked hospital. 2. antenatal and postnatal care by West Essex, non-team midwives but delivering outside of area. 3. antenatal and postnatal care by one West Essex team but delivering outside of area. *Data collection via:* • interviews • surveys (postal questionnaires) • clinical audit	92 midwives (including 2 Enrolled Nurses - [ENs]) surveyed. 83 responded. Response rates 95% (community) 84% (core). *Other staff* • 124 GPs (+ 19 controls). 78% response rate (n = 112). • 42 health visitors. 83% response rate (n = 35).	1077 women in the study group; 943 responded. 443 in the 3 comparison groups; 392 responded. Total responses = 1335; overall response rate = 88%. (Questionnaires returned by 'study' women represent 71% of total.) Groups in study similar with respect to parity; employment status; ethnicity. Significant differences between groups reported for: age; housing tenure; education; high/low-risk status.

Scheme	Authors of evaluation and date	Aim of the study	Methods and outcomes	No. of midwives involved	No. of women involved
		3. to describe user satisfaction and experiences. 4. to establish whether there are any changes in practice and their impact on clinical outcomes. 5. to identify the number of contacts between women and midwives.	• process and outcome forms completed by midwives *Outcomes* • audit of the number of antenatal and intrapartum midwife contacts. • clinical outcomes. • staff satisfaction survey. • women's views.		

Results: Community Midwifery Teams in West Essex: comparison with three other care groups

Implementation process
- Report suggests that consultation concerning both the pilot scheme (involving only one team) and the full scheme was very limited.
- Some dissatisfaction noted with allocation of midwives to teams: many midwives opting for core staff thought core = delivery suite and were not happy with ward allocation. Not enough midwives opted for community and some who had given it as second choice were therefore allocated there.

Midwives views:
- Some demographic differences between scheme and non-scheme midwives. Generally positive about the scheme but both groups were quite stressed and had not enough time.
- Midwives more likely to think that quality of care had declined than that it had improved with *loss* of continuity most common reason cited.

Scheme midwives wanted:
- Smaller caseloads.
- Smaller teams.
- Bringing teams up to complement.
- Cutting on-call/labour ward shifts.

Hospital midwives suggested:
- Employing more midwives.
- Correcting skill mix.
- Raising the profile of the hospital service in line with community.

GPs' views:
Pro community care but not convinced the system worked.
Size of team seen as critical.
Women may meet seven midwives from her team in pregnancy and then not be delivered by any of them therefore:

- Continuity reduced.
- More caregivers.
- More conflicting advice.

(NB some GPs thought that 'team midwifery' meant GP and midwife worked together as a team, or interdisciplinary team.)

- Some didn't know that they had a link midwife. Only 40% had met all of their team.
- More than half would go back to the old way of working because communication between midwife and GP was thought to be better.
- 50% of GPs thought the service had deteriorated as a result of teams because of reduced continuity for women.

Health Visitor's views:
- Similar to GPs.
- They especially preferred the old system because of better communication between health visitors and midwives.
- New system was thought to be worse because of lack of continuity.

Women's views:
Data collected when the baby was 10 days old. The study women were younger and less well-educated than women in comparison groups.

- Most women had five to nine antenatal checks.
- Over 75% of the *study* group reported seeing a different midwife each time whereas women in *comparison* group (group 2) saw just one or two.
- 10% didn't know that their midwives worked as a team.
- No difference in choice of location of antenatal care, but controls reported more choice of place of delivery (NB: this was a criterion for constitution of comparison groups).

Seeing more than two midwives antenatally was found not to foster the development of a relationship between a woman and her midwives.

Study group
- Study group most likely to report that it was 'not very important' to see the same midwife each time.
- Study group women more likely to report that looking back they would have liked more opportunity to discuss what might happen in labour.

Comparisons
Comparison group (group 2) women:
- Saw fewest midwives during the antenatal period; most likely to have named midwife.
- Felt best prepared.
- Most likely to form a relationship.
- Most satisfied with antenatal care.

Intrapartum care
Pain relief
Differences in use of pain relief were related to place of delivery.

Knowing the midwife
- Women in the study group were more likely than women in comparison groups to be delivered and sutured by a community midwife.
- 33% of study group women had previously met all the midwives who cared for them in labour; 33% had met some; 33% had met none.
- Comparison group women were less likely to have met any of the midwives who cared for them.
- The majority of those who had met a known midwife said that made them feel more at ease but majority of those who hadn't said it didn't make any difference.
- No difference was noted in the satisfaction with care during labour and delivery.

Postnatal care
- Overall one in four women reported conflicting advice while on the postnatal ward.
- No differences in satisfaction with hospital postnatal care.
- Study group women had the lowest continuity during the postnatal period (comparison group 2 had fewest midwives postnatally).
- No difference in (retrospective report of) antenatal intention to breastfeed but higher incidence in two of the comparison groups (groups 2 & 3).
- No difference in satisfaction with postnatal care at home.

Audit of contacts
- The mean number of midwives seen in pregnancy was six.
- Mean number of times the booking midwife was met again was 2.2.
- Prenatal testing: only 12 women (1%) had midwife with them for a scan (these may have been high risk women: 4 had midwife for 2 scans and 2 for 3 scans).
- Mismatch is noted between women's reports and audit on whether they were delivered by a known or a team midwife.

Tucker et al. (1996)

Scheme	Authors of evaluation and date	Organization of midwifery service	Aim of scheme and pattern of care provided	No, of midwives involved in the scheme	Midwives' grades	No. of women cared for per annum
The Scottish Antenatal Care Trial: Provision of routine antenatal care by GPs and midwives.	Tucker, J.S., Hall, M.H., Howie, P.W., Reid, M.E., Barbour, R.S., du V Florey, C., McIlwaine, G.M. 1996 *British Medical Journal* 1996; 312: 554–559.	Routine antenatal care in primary care setting. • care provided by GPs and midwives according to care plan and protocols for managing complications. • participating GPs and midwives linked to one of 9 urban or rural hospital centres. • hospitals' participating consultants agreed to accept low risk women booking for delivery who had received all routine antenatal care from GPs and midwives in the community.	*Aim* To compare routine antenatal care provided by GPs and midwives with obstetrician led shared care. • detailed care plans and protocols to deal with complications arising during pregnancy defined for both arms of trial. • protocols based on the Grampian integrated antenatal care schedule. • clinical content devised by expert consensus. • fewer visits scheduled for multiparous women than for primiparous women. • routine investigations including scans undertaken in primary care. • obstetricians remained responsible for recall of women identified as at risk by serum screening.	45 community midwives Other staff • 224 GPs at 51 practices.	Not reported.	1765 women (Feb. 1993 – Mar 1994).

APPENDIX C7B

Tucker et al. (1996)

Scheme	Authors of evaluation and date	Aim of the study	Methods and outcomes	No. of midwives involved	No. of women involved
The Scottish Antenatal Care Trial: Comparison between routine antenatal care provided by GPs and midwives and obstetrician led shared antenatal care. Recruitment to trial from Feb. 1993 to March 1994.	Tucker, J.S., Hall, M.H., Howie, P.W., Reid, M.E., Barbour, R.S., du V Florey, C., McIlwaine, G.M. 1996 *British Medical Journal* 1996; 312: 554-559.	To compare routine antenatal care provided by general practitioners and midwives, with obstetrician-led shared care.	Evaluation by multidisciplinary research team. *Methods* Multicentre randomized controlled trial of women at low-risk of antenatal complications who presented to participating GPs from Feb. 1993 to Mar. 1994. Comparison between women receiving community-based antenatal care from GPs and midwives and women receiving obstetrician-led shared care. • high-risk identified as ineligible according to 18 pre-defined criteria + history of previous caesarean section. • eligible women informed of trial by GP and referred to booking clinic with their notes flagged as eligible.	45 community midwives. Other staff • 224 GPs at 51 practices.	• 2642 low-risk women referred by GPs. • 2167 still eligible after booking. • 1765 (82%) consented to join the trial. • 9 women were withdrawn from the trial (4 women withdrew themselves, 5 women were withdrawn by medical staff: all 9 were included in the follow up). • Complete records were available for 1674 women: 834 in the GP + midwife group: 840 in the shared care group.

Scheme	Authors of evaluation and date	Aim of the study	Methods and outcomes	No. of midwives involved	No. of women involved
			• consent sought after booking for delivery and after eligibility checked by the research midwife. • randomization by telephone to a secretary who held trial allocations in a series of opaque non-resealable envelopes. • restricted randomization used to maintain equal numbers in both arms of the trial. • permuted block size of 14-20 used to prevent anticipation of the next trial allocation. • randomization not stratified. *Exclusion* criteria: • women booking after 18 wks. • women who attended the booking clinic who had seen an obstetrician before the research midwife. *Data collection via:* • medical records review (booking visit records; shared care cards; midwifery records after delivery). • audit of care. • audit of carer (no. of carers and professional group). • questionnaire to women: 6 weeks postnatal. *Outcomes* • clinical (sample size recognized to be insufficient to detect differences in maternal and perinatal mortality). • audit of health service use. • indicators of quality of care. • women's satisfaction. • staff satisfaction (not yet reported). • health economic analysis (not yet reported).		Comparison of demographic characteristics of the women with complete data showed no significant differences between the 2 groups.

Results: Routine antenatal care provided by GPs and midwives: multicentre randomized controlled trial with obstetrician-led shared antenatal care

Implementation process: not described.

Reliability checks:
Checks on data collected by research midwives in the nine hospital centres were carried out: 5% of clinical case notes were reviewed for intracoder and intercoder reliability.
- Intracoder reliability ranged from 97.8% to 100%.
- Intercoder reliability ranged from 97.3% to 99.3%.

Statistical analysis: using SPSS for Windows
- Analysis by intention to treat.

Health Service use:
Data from 9035 routine clinic visits for the GP + midwife group.
Data from 9735 routine clinic visits for the shared care group
- Significantly smaller proportion of the GP + midwife groups' visits were to obstetric specialists and more of their visits were supervised by GPs and midwives.
- Women in the GP + midwife group had significantly fewer routine clinic visits than those in shared care group. This remained true for women with and without antenatal complications and by parity.
- Only in the GP + midwife group did multiparous women have significantly fewer routine clinic visits than primiparous women.
- Women in the GP + midwife group had fewer carers, antenatal admissions, day-care episodes and non-attendances.
- There were similar proportions of women who made self-referrals in the two groups
- Significantly more women in the GP + midwife group were referred to hospital staff than women in the shared care group.
- Significantly more women in the GP + midwife group changed from their pre-determined style of care in the antenatal period: 17% before 37 weeks gestation and 21% between 37 weeks and 24 hours before delivery, compared with 7% and 18% in the shared care group.

Indicators of quality of care:
Antenatal care
- Overall, significantly more women in the shared care group (56%) experienced at least one pregnancy complication compared with women in the GP + midwife group (51%).

Significant findings	GP + midwife care (n=834)	Shared care (n+840)	P value
Pregnancy induced hypertension (sustained BP > 140/90)	37 (4.4%)	70 (8.4%)	0.002
Proteinurea (+ or more)	79 (9.6%)	116 (13.9%)	0.007
Pre-eclampsia (concurrent hypertension and proteinurea)	10 (1%)	34 (4%)	0.0005

- No significant differences between women in the two groups were detected for the incidence of transient hypertension (diastolic BP > 90 once only); anaemia (HB<100 g/l); multiple pregnancy; malpresentation or unstable lie; APH; gestational diabetes; hydramnios; hyperemesis (requiring hospitalisation); UTI (treated with antibiotics); other conditions.

Although the total number of 'failures of care' was small, there were significant differences between the trial groups.
- Significantly more of the rhesus negative women in the GP + midwife group did not have their antibodies checked at 34/36 weeks.
- More women in the shared care group were not treated when anaemia was found through blood testing (this did not reach significance ($p = 0.04$).

Intrapartum care:
- Significantly more women in the shared care group had their labour induced and fewer has spontaneous onset of labour.
- The groups were similar with respect to: preterm deliveries; mode of delivery; undiagnosed abnormalities at birth; number of liveborn babies in SCBU for >24 hours; number of babies who were ever breastfed in hospital.
- There was one maternal death in the GP + midwife group four weeks postnatally. This is reported as being unrelated to antenatal care.
- The two groups were similar with respect to: live births; still births, neonatal deaths, fetal losses <24 weeks and terminations.

Women's satisfaction:
78% of women responded to the postal questionnaire: (1335/1712): 668 from the GP + midwife group, 667 from the shared care group.
- Women in both groups demonstrated similarly high levels of satisfaction with care received during pregnancy.
- Women in both groups considered their allocated style of care to be acceptable.
- In the GP + midwife group significantly more women reported getting on 'very well' with their main carer (rather than 'well' or 'not at all') and more reported unreservedly enjoying their antenatal care.
- Significantly more women in the GP + midwife group expressed a preference for seeing the same person at every antenatal visit.

Klein et al. (1983)

Authors	Date	Study reference	Intervention assessed	Evaluation	No. of women studied	Main outcomes
Klein, M. Lloyd, I. Redman, C. Bull, M. Turnbull, A.C	1976	Two consecutive papers in the *British Journal of Obstetrics & Gynaecology* (1983) vol 90 pp. 118-122 I. Obstetrical procedures and neonatal outcomes. pp. 118-122 II. Labour and delivery management and neonatal outcome. pp. 123-128	A comparison of low-risk pregnant women booked for delivery in two systems of care: shared care (consultant-led) and integrated general practitioners' unit (GPU). *The GP Unit* • the Oxford GPU is located within the specialist obstetric unit. • community midwife seen as the 'key figure': midwife uses the GP and consultant team for support, gives antenatal care and usually attends deliveries. • women discouraged from using epidurals. • electronic fetal monitoring was not used in the GP Unit. • immediate access available to anaesthetist, obstetrician and paediatrician in both systems. *Shared care:* • antenatal care by GP and midwife. • minimum of 3 hospital antenatal visits.	Retrospective case-note comparison of women booked for shared care with women booked for the integrated GP Unit. *Entry criteria:* low-risk women: • primips between 18 and 30 years of age; • multips with parity <3, aged 18-35 years were included. *Exclusion criteria:* past history of: caesarean section; neonatal death; stillbirth	Of the 5,005 births in the study unit in 1976, 1436 women met the 'low-risk' criteria. • 1188 booked for delivery in the consultant unit • 247 booked for delivery in the GP Unit	• intervention rates at delivery • neonatal outcomes • presentation and length of labour • management of labour pain

Authors	Date	Study reference	Intervention assessed	Evaluation	Number of women studied	Main outcomes
				or low birthweight infant <2500gms; height <152 cms; significant medical history; currently on long term medication: diagnosed with malpresentation; multiple pregnancy; antenatal BP of >140/85 mmHg. NB: The GP Unit and consultant unit use the same records, allowing for retrospective comparison of outcomes with the same system of record keeping.	The second paper deals only with a subset of these women, (those admitted because they were in spontaneous labour, or thought that they were). The notes of 63 multips and 63 primips from each of the two settings meeting these criteria were reviewed (ie N=252).	

Results: A comparison of low-risk pregnant women booked for delivery in two systems of care: shared-care (consultant-led) and integrated general practitioner unit care

General Practitioner Unit (GPU)
Characteristics:
- primips in the GPU had slightly lower diastolic blood pressure, were slightly taller and younger than the multips.

Transfer rate:
- 48% of primips and 25% of multips were transferred to the consultant unit in pregnancy, labour and the puerperium. In the sub-sample for the second paper, these figures were 29% and 5%, reflecting the more highly selected group. The reasons for transfer and subsequent outcomes are not identified.

Obstetric outcomes:
From the first paper:
- 27% of multips receiving shared care were induced compared to 10% in the GPU.
- Epidural as a form of analgesia was used more frequently by both multips and primips in the shared care group compared to the GPU.
- Forceps delivery was more common in the shared care group.
- Similar numbers of primips had emergency caesareans in the two types of care, no multips in the GPU had an emergency caesarean section.
- There was no significant difference in birthwieght of infants in either group.
- In multips, the rates of intubation and asphyxia requiring admission to special care baby unit were slightly higher in the shared care group of women.
- Both primips and multips in the GPU group were more likely to be breastfeeding at discharge than women in the shared care group. This assessment was actually made at different times for the two groups: mean 4.3 days in shared care group and 2 weeks for GPU women, thus underestimating the extent of the difference.

From the second paper:
- Home visiting in early labour was part of the GPU policy, as a result of which GPU women arrived at the hospital in a more advanced stage of labour and the mean length of time from arrival to delivery was reduced by approx. one third.
- Although GPU primips had significantly longer first stage of labour than primips booked for shared care, they were significantly less likely to use pethidine or epidurals.
- GPU women were considerably less likely to have electronic fetal monitoring

Conclusions:
The authors found higher intervention rates in low-risk women booked for the shared care system. The authors acknowledge that that this type of study does not define these differences in any detail and that unknown biases may be present.

They do, however, conclude that newborn short-term outcomes in an integrated GPU are as good as for those infants of comparable low-risk women in a shared-care system.

Differences in the use of electronic fetal monitoring and pharaceutical pain-relief reflect unit policies, which would have been known to women at booking. They may, therefore, reflect women's pre-exisiting preferences, i.e. women wanting these things would be less likely to choose a GPU booking. The Discussion of paper 2 indicates that women booked for shared care lived further from the hospital which is likely to effect the management of early labour.

Chapman et al. (1986)

Authors	Date	Study reference	Intervention assessed	Evaluation	Number of women studied	Main outcomes
Chapman, M.G. Jones, M. Spring, J.E. De Swiet, M. Chamberlain, G.V.P.	?1984	*British Journal of Obstetrics and Gynaecology* 1986 93, pp. 182-187.	The use of a birthroom compared with delivery on the standard labour ward. The birthroom was adjacent to the labour ward, had wallpaper and carpets and was furnished like a bedroom. Epidurals and electronic fetal monitoring were not available. All women in the study were delivered by their community midwives.	Randomized controlled trial. *Eligibility criteria:* multiparous women with normal previous pregnancies and deliveries. All were under the care of Queen Charlotte's Maternity Hospital community midwives; all had asked for early discharge and lived within 5 miles of the hospital.	253 parous women were eligible, but only 148 agreed to take part. 76 were allocated to the birthroom, 72 to the labour ward, but 35 were subsequently withdrawn leaving 54 and 59 respectively.	Events of labour and delivery were recorded on specially designed forms. Postnatal events, method of infant feeding and complications were noted. Information was also collected by questionnaire from mothers at 6–8 weeks postpartum.

Results: The use of a birthroom compared with delivery on the standard labour ward

Reasons for refusal: 105 women (41%) declined to be in the trial: 86 refused because they wanted an epidural and 13 because they wanted monitoring (=99, therefore six refused for other reasons). Subsequently two more withdrew (included below) because they wanted an epidural.

Withdrawals: Thirty-five women (23.6%) were withdrawn from the study, mainly because they developed complications. Therefore analyses were based on only 54 women in the birthroom and 59 women in the labour ward. Twenty-two women were withdrawn from the birthroom group, (11 before labour, 11 during) and 13 from the labour ward group (10 before labour, 3 in labour). There were significantly more withdrawals from the birthroom group than from the labour ward group (p<0.01). Two of the women withdrawn from the birthroom group were withdrawn only because they wanted an epidural. This introduces a bias because this would not have excluded them from the other group. Two of the withdrawals were because women were misdirected by hospital staff to the labour ward instead of the birthroom.

Outcomes:
- No difference in women's ratings of the difficulty of this labour compared with previous labours for the two groups.
- Birthroom women used less analgesia (6 in labour ward had an epidural); 31/54 in the birthroom (57%) and 17/59 in the labour ward (29%) had no analgesia.
- Length of labour was no different between the groups but the admission-to-delivery interval was shorter for birthroom group.
- Birthroom group felt they had more freedom of movement.
- Similar rates of perineal injury but less suturing in birthroom group. Therefore there was either less severe injury or different thresholds for suturing.
- No differences in method of feeding – 85% breastfed in both groups.
- Birthroom mothers were more likely to think that the birth had had a positive effect on their relationship with their baby.
- Women in both groups would prefer the birthroom next time.

Methodological comments
Women in the two groups had care from the same group of (community) midwives. Thus, the setting led to differences in outcomes either through a direct effect on the mothers or because midwives behaved differently in the two settings. Unfortunately the study did not report midwives' view.

Unlike most RCTs, this study was not analysed on the basis of 'intention to treat', and women were withdrawn from the study if they developed any complication or if they were otherwise not delivered in the intended setting. There were significantly more withdrawals from one group than the other and, furthermore, exclusion criteria were not strictly comparable between the groups. Thus, even though the two groups as *randomized* were comparable, we cannot be sure that the two groups as *analysed* were.

Currell, R (1985)

Authors	Date	Study reference	Intervention assessed	Evaluation	No. of women studied	Main outcomes
Currell, R.	October 1979 – June 1985	'Continuity and fragmentation in maternity care', unpublished MPhil. dissertation, University of Exeter, 1985. Details in this table are taken from Currell, 1990 and MIRIAD 1994 pp. 308-9.	Different systems of care (consultant unit, GP Unit and home delivery) were studied in two areas in the south of England.	A comparative study using non-participant observation and semi-structured interviews. Interviews were analysed using categories developed at the pilot stage and others that emerged from the data. In the observational episodes, all mother-staff contacts were counted and coded according to pre-defined categories. It was hypothesized that the organizational patterns of maternity care would be found along a continuum with continuity of care at one end and fragmented care at the other and that women who received the greatest degree of continuity would be the most satisfied and vice versa.	117 mothers and 95 midwives.	Illustration of fragmentation of care. Women's satisfaction. Women's and midwives' accounts of care.

Results: Continuity and fragmentation in maternity care

The study showed considerable fragmentation in all patterns of care, except for a very small number of the women who had home deliveries. Satisfaction with care, for both mothers and midwives, in all groups, appeared to be related to successful problem solving and the giving of 'focused care'. Neither the use of technology nor organization size appeared to have a direct effect on women's experiences of care. The hypothesis that women who received the greatest degree of continuity would be the most satisfied and vice versa was not supported. Both praise and criticism of midwives and their care were found in all the patterns of care, and there were no significant differences between groups.

Midwives appeared to find difficulty in reconciling the medical 'cure' aspects of maternity care with the less specific 'care' aspects of midwifery. They appeared to be able to combine cure and care most successfully with women in labour and least successfully in antenatal care. The author suggests that the concept of continuity of care should be replaced by a concept of unity in care, with care centred on each woman rather than on the organization or the providers of the service.

Walker et al. (1995)

Authors	Date	Where published	Intervention assessed	Entry criteria	Number of women studied	Outcomes measured
Walker, J.M. Hall, S. Thomas, M.	1995	Walker, J.M., Hall, S., Thomas, M. (1995) The experience of labour: a perspective from those receiving care in a midwife-led unit. *Midwifery*, 11: 120-129.	Care in a midwife-led unit (Bournemouth). • midwifery-led unit sited in DGH that does not have a consultant obstetric unit. • care provided by permanent Midwifery Development Unit staff. • 24 hour obstetric emergency service is available within the hospital but policy is to transfer women to nearest consultant unit.	*Methods* Retrospective in-depth interviews with women. • purposive sample of women who had delivered in the midwife-led unit and women who had not delivered in the unit but had antenatal or postnatal care there. • interviews carried out during the postnatal period or between 3-4 months after delivery.	• 32 women and six partners • of these, 11 women had not delivered in the midwifery-led unit.	• women's perceptions about control and support in labour. • women's perceptions about informed choice and options available. • women's perceptions about supportive environment. • women's perceptions about continuity of care.

Results: The experience of labour, perspectives from those receiving care in a midwife-led unit

A grounded theory approach was used to identify common categories, issues and experiences

- Core category to emerge was the balance between personal control and support.
- Control came from being able to have 'support' (i.e. midwife's presence) when a woman wanted it and not when she did not and being able to hand over control or let the midwife take control when appropriate.
- Staffing levels therefore need to be adequate to ensure access to a midwife throughout labour.
- Women who experienced difficult or prolonged labour or transferred to a consultant due to a high-risk factor were more likely to express the need for continuity of care.
- These women were, however, less likely to receive continuity of carer and are likely to be the women in greatest need from this type of support.

APPENDIX C12

Drew et al. (1989)

Authors	Date	Study reference	Intervention assessed	Evaluation	Number of women studied	Main outcomes
Drew, N.C. Salmon, P. Webb, L.	1989	*British Journal of Obstetrics and Gynaecology* 1989; 96: 1084-1088	Mothers', midwives' and obstetricians' views on the features of obstetric care which influence satisfaction with childbirth.	Descriptive survey of the views of three groups: 1. Women who delivered a healthy single baby in a specialist obstetric hospital. Approached on the postnatal ward 18-96 hours (1-4 days) postnatally. 2. Midwives. 3. Obstetricians. Methods: • Pilot stage: A questionnaire containing 40 questions was initially given to 15 women to elicit features of their care and the hospital environment. • Self completion questionnaire: ratings of the 40 items were on a 7 point scale from irrelevant to essential.	224 women (183 responded; 82%) • ages ranged from 16-45. • 53% were primips. • 11% unmarried. • 25% had caesarean deliveries. • 21% had instrumental deliveries. 28 midwives' questionnaires returned which represented 54% of the population and 71% of those staff on the wards participating in the study. 67% were qualified midwives the rest were students. 52 obstetricians from a variety of hospitals.	• the importance of certain criteria to women particularly in relation to labour and postnatal care.

Results: Satisfaction with childbirth, the views of mothers, midwives and obstetricians

- Respondents tended to rate items more at the 'essential' end of the continuum rather than 'irrelevant'; only six items were scored at less than the midpoint (3.5) by mothers and obstetricians and only one by midwives.

Mean scores for each item were calculated and they were then rank ordered.

- Having a healthy baby and communication, receiving adequate information, having a friend/relative at delivery with staff were rated highly by women, midwives and obstetricians.

- Being attended by the same doctor throughout pregnancy was ranked 23 by both women and midwives.

- There appeared to be no difference in the ratings given by women who had had different types of deliveries.

Lee, G. (1994, 1995)

Authors	Date	Study reference	Intervention assessed	Evaluation	Number of women studied	Main outcomes
Lee, G.	?1992	Lee G. (1994) A reassuring familiar face? Nursing Times 90: (17) 66-7 Lee G. (1995) "Free speech": the named woman. Midwives 108(1288): 162 Based on a dissertation submitted to the University of Sheffield, 1993.	Community team midwifery in one Health District.	The study was based on interviews with 12 midwives (half of those in 4 teams of 6) and 32 women, some of whom had had care from the teams. The scheme catered for women of all risks. Midwives worked a 24-hour on-call system, and carried bleeps. Reports are very brief and give no details of the methods used.	32 women and 12 midwives.	The value and meaning of community team midwifery for women and midwives. Women's rankings of an ideal system and of the characteristics that they valued in a midwife. Women's satisfaction.

Results:

Women
Women were asked to rank characteristics of an ideal system. Being able to reach the midwife by bleep was ranked top of the list, followed by knowing the labour midwife. However, when women were asked to rank the qualities that they wanted in a midwife, 'inspires confidence and trust' was top of the list, followed by 'safe and competent care'. 'Is known to you' came only half way down. A 'small majority' would prefer a good midwife that they had not previously met to one who was known but was neither very good nor very bad. Most women (81%) had previously met their labour midwife and they were significantly more satisfied than those who had not.

Midwives
Midwives thought that their bleep system was good but reported an adverse effect on their social life of being on-call. Relationships with and support from colleagues was highly rated and all but one midwife expressed high job satisfaction. Two-thirds thought that it was more important to get to know a woman well, even if they then did not deliver her, than to deliver a woman they had met but did not know well. They felt that feeling comfortable with a woman did not mean having to have met her before.

APPENDIX C14

Gready et al. (1995)

Authors	Date	Study reference	Intervention assessed	Evaluation	Number of women studied	Main outcomes
Gready, M. Newburn, M. Dodds, R. Gauge, S.	1995	The full report of the study is an internal publication from The National Childbirth Trust entitled: Choices: childbirth options information and care in Essex during antenatal, labour and early postnatal period.	No intervention. Survey of childbirth options, information and care in Essex during antenatal, labour and early postnatal period.	Evaluation by the National Childbirth Trust. *Methods* • postnatal questionnaire to women: all women resident within the health authority area who gave birth in one of 3 consultant units between 14 November and 25 December, 1994 plus those who gave birth at home or in one of 4 GP Units up to and including February 5th 1995. NB: To increase the sample size for statistical purposes, women having home deliveries or delivering in a GP Unit were recruited for a longer period. • focus groups: 7 groups were developed to include women with special needs. • user representatives' questionnaire: questionnaires were distributed to: 3 MSLCs, 2 CHCs, 1 maternity user group and 1 women's services group	• potential sample of 1195 women who gave birth within the qualifying dates. • 797 women responded, but 5 too late for inclusion. Of the sample: • 42% were having their first babies • 58% their second or subsequent babies. • 98.3% of the women who responded were white • 1.11% Irish • 0.4% Black (including African-Caribbean and Black African) • 0.7% Asian • 0.3% Chinese • 0.4% Other	• continuity of carer • women centred care • communication and information • involvement in decision making • dignity and personal comfort

Results: 'Birth Choices, Women's Expectations and Experiences'

Analyses were calculated using the chi-squared test based on 95% confidence interval.

Results from user representatives

Response rate:
Thirty questionnaires were distributed to assess involvement on the committee(s); how effective they thought the committees were in facilitating change and providing training and support.

- There was a 67% (N=20) response rate.
- 47% of responders thought that the user representation on their committee was good.
- 37% thought their committees required more and younger user representatives.
- 79% of all responders stated that the times of meetings and frequency were inconvenient, there was frequently no crèche facility available which added to the problem.
- Several people alluded to the fact that purchasers and providers were '...actively seeking users' views' and 46% felt 'respected' by purchasers and providers. 60% felt confident to participate in the meetings.

Use of research based evidence:
- Research based outcomes were rarely mentioned. This is an important finding in that the Choices project intended to identify what recommendations for change had been made by the users' committees, based on evidence.
- Some had carried out users surveys but none of the representatives mentioned using clinical research or the Pregnancy and Childbirth Database. They were aware of research being undertaken in certain areas of maternity care e.g. breastfeeding, fetal monitoring.
- Of those who were aware of research evidence, many did not feel they had the training or access to interpret this research.
- A very small group (n = 3) were aware of Effective Care in Pregnancy & Childbirth.

Priorities for change:
- Providing women with more information about choices available to them.
- Improving support and information.
- Giving midwives the opportunity to provide midwife-led care.

Conclusions drawn:
- The authors concluded that purchasing authorities need to provide 'unequivocal support'. User representatives will need to be more aware of research based evidence and ensure that this is placed high on the agenda in discussion with both providers and purchasers.

Women's perspectives

Antenatal care:

- 92% of women felt that either a doctor or midwife remembered them and their progress from visit to visit.
- 90% of these women felt fully involved in all or most of the decisions about their pregnancy compared to 82% of those who did not report such continuity (p=.005).

Labour:

Place of delivery

Consultant unit	90.5%
GP Unit	8.5%
Home	1.0%

Obstetric outcomes

Vaginal births	88.0%
Caesarean rate	12.0%
planned	40.0%
emergency	60.0%
Assisted deliveries	9.5%
Twins	1.0%
ARM	57.0%

Episiotomies:

696 women had vaginal deliveries.

- 27% had an episiotomy (the numbers were similar in each unit).
- 69% of women had either an episiotomy or tear.
- 15% of primips did not have stitches.
- 68% of women delivering at home had an intact perineum as did 64% of women. who delivered in a particular consultant unit.

Women's responses to key questions

(total n=791)

Labour

	%	n
Women who had a midwife with them all the time	45	729
Women who were left alone	17	735
Women who had met one of the midwives who cared for them in labour	31	740
Women who did not see a doctor during labour	44	783
Those who had met the doctor previously	47	710
Women cared for by the same midwife during labour	54	736
Women who had 4 or more midwives caring for them during labour	11	735

Women who felt that:	%	n
Enough was explained to them about what was happening	78	730
They were told enough about why things were necessary	79	726
Notice was taken of their views and wishes	81	722

	%	n
Pain relief in labour (vaginal deliveries):		
Epidural	11	694
Pethidine	45	694
Gas & air	80	694
TENS	22	694
Natural methods	49	694

Postnatal care:	%	n
Women who stayed in hospital for 24 hours or less	28	766
Women who stayed in for more than four days	21	766
Women who had met at least one midwife caring for them postnatally	43	770
Women who felt that midwives in hospital were always able to spend enough time with them	30	769
Women who felt their stay in hospital was just the right amount	84	765
Women visited by midwives at home every day – up to 10 days	41	782
Women who felt they had enough support from the midwives	96	783
Women who had a midwife's contact number	95	787
Women who phoned a midwife	59	744
Women who had 4 or more midwives care for them at home	12	777
Women who knew at least one of the midwives well	44	780
Women who felt fully involved in decisions about their care	85	785

Feeding:		
Women who breastfed within 2 hours of delivery	80	518
of these, incidences where a midwife was available for the whole feed	37	515
Women who exclusively breastfed in hospital	49	753
Women who fed their baby on demand	85	790
Women bottle fed who had help and support from the midwives	78	232
Women who had major problems with feeding	6	787

Knowing the midwife who gives postnatal care in hospital:
- 10% of women felt that knowing the midwife well 'mattered a great deal'. The main reasons being it gave the women more confidence (42%) and made them more relaxed (23%). 16% said it 'mattered', 39% 'it didn't matter much', 35% 'it didn't matter at all'. The main reasons given for this response was that women found all the midwives 'friendly and helpful' (60%) and competent (15%).

Care at home after the birth:
- 43% knew at least one of the midwives well.
- 45% had met at least one before.
- 12% had never met any of the midwives.

Women were asked if it mattered to them if they knew the midwife who cared for them at home.

- 48% said it 'mattered a great deal'.
- 31% 'it didn't matter very much'.
- 22% 'it did not matter at all'.

- Of the women who had not met any of the midwives before, 51% said it did not matter at all, but 18% of women who had previously met one of the midwives who cared for them at home held this view.
- The greatest continuity of care was experienced by women who gave birth at home and the women who gave birth within a GP unit. Positive outcomes were associated with continuity of care and.... 'a sizeable number of women value it'.

Overall care:

	%	n
Women who felt that their GPs, midwives and hospital doctors' were working together	73	762
Women for whom the maternity service provided the service they wanted	92	759

Continuity of carer
- 23% of women had experienced continuity of carer at all stages of their care. The results varied depending on where the women delivered. 92% of women stated that either a doctor of midwife remembered them at each antenatal visit.
- This was more common in women having 2nd or subsequent babies. There was no difference in the different units i.e. GP or hospital clinics.
- The small numbers of women who found that they were not remembered were less likely to say that they had enough information in pregnancy on adopting and leading a healthy lifestyle.
- Women who had experienced continuity felt more involved in decision making.

Continuity of care in labour:
- Of the 743 women who went into labour, 31% had met at least one of the midwives before and of these 55% had met the midwife in the antenatal clinic. This number was lower in primips.
- 54% of women had one midwife throughout labour, but this figure differed between the consultant units.
- 69% had two or more midwives but this also differed between units.

- 389 women had a hospital doctor with them during labour.
- 70% had not met this doctor before.

Women who had met either the midwife or doctor previously...'were significantly more likely to feel that health professionals always explained enough about what was happening in labour'. These women also felt more involved in decision making in relation to their care.

- 53% would 'not really' have liked to get to know the doctors/midwives more before delivery, 33% 'possibly', and 14% 'definitely'.

GP Units:
- Women who gave birth at one of the GP Units experienced higher levels of continuity of carer and stated that GP Units were more comfortable, quieter, more private and relaxing.
- Women who gave birth at a GPU were more likely to say that they had enough help and advice on the ward postnatally than women in consultant units.
- They also felt more involved in 'all' decisions postnatally: 91% v 84% of women in consultant units.

Women acknowledged that if they developed complications which required specialist care they would be happy to go to a specialist unit.

Home births:
- Women who had delivered at home had met at least one of the midwives who cared for them.
- 20 women had a home birth (18 were planned).
- Some women requesting a home birth had experienced difficulties and negative views from some doctors and midwives.
- Lack of appropriate training of some staff had also restricted women's choice for having a home delivery.

Women and user groups request and suggest that more information should be supplied for women in order to make an informed choice about where to deliver.

Women who delivered at home had the best continuity of carer and 100% were satisfied with their involvement in decision making in labour and postnatally, 95% antenatally.

- 84% of women knew the midwife who delivered them at home.
- in 75% of cases, a midwife stayed with them all the time in labour.
- 97% of women were very satisfied with their care from both the doctor and the midwife.
- 87% were happy with the pain relief they had compared to 68% in GP Units.

Special needs:
Black women from Harlow:
- were unclear why the race of both partners was relevant at booking as it was not explained.
- had concerns about antenatal screening, especially blood tests.

Women from service families felt that:
- Many husbands are away from home and therefore a rapid assessment is required at times to ensure that husbands can be present for the birth.
- An early discharge may be preferable for women when their husbands are home on leave.

Women with disabilities:
Women felt that health care professionals required:
- An increased awareness of the needs of women with hearing and other disabilities. For example, antenatal classes for hearing impaired women can be a problem, as can security systems that are dependent on intercoms.

Recommendations in report:
- All women should be provided with appropriate information to ensure that they are aware of and informed about the choices available to them in the type of care they receive. The authors recommend that all women should be provided with a copy of the HEAs The Pregnancy Book and the Maternity Services Charter.
- Women should carry their own maternity notes and there should be a reduction in the amount of conflicting advice given by professionals.
- Professionals, through training, should be made more aware of issues in relation to race, culture, disabilities, dignity etc.
- Authorities should develop and adopt agreed policies for certain procedures e.g. breastfeeding, cord care, babies' sleeping positions.
- Current work patterns should be addressed to maximize continuity of carer and further research undertaken to look at the 'effectiveness' of midwives being allocated a specific caseload.
- Clinical audit and effectiveness of care should be incorporated into all procedures and women and user representatives kept informed and involved in the process of dissemination of findings.
- Research evidence should be more readily available for users, purchasers and providers.
- Units should work within a 'research based framework'.
- User representatives on groups and committees should be involved and made aware of procedures and the terminology used in meetings and discussions.
- The authors recommend that further research is undertaken to look at ways of improving the 'effectiveness of MSLCs'.

APPENDIX C15

Flessig and Kroll (1996)

Authors	Date	Study reference	Intervention assessed	Evaluation	Number of women	Main outcomes
A Fleissig, A Kroll, D McCarthy, M.	Scheme in operation from July 1993 Evaluation from November 1993 – April 1996	The full report of the study is an internal publication from University College, London, entitled: Evaluation of community-led maternity care in South Camden, London. 1996 Extracts have been published in: *Midwifery* 1996; 12:191-197	Provision of community led maternity care to all childbearing women in South Camden, London. • 3 community teams of 8 midwives (24 whole time equivalent) organized into pairs. • within each team, G or H grade midwives are responsible for defined caseload and for providing 'mentorship' to F grades. • annual caseload of approximately 1,000 : caseload per team no more than 350 per annum. *Antenatal care* • women booked with named midwife in GP clinic. • all women booked under consultant unit (GPs did not provide intrapartum care).	Independent evaluation *Methods* Retrospective evaluation. There was no comparison group 'as the community-led service was offered to all local women'. 1. Review of case notes and records to describe the care and continuity of care provided. 2. Postal survey of women's views and experiences. 3. Survey of community midwives', GPs', consultant obstetricians' and labour ward midwives' opinions.	• 524 women initially recruited. • 14% moved out of the area. • 453 women remained in the study. • adequate data were available on 449 of these women. • 381 (85%) planned to have community-led care.	• patterns of care audit • staff's views • women's views

Authors	Date	Study reference	Intervention assessed	Evaluation	Number of women studied	Main outcomes
			• low-risk community care shared between named partnership + GP. • minimum of 2 hospital antenatal visits at approx. 12 weeks (scan) and term. • women wanting /needing hospital only antenatal care transferred to hospital team. • in patient care provided by hospital midwives. *Intrapartum care* • teams provided 24 hour on-call cover over two shifts to provide intrapartum care for women. • hospital midwives provided intrapartum care when team midwives not available. *Postnatal care* • community midwives remained prime carers for normal and uncomplicated instrumental deliveries – in between team visits, care provided by hospital midwives. • postnatal care for caesarean sections and complicated instrumental deliveries by hospital midwives. • postnatal care in community 'ideally' given by named partnership.	NB: the evaluation specifically excluded: • comparison of outcomes or costs of the service with other models of care. • audit of clinical outcomes (numbers were too small). • assessment of the cost effectiveness of the service.	*Other staff* • 28 community midwives: 25 responded (89%). • 8 core staff on labour ward: 100% response. • 60 GPs; 49 responded (82%). • 6 consultant obstetricians: 100% responded. (no information is provided re. hospital midwives providing care in antenatal clinic or antenatal + postnatal wards).	

Results: Community-led maternity care in South Camden

- Teams were organized by geographical area and allied to GP practices.
- Each team referred to particular hospital consultants.
- H grade midwives paired with a G grades: The other G grades paired with F grade midwives.

Implementation:

- Eight hospital F grade posts were transferred to the community sector.
- Originally the plan was for the community midwives to provide *total* antenatal and intrapartum care either in the hospital or the community. Modifications occurred due to staffing levels and a shortage of space.

Characteristics of women in scheme: population characteristics

- Diverse ethnic and socio-economic backgrounds. Areas of high unemployment and poverty.
- Highly mobile population, many live in poor housing or temporary accommodation.
- Relatively large numbers of people from Bangladesh, Cyprus, Ireland and the West Indies. Also refugees from other countries.

Analysis of case notes and records: data collection

- Retrospective review of records using data from maternity care plan completed by the community midwives specifically for this study.
- The computerized Patient Information System.
- The hospital notes (usually held by the woman) and
- The midwifery cardex
- Information from midwives on duty.

Staffing levels

Low staffing levels and shortage of space resulted in modifications to the service. During the period of the study (Oct 93– Oct 94):

- Three community midwives left.
- Three were on full-time study leave.
- Three on maternity leave.
- Three off sick for at least one month.

The full complement of three midwives on call was not achieved for 17% of shifts during the study period.

Women included in the study

- More than 75% of the women for whom data was available had no medical or obstetric complications at their first booking visit.
- 18 women planned to have a home delivery.
- One consultant saw his patients at 34 weeks, in addition to the schedule.
- 36 women had either multiple pregnancies, a previous positive cervical smear or high blood pressure. Their antenatal care was still community-led with additional visits to the hospital obstetric staff.

- 45 women had existing medical/obstetric histories and received full hospital care.
- 23 women, for various reasons including personal request, received care from the hospital team and their GP without the community midwives being involved.

Actual antenatal care of women who planned to have community-led care
Women without complications:
- Over 50% of women without complications had *all* their antenatal care in the community until term.
- 29% had most of their care in the community with occasional referrals to hospital, most commonly because of concern about fetal growth (20 women, 6%).
- 11% attended hospital regularly (fetal growth, induced hypertension, malpresentation and reduced fetal movements) but still planned to have intrapartum care from community midwives.
- 3% transferred to full hospital care.
- 2% did not attend regularly for antenatal care.

Women with complications:
Most had community-led care with occasional extra visits
- 70% had 50% of their checks in community antenatal clinics.
- 50% attended hospital regularly by the end of the pregnancy but planned to have intrapartum care from the community midwives.
- Three transferred to total hospital care.

Referrals to labour ward/day unit during pregnancy:
- 52% were referred to labour ward or the day unit.
- 25% on one occasion.
- 11% twice.
- 16% three times or more.
- 18% of women were referred by the community midwives: 8% for fetal growth and 5% for pregnancy induced hypertension.

Referrals to hospital
Main reasons during the antenatal period:
- Concern by midwives about fetal growth.
- Pregnancy induced hypertension.
- Malpresentation.
- Perceived reduction in fetal movement.

Continuity of antenatal care
- 97% of women were booked by the community midwives for community-led care. In 81% of cases the booking midwife was the named midwife or partner.
- 93% of women were booked at home.
- On average, women saw three different community midwives for eight antenatal visits.
- Only 34% saw their GP routinely for antenatal care.

Intrapartum care

Continuity of carer was not achieved because of staff shortages, annual leave and demands on midwives' time made by women with complications.

- Only 50% of women were visited at home by a midwife in early labour.
- 33% of women were cared for throughout labour by a midwife from the named team.
- Continuity of care for women who needed a cervical smear or were induced was poor.

Postnatal care
Postnatal care at home

- Only 12% of women had their postnatal care at home from their named midwife or intrapartum midwives as planned.
- 80% were visited by at least one midwife who they had not met during antenatal or intrapartum care. (Although they may have been met at classes, social meetings/ previous pregnancies.)

Discussion

- The services were flexible enough to provide for those women who required additional hospital care without the loss of support from their known community midwives.
- The source and reasons for referral were not always recorded in the notes.
- Approx. 50% of women were referred to hospital during the antenatal period and the community service required that they were returned effectively to community based care.
- The midwife teams met frequently to enhance continuity of care and for transfer of information. Continuity of carer may not always have been achieved but continuity of care was not felt to have been compromised.
- Continuity of carer in the postnatal period was rarely provided exclusively by the named midwife.

Postnatal survey of women

A systematic 1:2 sample was selected. Women were asked about their views on:

- antenatal, intrapartum and postnatal care
- choice
- continuity of care
- information and advice.

The questionnaires were sent out at six weeks with two reminders for non-respondents. Women who required interpreters were telephoned and offered home visits.

Respondents

- The original sample of 242 women was reduced to 195.
- 44 women cancelled bookings or moved out of the area.

- Three others were excluded due to severe psychiatric problems or because babies had died.
- Parity and ethnicity did not make a difference to response rate.
- Women under 25 years of age at booking were less likely to respond than older women.

Women's views on antenatal continuity of care (either from the same doctor or midwife)

not important	11%
important	69%
quite important	24%

- 89% of women were given the name of their named midwife.
- 75% saw their named midwife regularly.
- Women who saw their named midwife regularly during pregnancy were more likely to say that they were given the opportunity to talk to staff about things (98% compared to 82%).
- 93% of women who saw their named midwife regularly were also more likely to say that their antenatal care was good, compared with 79% who did not.
- Women who had local antenatal care were more likely to see their named midwife (82% to 55%).

Intrapartum care
- 85% of woman had discussed issues around home births.
- 39% stated that they did not have a choice about the place of delivery.
- 50% of women had previously met at least one of the midwives who cared for them in labour.
- Knowing at least one of the intrapartum midwives was not associated with more positive feelings about the way labour was managed or associated with improved perceptions about positive staff attitudes.
- 82% of women who had met at least one of their intrapartum midwives before said it made them feel more at ease.

Postnatal care
In hospital
- 73% of women spent 3 days or less in hospital.
- 73% were happy with their length of stay.
- 22% felt they were sent home too early.
- 22% of women while in hospital would liked to have had more time to speak to staff about how to look after themselves and their babies.
- One in six women were confused having received conflicting advice. Primips were likely to be more confused than multips (31% to 7%).
- Women visited in hospital by their named midwife were as likely to be confused as other women.

At home
- 32% of women telephoned the community midwife for advice.
- 81% said that having previously met the midwife had helped.

- 84% of women who had previously met the midwives were likely to say that their postnatal care was good, compared to 57% of other women.

Community midwife survey and responses
- Midwives who had worked in the community for at least three months before the study commenced were surveyed.
- Questionnaires and two reminders were sent approx. 18 months after implementation of the new service.
- Midwives who had worked in the community prior to commencement of the new service were also asked to compare the new service with the pre-existing service.
- Some midwives found the new service stressful, but most were coping and found their work rewarding.
- They liked the autonomy and the direct relationship with the hospital staff.

They wanted:
- More support from their managers and thought that professionals needed a better understanding of their role.
- To provide both continuity of care and carer. They were disappointed at the levels of continuity achieved, particularly in the intrapartum and postnatal periods.

Obstacles to continuity of care
- Staff turnover.
- Absence, annual leave, study leave or sickness.
- Additional workload created for team midwives by women with greater social needs.
- The midwives in the study commented on the difficulty of providing antenatal continuity to women who developed complications.

Midwives expressed diverse views on the best way to organize care. This may have reflected their domestic circumstances and previous experience.

GP survey
Sixteen months after the new service was implemented, individual GPs were asked to complete a postal questionnaire. GPs who did not provide antenatal care or those who had moved into the area less than six months earlier were excluded. Two reminders were sent.

Antenatal care
- 79% of GPs offered women a choice between shared care and hospital antenatal care.
- 88% of GPs were satisfied with the current booking arrangements.
- 81% were satisfied with the new service.

Problems:
- Communication.
- Not having a midwife based at the surgery.

Home births
- 44% of GPs routinely offered women a choice of home birth.
- 77% would refer the woman to the midwives.
- Involvement in intrapartum care was usually limited to the post delivery check.

Discussion
- Most GPs did not want to increase their involvement in intrapartum care.
- GPs also complained about lack of communication from midwives if the woman was referred to the hospital.
- Where the midwives held clinics in surgeries, the GPs were more likely to acknowledge and complement their roles. 'Trust and co-operation were obviously enhanced by contact between GPs and midwives'.

Consultant obstetricians' survey
'On the whole, the consultants acknowledged that community-led care was acceptable for local women. But, most did not think that care had improved as a result'.
Concerns:
- Reduction in medical involvement and influence.
- Low staffing levels of hospital midwives, which they thought was due to the expansion in the number of community midwives.
- They differed in their views on the number of antenatal visits women should make.

Views from core labour ward staff
Staff thought that:
- Community-led care had improved continuity of intrapartum care but
- Organizational problems needed to be resolved.
- Communication between hospital and community staff had improved.

Main concerns:
- Staffing levels
- Skill mix
- Role of community midwives on the labour ward
- Responsibilities need to be clarified to improve staff relations.

Conclusion
- Community-led care can be provided to the majority of women even those with complications but certain organizational issues need to be addressed.
- Access to specialist advice and facilities must be available when necessary.
- Attempting to provide continuity raises issues around equity for women and resource implications together with demands on the midwives' time and capabilities.
- Women need to be made aware of the role of the midwife and the reality of being delivered by the named midwife. This would prevent women's expectations being raised unnecessarily.
- Antenatal-intrapartum continuity of carer may not be essential for all women. Satisfaction in labour was not dependent on the woman knowing her midwife.

Providing care for women with complications
- If midwives are to take on this role, further education, training and support may be required.
- The most appropriate individuals to provide this type of care and the types of systems needed have still to be identified.

Organization
- The size and balance of midwives' teams needs to be addressed to ensure that disruption to the structure of a team is not caused by study leave, annual leave, sickness etc.
- Location of teams and on-call arrangements also needs to be evaluated.
- Problems with communication between women, community midwives and hospital midwives together with GPs needs to be resolved.
- Team working needs to be developed.

APPENDIX C16

Murphy-Black (1993)

Authors	Date	Study reference	Intervention	Evaluation	Number of women studied	Main outcomes
Murphy-Black, T.	1993	'Identifying the key features of continuity of care in midwifery' Nursing Research Unit, University of Edinburgh, March 1993	No intervention.	Report prepared for the Scottish Office Home and Health Department. Group interviews with midwives from four Scottish maternity units. Criteria for selection: • considered by Supervisor to be expert in their current post • currently in clinical practice, any grade • from any ward or department except special care baby unit • day or night duty, full or part-time • at least one from a team, where team midwifery in use. Convenience sample of mothers from the same units, invited by the Supervisor of Midwives. Also group interviews. Interviews transcribed and subjected to content analysis.	19 mothers and 37 midwives. Although it was intended that the mothers should have recently given birth, in one unit half the mothers had not yet had their babies.	Purpose was to elicit midwives' and mothers' ideas of the key features of continuity of care. Both were asked to give: • their ideal of continuity of care in midwifery • the reality as they experienced it • which aspects they considered essential • which aspects they considered desirable but not essential.

239

Results: Identifying the key features of continuity of care in midwifery

Midwives

The midwives worked predominantly in hospitals. Of the four units, two were rural and small and two urban and large. This made an important difference to the practicalities of their work, e.g. being 90 miles away from the consultant unit.

Ideal of continuity:

All midwives agreed that the ideal was continuity of *carer*, but all identified constraints that prevented them from giving such care. They distinguished the process of care from the structure and considered process to be more important. The central aspect was seen as the relationship with the mother. This was particularly identified by those practising team midwifery. Continuity of *caring* was recognized as second best if continuity of *carer* was not possible. The key element here was policy, but good record keeping was also highlighted as essential so that a midwife taking over would know what had gone before.

Midwives considered that continuity of care could not be achieved without individualized care and that an essential element was therefore the woman's active partnership in the care process, i.e. being prepared to discuss her wishes and needs.

The final key element was seen to be flexibility on the part of the midwives themselves.

Mothers

Mothers discussed continuity mainly in terms of outcomes of their care, e.g. a known midwife in labour, a named midwife, conflicting advice. In only one of the units were women likely to know the staff who cared for them in labour. However, this was not necessarily seen as a problem. 'After 5-10 minutes, it feels like they always knew you – they mother you, especially the older ones'. Mothers did appreciate seeing a familiar face for their postnatal care, even if they did not necessarily have a named midwife. Mothers also gave examples of midwives acting as their advocates, for example regarding place of delivery. Nearly all of the mothers in all units said that their care had met or exceeded their expectations.

Mothers also mentioned some issues do to with the process of care such as social visits from midwives and shift-to-shift continuity and communication between staff, echoing the point made by the midwives about documentation.

Conclusions

The author concludes that, for the midwives who took part in this study, their ideal would be to work as independent midwives do, with their own caseloads and with all care given locally. However 'the reality is that the midwives have not yet reached the ideal and are compensating with continuity of caring'.

APPENDIX C17

Sikorski et al. (1996)

Authors	Date	Study reference	Intervention assessed	Evaluation	Number of women studied	Main outcomes
Sikorski, J. Wilson, J. Clement, S. Das, S. Smeeton, N.	June 1993 – July 1994	Sikorski, J., Wilson, J., Clement, S., Das, S., Smeeton, N. (1996) A randomized controlled trial comparing two schedules of antenatal care visits: the antenatal care project. *British Medical Journal*; 312: 546-553 + full report of the study internal publication by Dept of Public Health Medicine, Guys & St Thomas' UMDS	A reduced schedule of antenatal care visits for low-risk women.	Evaluation undertaken by multidisciplinary research team. *Methods* Randomized controlled trial. Low-risk women were randomized into one of two groups: • traditional care pattern of 13 antenatal visits • 'new' care pattern of reduced antenatal visits: 7 for nulliparas and 6 for multiparas. Randomization: at booking visits with random permuted blocks of 8 & 16. • stratification at the 6 offices where the recruiting midwives were based. • non-resealable opaque envelopes were sequentially numbered, and contained either traditional or the new style of care. • the woman's maternity notes were then 'tagged' to identify her number and the type of antenatal schedule.	Women eligible for the study were those assessed as low-risk, booking for maternity care at Lewisham or Guy's Hospital, or in communities within the catchment areas between June 1993 and July 1994. • potential study population of 3252 women. • 2893 women eligible.	• Fetal and maternal morbidity. • Health service use. • Psycho-social outcomes. • Maternal and professional satisfaction.

Authors	Date	Study reference	Intervention assessed	Evaluation	Number of women studied	Main outcomes
				Data collection • from women's notes by 2 research midwives. • 2 x questionnaire to women (antenatal + postnatal). • health professionals' questionnaire.	• 97 of these were lost to follow up. • a further 2 withdrew. • 2794 women included in the study. • data not available for 36 of these women. *Other: staff* 464/475 GPs (98%) agreed to participate.	

Results:

The Antenatal Care Project

Implementation process: Before the project started, interested people including clerical staff working within the maternity service were informed of the project and various discussions took place. Planning and training meetings were held with a number of professionals both in the Trust and the community. At each of the hospitals' antenatal clinics, a midwife was nominated as the 'link' between the midwifery staff and the project team.

Of 105 GP practices involved, 83 were visited by the research midwives prior to the project starting.

For the study, a visit was defined as... 'an encounter between a pregnant woman and a midwife or doctor for the purpose of assessing maternal or fetal well-being'.

Day or inpatient visits for ultrasound or blood tests were not counted.

Data collection
- Women's questionnaires were sent at 34 weeks and six weeks postnatally to obtain their views and measure psychosocial effectiveness. These included the Edinburgh Postnatal Depression Scale and the Cambridge Worry Scale. Items from the OPCS survey manual on women's experiences were also used.
- A questionnaire was given to women who did not want to participate in the trial to assess their views.
- Health professionals received a questionnaire before the trial and during its last few weeks.
- All questionnaires were piloted and reminders sent fortnightly to women and health professionals who did not respond.

Analysis: was by intention to treat.

Results

Women from ethnic minorities and first time mothers were less likely to participate.

- They did not want fewer visits as they wanted reassurance and time to talk. A small minority were concerned about safety. 4% saw it as a health service cutback and 4% wanted traditional care.

Response rate to maternal questionnaire
- 70.2% (antenatally) and 63.2% (postnatally), the authors state that these are high for an inner city area.

Mean number of visits
- Difference was smaller than expected, 10.8 v 8.6, but was statistically significant (p<0.001).
- Women in the traditional group had on average 1.65 fewer visits, and the new style group 2.60 more visits than intended.

Clinical variables

Information from the Notes	*Difference between New & Traditional style care*
Pre-eclampsia	No
Induction rate	No
Caesareans	No
Admitted for blood pressure	No
Labour & delivery	No
Pain relief	No
Length of labour	No
Type of delivery	No
Fetal distress	No
APGAR score	No

Information from Questionnaires	*Difference between New & Traditional style care*
Antenatal or postnatal depression	No
Amount of information received	No
Breast feeding rates	No
Women smoking late in pregnancy	No
Worried about their babies before & after birth	Yes
More time to talk to caregivers	Yes
Less conflicting advice	Yes
Less likely to be remembered at each visit	Yes
Preference of health care givers	Yes

Continuity of caregivers
- Women in the new style group saw fewer caregivers and also saw caregivers less frequently.
- Continuity of caregivers was maintained but women felt that they were less likely to be remembered.

Information
- Women in both groups received similar amounts and types of information and were happy with the advice, information and explanations given.
- Responses in the postnatal maternal questionnaire indicated that women would have liked to have known more about feeding their baby.

Social support
- Women in the new style group would have liked more time to talk at each visit. They were more worried about: coping with their baby postnatally; whether the baby was 'thriving' antenatally.
- Women in the new style group felt more negative attitudes towards their fetus, more detached, concerned and uncertain, this continued into the postnatal period.

Acceptability of visits for women
- Women in the new style group indicated higher dissatisfaction with their care and the number of visits they received. This dissatisfaction was more common in early pregnancy but was also present in the postnatal period.
- Women in the new style group also reported that their partners were less satisfied. Some women also felt that the period between each visits was too long, but women would opt for this type of care again.

Acceptability of visits for professionals
- The majority of professionals would like to see a reduction in the traditional number of visits but felt that the traditional method met the 'non clinical needs of nulliparous women better' than the new style: 53% v 22%.

Discussion
The authors recognize that....'the sample size precludes examination of rare but serious events such as perinatal loss, eclampsia, and maternal mortality'.

Economic implications of alternative patterns of antenatal care were not considered. The authors suggest, however, that a reduction in the number of antenatal visits should make available more time for professionals to provide a flexible service that identifies and meets the needs of individual women.

The new style care appeared to be as effective in terms of clinical variables as the traditional style of care. Women in the traditional group received more ultrasound and day admissions for possible small-for-dates diagnoses. This increased use of resources did not appear to be cost effective as no significant clinical effect was identified.

Fewer visits appears to be less effective psychosocially and less acceptable for women. The authors comment that women may find it difficult to ask for extra visits to discuss issues that are not clinically based and may feel that this places extra demands on the professionals' time.

Sandall (1997)

Authors	Date	Study reference	Intervention assessed	Evaluation	Number of women studied	Main outcomes
Sandall, J.	June 1994 – Feb 1995	Sandall J. (1997) Midwives' burnout and continuity of care. *British Journal of Midwifery* 5:106-111.	The impact of different ways of organizing midwifery services on midwives' work and personal lives.	Study carried out by University-based sociologist/midwife. Multiple site case study: each of the 3 case study sites represented a different, community-based model of continuity of carer along a continuum from complete one-to-one continuity to continuity within a team. These are described as: • traditional model of GP-attached community midwives • a community team • a midwifery group practice. *Methods* • observation of midwifery work. • collection of some policy and audit documents. • interviews with a sample of midwives (n=48). (This report is part of a larger, unpublished, doctoral study which examines the impact of *Changing Childbirth* on midwives' work and personal lives.)	Study did not include childbearing women. No. of midwives interviewed = 48.	Identification of key factors necessary to sustain models of midwifery service organization which aim to provide continuity of carer. These are described as: • occupational autonomy. • social support. • developing meaningful relationships with women.

Results: Midwives' burnout and continuity of care:
Data analysis
Interviews were transcribed and analysed using a computerized qualitative data analysis package.

Definition of burnout:
> 'a syndrome of emotional exhaustion and low personal accomplishment at work. At the extreme, dehumanisation of clients which includes a "blame the victim" attitude and a desire for minimal human contact both at work and home occurs along with a disillusionment with work and life in general'. (Maslach, C., Jackson, SE. (1986). *Maslach Burnout Inventory*. Palo Alto, California: Consulting Psychologists Press)

- Nine out of the 48 midwives from all three sites identified themselves as experiencing burnout.

Occupational autonomy
- Having a level of control over work was cited by all midwives as an essential component of managing work and integrating domestic circumstances successfully.
- The self-employed midwifery group practice midwives and some GP attached midwives were able to work more flexibly and had more control over their work.
- Living in close proximity to work was seen as important.
- Midwives who had greater control over their work reported less burnout.
- Stress was perceived as relating to lack of control over work rather than to the actual workload itself.
- The way that work was organized in each site either mitigated or enhanced the midwives' perceived stress.

Developing meaningful relationships with women
- Providing continuity of care was a major source of satisfaction to all midwives.
- The inability to develop meaningful relationships with women was a source of frustration and stress for midwives.
- Midwives carrying personal caseloads for which they were the named midwife experienced high levels of satisfaction.
- Team midwives found it difficult for midwives and women to get to know each other well and this increased stress and reduced job satisfaction. Nevertheless, when a good relationship was established, this was one of the most important sources of satisfaction.
- Unachievable ideals of continuity of carer within teams can precipitate disillusionment.
- GP attached community midwives were able to develop meaningful relationships with women despite their large caseloads. They experienced good job satisfaction but at the expense of not attending the births of the majority of their caseload.
- The type of caseload in the three sites either enhanced or reduced the opportunities to 'know' women which influenced the midwives' experiences of stress and job satisfaction and their work-flexibility.

On-call
- Being on-call was stressful, to a varying extent, for all midwives.
- Some midwives emphasized the difficulties of integrating on-call into family life.
- The midwifery group practice midwives felt that stress resulting from the uncertainty of on-calls was reduced by the considerate and supportive attitude of the women that they had got to know well.
- Team midwives cited on-calls as the most stressful aspect of their work; this was associated with not 'knowing' the women, a problem compounded by larger caseloads.

Social support
- The establishment of organizational practices that fostered team building and collegial support helped to guard against burn-out.
- Midwives in all sites cited social support from colleagues as one of the greatest stress reducers.
- When group dynamics were poor, this became an important source of stress in all three sites.
- The presence or lack of emotional and social support at home was also an important factor in stress experienced by midwives in all three sites.
- It was unclear whether the presence of children was an additional stress factor or a buffer against stress.

Implications for practice and future research:
> 'The implications are that continuity of care is as important to midwives as it is to women and that personal caseloads that incorporate regular time off may be more sustainable in terms of less burnout and greater personal accomplishment than team caseloads.'

In addition:

> 'The success of caseload midwifery depends on a reasonable caseload size and adequate cover for sick and maternity leave.'

Pankhurst (1995)

Authors	Date	Study reference	Intervention assessed	Evaluation	Number of women studied	Main outcomes
Pankhurst, F.	Pilot scheme in operation from March 1995– November 1995	The report of the pilot study is an internal publication from the Centre for Nursing & Midwifery Research, University of Brighton (Nov. 1995) entitled: Great Expectations: The impact of caseload midwifery on women, practitioners and practice. Part 1: The first nine months.	Provision of care by two midwifery group practices to women (low and high-risk) registered with GP practices covered by the scheme: • 1 urban (Redham) • 1 rural (Greenfields) Both used the same (Bluebell) hospital. • No. of midwives varied: 8–10 midwives in 8 full time equivalent posts. • Midwives worked in teams of 2 within each group practice. • Each team carried a caseload of approx. 35–40 women p.a • Midwives attempted to provide antenatal, intrapartum and postnatal care in both hospital and community.	Independent evaluation *Methods* Retrospective • Interviews. • Women's questionnaires. • Audit of on-call rotas. • Group practice midwives' call-out logs. • Audit of caseload women on labour ward. • Logs for midwives to trace continuity of care and postnatal outcomes. • Participant observation in clinical arena, in meetings and in women's homes	Number of women involved not known. *Characteristics* of women in the childbearing population: not known.	• women's perspectives • professionals' perspectives: managers, supervisors, hospital midwives, community midwives, caseload group-practice midwives, GPs and hospital doctors. • assessment of level of staffing and support required from core hospital staff for intrapartum care of caseload women.

Summary of results

Implementation process

In the initial aim to increase choice, continuity and control for high and low-risk women within a scheme that was also advantageous for midwives, it was planned that midwives would provide a one-to-one service in which a named midwife would attempt to deliver all the women on her caseload.

The scheme evolved throughout the pilot period: 'the reality of delivering the service was not practicable and an amelioration of their practice from caseload into team midwifery began'.

- Group practice midwives were recruited from existing community staff and six midwives from hospital (process not specified). Dissatisfaction with recruitment is reported; perceptions of exclusion from teams by hospital midwives.
- Chronic staff shortages among hospital midwives: one ward had been closed due to a shortage of 14 midwives.
- No induction into the scheme for participating midwives.

Characteristics of the teams

Urban group:
- Four midwives, all full-time (1G, 2F, 1E grade).
- Group based at one GP practice, 4 miles from the hospital.

Rural group:
- Four full time equivalent midwives:
- At the beginning of the pilot scheme 1G+1F+1F working full time plus 1G+1E working part time.
- At the end of the pilot period 1G+1F+1 acting F working full time + 1 acting F working part time.
- Midwives based at the Greenfields cottage hospital, 13 miles from Bluebell hospital.

Rota system

- *Urban group:* midwives worked 7½ hr day. First midwife on-call for 24 hours. Second midwife on stand-by.
- *Rural group:* midwives worked 7½ hr day. First midwife on-call for 24 hours. Second midwife on back-up on-call (2nd on-call for home deliveries only for last three months of pilot scheme). Rural team midwives either first or second on call for practically every day they were on duty.

Cross-Border issues

- *Urban group:* no cross-border women.
- *Rural group:* compromise position reached in which group midwives offered antenatal care and labour assessment at the Cottage or Bluebell hospital for women living beyond the boundaries; postnatal care relinquished to the neighbouring Trusts.

Characteristics of care
Antenatal care
- Women admitted to hospital antenatally were visited by group practice midwives.

Urban group:
- Each pair of midwives ran two clinics per week in a room in the GP practice
- The group practice ran a parent education class one evening per week for six weeks in rotation.

Rural group;
- Each midwife allocated to one of five General Practices in the geographical area: midwives responsible for running a separate clinic for their women at that surgery
- Group practice provided weekly drop-in parentcraft session at the Cottage hospital + evening class provided by the midwives on six weekly rotation.

Intrapartum care
- Provided by named midwife or on-call midwife from group when possible.
- Relief provided by hospital midwives.

Postnatal care
In hospital: care by group practice midwives to women in their caseload plus hospital based midwives. Rural group practice midwives also responsible for care in the Cottage hospital (2 beds only).

Response from staff
Initial feelings were mixed. Hospital staff were concerned about the possible increase in workload and some felt threatened by the implementation of the new scheme. These feelings were more common amongst hospital staff, partly because pre-existing organization of work encouraged specialization in certain areas. There were some misunderstandings about the level of commitment necessary to be involved in the scheme.

Some early decisions by the project team in relation to caseload midwifery also created some bad feelings (work undertaken prior to the scheme in evaluating existing research was not felt to have been valued).

The start of the scheme coincided with a busy time in the hospital and this caused resentment, particularly as six of the midwives recruited from the hospital began their work in the community before replacement midwives were in post.

It was felt that the caseload midwives got preferential treatment. Concern was expressed about E grades working in community.

Reality of caseload midwifery
The provision of one-to-one care was not practical. The staffing level of four full-time equivalents in the rural group practice, in particular, was felt to be inadequate.

The result was that the scheme evolved into a system of team working rather than caseload midwifery practice.

Group dynamism – the urban group

- The urban group shared similar values and philosophies which helped them 'gel'. This was also evident to outsiders. Women were said to feel that they knew the midwife who delivered them within the group even though they may not have met her before. The midwives had a good relationship with the GPs.
- The midwives were attached to one GP practice, they arranged clinics at the same time and established new ways of communicating with the consultants and each other.

Adjusting to new roles

- The hospital midwives had to adjust to a new way of working.
- The group practice midwives had to cope with longer hours on the labour ward. It was agreed that six hours would be the maximum time spent by urban group practice midwives on the labour ward at any one time. The midwife would then be relieved by the 'standby' midwife. Occasionally they would be relieved by the labour ward staff. This relationship was 'usually' good. Some labour ward staff were concerned that the team were exhausted and therefore not able to function properly.
- The team adopted a flexible approach to working and provided care to meet the needs of their client group. This included providing antenatal classes on a Saturday morning. They constantly evaluated the pattern of care provided and the needs of women in their caseloads.

Group dynamism – the rural group

- The midwives expected research evidence to provide guidance on size of the group practices and organizing off-duty rotas. However this support was lacking. They also expected a structured orientation programme and induction to the hospital and community. Staff shortages meant that the induction programme had to be cancelled.

Adjusting to new roles

- Initially the group worked well, later it became more difficult for midwives to attend meetings. The rule was that three midwives had to be present at a meeting to agree any changes in planning, but decisions were not always accepted by the other midwives.
- The method of allocating women within the urban group practice was not ideal and some midwives had a caseload of 50 women while others had very few. The number of GPs and General Practices imposed limitations on the midwives' freedom to practice.

Differences in circumstances of urban and rural group practices: Factor	Urban	Rural
Midwives grades	G,F,F,E (4 full time equivalents)	G,G,F,F,E (4 full time equivalents)
Part-time midwives	No	Yes
Turnover of staff	No	Yes
Group dynamics	Good	Problematic
Type of area	Metropolitan	Rural
Miles from core unit	4	13
Cross boundary cover	No	Yes
Office base	No	Yes
Number of GP practices	1	5
Number of GPs	7	11
Relationship with GPs	Good	Mixed
Relationship with core unit	Mostly good	Mostly problematic
Support needed from core unit	Low	High
Number of commitments e.g. classes, clinics per week	5	7-8
Responsible for postnatal beds	No	Yes

GPs responses to caseload midwifery
- Responses were mixed. Some GPs were unclear as to their role in this type of care, others saw it as an opportunity to rethink their role.
- GPs initially thought that home deliveries would increase.
- Many were concerned about the welfare of the midwives.

Pros and cons of Caseload Midwifery
Advantages – midwives
- Increased continuity of care and increased use of skills.

Advantages to women
- Women appeared very satisfied with their care and were positive about the scheme.
- Women in the rural group practice area particularly valued being assessed at home.
- The majority of women felt it important to know the midwife who delivered them.
- The women did not find it a problem meeting more than one or two midwives. Most women appreciated the difficulties and impracticalities of seeing only one midwife.

Disadvantages – midwives
- Emotionally draining for midwives.
- Pressure of work for some midwives.
- Working in a group practice could also mean that situations where personality clashes occurred between the women and the midwife were less easy to avoid.

Implications for extending the scheme
- Recruitment.
- Quality of care in antenatal and postnatal wards: issues of continuity vs quality.
- Relationships with labour ward staff: time needs to be invested in 'building relationships' and involving all staff in the implementation and evaluation of new schemes.

Impact on deliveries for students and junior doctors and skills and experience of caseload midwives: caseload midwifery had begun to impact on the students trying to gain experience in deliveries. This also had the potential to impact on junior doctors. These issues need to be addressed.

NB: future data collection to include:

- Evaluative data from women via interviews and questionnaires.
- Data on continuity of care and some postnatal outcomes collected by midwives.
- Data on clinical outcomes via Euroking database.
- Case study of the caseload group practice midwives.

Kean et al. (1990)

Authors	Date	Study reference	Intervention assessed	Evaluation	Number of women studied	Main outcomes
Kean, L.H. Liu, D.T,Y Macquisten, S.	1990	International Journal of Health Care Quality Assurance 9/5 (1996) 39-44	No intervention. The study was 'to examine the community-hospital interface in the care of low-risk woman' and to identify problems arising in those women with *no* identifiable risk factors. At the time of the study, women in Nottingham received shared care including: • 1 hospital booking visit before 20 weeks and a scan. • Care shared between midwife and GP. • Women delivered in the maternity hospitals.	*Methods* Retrospective analysis of the notes of women assessed as being at low-risk in 2 hospitals in Nottingham in the year 1990. • a random sample of 1 in 12 files was coded independently to compare coding for women identified as low-risk. • Clinical data were obtained from the maternity computer system and the Patient Administration System for admission data. • risk categories were identified by the consultants involved: only those women identified as low risk at booking were eligible for inclusion in the study.	4579 women who delivered during the study year. Of these: • 1976 were identified as low-risk (43%) • 1130 (57%) were primiparous • 836 (43%) were multiparous.	• identification of problems arising in women assessed as low-risk for whom problems were not anticipated.

Authors	Date	Study reference	Intervention assessed	Evaluation	Number of women studied	Main outcomes
				• each consultant was interviewed personally on their indicators for risk markers. • The risk markers identified were combined to provide the safest limits and then these applied to the study population, to identify those women suitable for community based care. Any change in lead professional was also noted in relation to the risk factor.		

Results: Pregnancy care of the low-risk woman: the community-hospital interface

Antenatal period

- 501 women required at least one admission prior to labour.
- 474 (24%) had problems in pregnancy requiring a change in risk categorization
- 128 women who remained low risk throughout pregnancy were induced. The most frequently noted reason was post-maturity; induction following maternal request was not uncommon. These women were assumed to have had an obstetric intervention.
- 1374 (69.5%) of women in the low risk group remained low risk prior to labour and reached at least 36 weeks. Of these:
  - 742 (65.6%) were primips and 632 (74.7%) multips.
  - 210 had required hospital attention at some point during the pregnancy but the problems did not warrant a change in risk status. In 88 women the admission was due to a false alarm.

Frequency of admissions requiring a change in lead professional

No. of admissions	Reason for admission
91	Pregnancy induced hypertension
76	Antepartum haemorrhage
40	Reduced fetal movements
26	Threatened pre-term labour
14	Medical problem
12	Inter Uterine Growth Retardation (suspected)
7	Unstable lie
2	Placenta praevia

Admissions not requiring a change in lead professional

No. of admissions	Reason for admission
128	Suspected labour (false alarm)
83	Non-specific abdominal pain
60	SRM (suspected)
54	Reduced fetal movements
24	Urinary tract infection
11	Accidents or faints
49	Others
20	Unknown

Labour

- 371 primips (50%) and 523 multips (84%) had no complication throughout labour.

The most common complications were:
- Fetal distress (20.5% in primips and 6.6% in multips).
- Failure to progress in either first (7.4%) or second stage (19.1%). This occurred in 2.4% of primips and 3% of multips.

Major complications were rare. There were:
- Seven cases of sever shoulder dystocia, six in multips.
- Three cord prolapses, two in primips and one in a multip.
- 14 postpartum haemorrhages, six in primips and eight in multips.

Fetal outcomes
- Four babies were admitted to the neonatal unit, two of whom died from unrecognized major congenital abnormalities.
- 12 had APGAR scores of less than seven at five minutes.

- Only 894 (45%) of women went through pregnancy and labour without complications which needed a change in the lead professional (371 primips and 523 multips).
- 110 required at least one hospital admission for problems that did not change their risk status.
- **40% of the women initially categorized as low-risk did not need hospital obstetric contact during pregnancy or labour (328 primips and 456 multips).**

Conclusion
- The number of women considered as suitable for community care was under 50%. Past obstetric complications were the main reason for exclusion.
- Although staffing levels in the community may need to increase, there may be very little change in the demands on hospital-based staff.
- Primips are likely to need the assistance of a member of the hospital team at some point: in this study, nearly 70% of primips who were considered low-risk at booking needed hospital obstetric advice or care at some point during pregnancy or labour.
- 60% of women who were initially diagnosed as being of low-risk will require hospital services at some point during labour and pregnancy.
- Of the total population of women assessed at booking to be low-risk, 80% will need some obstetric input.

Murphy-Black, T. (1992)

Authors	Date	Study reference	Intervention assessed	Evaluation	Number of women studied	Main outcomes
Murphy-Black, T.	November 1990 – April 1991	Murphy-Black T. (1992) Systems of midwifery care in use in Scotland. *Midwifery*; 8: 113-124	No intervention. Survey of systems of midwifery care in use in Scotland.	Postal questionnaire to all Supervisors of Midwives in Scotland, followed by a second system-specific questionnaire for more detailed information. There were replies from Supervisors of Midwives in 38 hospitals with maternity beds and 43 community units. Twenty-eight of the community units were integrated with the local maternity hospital. The integrated units undertook approx. 83% of deliveries in Scotland.	All Supervisors of Midwives in Scotland (N=55). 41 responded after one reminder (74%).	Systems of midwifery care in use in Scotland. Five were specifically enquired about: • individualized care plans • nursing/midwife process • DOMINO • patient allocation • team midwifery.

Results: Systems of midwifery care in use in Scotland

Results are based on 81 hospital and community units represented by respondents. The table shows the number using each system of care.

Systems	In operation	Planned	Total	%
Individual care plans	58	13	71	88
Patient allocation	43	10	53	65
Nursing/midwife process	41	12	53	65
DOMINO	44	6	50	62
Team midwifery	17	24	41	51

The majority of units were using one or more of these systems of care. Team midwifery was the least frequently used. Nearly a fifth of the units were either operating or planning all the five systems of care. The larger integrated units were more likely to have implemented systems to reduce fragmentation of care.

Advantages/disadvantages of each system of care: Respondents to the second questionnaire cited a wide range of advantages and disadvantages to the different systems. 'Continuity of care' was cited as an advantage for every system, although only one respondent elaborated on what this meant.

Swan (1993)

Authors	Date	Study reference	Intervention assessed	Evaluation	Number of women studied	Main outcomes
Swan, Mary	Pilot study in operation from July 1990. Evaluation completed August 1991. Gradual phasing in of district wide teams: total team midwifery care began January 1993.	Team Midwifery – The Scunthorpe experience. Journal of Management in Medicine (1993) 7(5): 55–61.	Team midwifery in Scunthorpe • District wide scheme. constituted 9 teams attached to GP practices. • Case load 240-280 women per annum. • Hospital team also established. *Antenatal care* • team midwives provided care in the home or clinic. • team provided parentcraft and informal pop-in sessions. • aquanatal classes introduced. *Intranatal care* • care provided by team members. • home bookings introduced. *Postnatal care* care provided by team members.	Evaluation by research midwife in provider unit. *Methods* Not specified.	Number of women involved in evaluation not known. *Characteristics* of population of childbearing women: mixed urban and rural including women from all social classes.	Not clearly indicated.

Results: Team midwifery in Scunthorpe

NB: Although the paper claims to present the results of evaluation and conclusions drawn from these, neither data nor information about the evaluation process are given. The interpretations offered by the author must therefore be read with caution.

Implementation
- Scheme began as a pilot with one team of midwives providing care in a defined geographical area of Scunthorpe (Winterton).
- Pilot scheme: 140 women per annum.
- Site for pilot chosen because majority of clients would be registered with a practice of 'supportive GPs'.
- Pilot scheme: four midwives initially with a fifth appointed to reduce pressure of on-call.
- Team midwives described as 'enthusiastic, dedicated and innovative and committed to achieving high standards' (selection method not specified).
- Each midwife completed a personal development programme before teams became operational.

Pilot Scheme: the author suggests that the team had:
1. Personalized the service by their holistic approach to care: postnatal comments indicate that clients and their families were greatly appreciative of this fact.
2. Enabled informed choice and continuity of care for their clients and families.
3. Reduced hospital bed occupancy through antenatal care in the home where appropriate, labour assessments prior to admission in labour and early postnatal discharge.
4. Improved job satisfaction for the team members through better utilization of midwifery skills.

In addition, the team was reported to have:
- Reduced medical intervention.
- Increased breastfeeding success: 80% of mothers were still breastfeeding on transfer to the health visitor (compared with 30% of the remainder in Scunthorpe).

After final audit was presented to the Health Authority and Operational Policies Board in August 1991, the scheme was expanded throughout the district.

District wide teams:
- Nine teams of five or six midwives.
- In establishing team midwifery, midwives were consulted re. team allocations.
- Case load 240-280 women per annum.
- Three team co-ordinators provided managerial and clinical backup.

Effects of Team Midwifery on practice and services

Advantages to the mother

1. Personalization of the service.
2. Continuity of care and carers.
3. Known carer in labour helps to reduce anxiety levels and possibly relieve pain.
4. Less conflicting advice.
5. Labour assessment and much of the care in the first stage of labour conducted in own home, if appropriate.
6. Reduced unnecessary admissions.
7. Reduced length of hospital stay.
8. Midwives who are aware of personal circumstances and possible impact on care.
9. Midwives in the team who appreciate all aspects of care.

Advantages to the midwives

1. Increased job satisfaction and full utilization of skills.
2. Flexible working patterns.
3. Peer group support and teamwork, especially during stressful periods.
4. Improved communication within teams.
5. Understanding of both hospital and community care.
6. Awareness of clients' progress in pregnancy, social background and possible impact on care and care uptake, allowing for a more reliable, holistic approach to care.
7. Increased confidence and accountability.
8. Good all-round experience.

Advantages to the organization

1. Increased client satisfaction and quality of care, which have led to reversal of outflow of women from the District to neighbouring units.
2. Reduced bed occupancy.
3. Reduced unnecessary admissions.
4. More evenly distributed workloads.
5. Midwives competent in all aspects of care.
6. More community based care.

Issues remaining:

- Postnatal care in the hospital fragmented at times.
- Attention needs to be given to maintaining the level of skill of hospital-based midwives.
- Attention needs to be paid to the antenatal and postnatal care of women booking for delivery outside of the District.

Midwives experiences of team working

- Midwives report feeling tired and stressed.
- They nevertheless prefer team working and would chose to continue with the scheme.
- A range of services have evolved with team working including: aquanatal classes; grandparents' classes, team-parentcraft classes in local venues; ethnic parentcraft; teenage parentcraft; bereavement support; informal pop-in sessions; mothercare pop-in sessions. Others are planned.

Barnsley DGH NHS Trust (1995)

Authors	Date	Study reference	Intervention assessed	Evaluation	Number of women studied	Main outcomes
Barnsley DGH NHS Trust Obstetrics and Gynaecology CMT	Pilot scheme November 1994 – July 1995	The report of the study is an internal publication from Barnsley DGH NHS Trust Obstetrics & Gynaecology CMT entitled: An evaluation of the Penistone Pilot Project in Team Midwifery. December 1995	One team of 7 full time midwives serving Penistone, Dodworth and Gilroyd and surrounding rural area. • Team based at central health centre. • Workload: equivalent to 25 births per midwife for duration of scheme (32 births per midwife per year). *Antenatal care* • bookings carried out in community either at a clinic or in home by team midwife. • antenatal care largely followed shared care model. • team midwives accompanied women to hospital for antenatal consultant appointments, scans etc.	Evaluation: not clear by whom the scheme is evaluated. Questionnaires designed by midwifery staff in collaboration with the clinical audit department. *Methods* • questionnaires for women who delivered during the period of the pilot. • clinical data collected by midwives via internal audit forms developed for the project.	145 women who delivered in either Barnsley DGH or at home during the operation of the pilot scheme. Evaluation concerns 82 completed data sets (57% of women delivered by team midwives). *Characteristics* of population of childbearing women: • Penistone area described as 'affluent' with a generally motivated and informed population.	• audit of care • cost estimate • description of women's perceptions • description of midwives' perceptions.

Authors	Date	Study reference	Intervention assessed	Evaluation	Number of women studied	Main outcomes
			• team midwife rostered in hospital provided care and support to team's women in antenatal clinics and scan dept. *Intrapartum care* • women in labour had option of being assessed at home by team midwife. • intrapartum care provided for all women by team midwife. • team midwife rostered to work in hospital provided care for team's women in labour suite. *Postnatal care* team midwife rostered to work in hospital provided care for team's women in postnatal wards.	• survey of views and perceptions of midwives not in team undertaken at 2 points: shortly after outset of pilot and shortly before its completion. • views of pilot team at several review sessions during the pilot scheme. • diaries: kept by team midwives. • retrospective study of 69 sets of midwifery notes re. infant feeding behaviours (no information is given regarding sample generation).	• rural areas: have widely dispersed population. Suggestion of lower birth weights for babies born in the Pilot area compared with the rest of the Borough.	

Results: The Penistone Pilot Project in Team Midwifery

Implementation process
Not described.

- After the initial three months, when the number of midwives in the team was increased, the catchment area and workload was also increased: one additional GP practice was included serving two more areas (Dodworth and Gilroyd).
- Initially six full time midwives. Increased to seven after three months: 2G grade (previously community midwives), 1F (previously relief community midwife), 3F (previously hospital midwives on E grades, temporarily regraded for the Pilot study), later addition of 1 more G grade (a community midwife).

- 24 hr shift system developed.
- System of message books developed + use of mobile phones to aid communication between team midwives.

Information about the GP practices providing the community base for team midwives is summarized:
- Penistone area served by single group practice of seven GPs.
- The two community midwives worked here already.
- Pre-existing patterns of care: GP and GP-consultant shared care.
- When the project was extended, a second practice with three GPs based in Dodworth became involved.

Cross-border issues:
18 women receiving team care gave birth outside of the area.

Types of Delivery (Barnsley DGH)

Type of delivery	Total	Project midwife present		Project midwife not present	
Normal	106	94	(89%)	12	(11%)
Labour suite c/s	24	20	(83%)	4	(17%)
Ventouse	4	3	(75%)	1	(25%)
Neville Barnes forceps	5	5	(100%)	-	
Wrigley's forceps	1	1	(100%)	-	
Total	140	123	(88%)	17	(12%)

Evaluation measured against Changing Childbirth '10 indicators of success'
Project not intended to address all indicators of success: relevant indicators:
- All women should be able to carry their own case notes.
- Pilot women carried duplicate copy of case notes.
- 45 women chose to do so 43 (96%) said they were happy to do so: two women expressed negative views associated with format of notes (smaller co-operation cards preferred).

- No notes were lost.
- **Every woman should know one midwife who ensures continuity of care.**
- Every woman had 'named midwife' in the team.
- Named midwife to ensure continuity not necessarily to provide that herself.
- Scheme aimed to make women familiar with all members of team.
- 82 women surveyed: 62 (76%) knew their named midwife, 11 (13%) did not, 4 (5%) did not respond, 5 (6%) had postnatal care only by the project and therefore did not have the opportunity to experience continuity of care under the scheme.
- **At least 75% of women should know the person who cares for them during the delivery.**
- Data from 70 women delivered at Barnsley DGH or at home: 52 (74%) delivered by a team midwife: a further 13 (19%) delivered by a doctor but with a team midwife present: 5 (7%) delivered by a hospital midwife.
- 12 women delivered out-of-area, not attended by team midwife.
- Did women know the team midwife who attended them at delivery? 48 (59%) women had met five or more of the team members before delivery, 71% of women could name five or more midwives in the team, 59% could name six of the seven midwives.

Evaluation measured against Health of the Nation Targets
Breastfeeding targets:
- Feeding behaviour of mothers at 28 days: retrospective study of 69 sets of midwifery notes (sample generation not specified): Penistone area rate at 28 days = 54%: Pilot project rate (for 44 women) = 86%.

Measures of client satisfaction
Preferred patterns of care
- 87% of women would prefer to be cared for by the team of six midwives before, during and after the delivery.
- 11% would prefer antenatal and postnatal care from a community midwife and intrapartum care from hospital midwives.
- 2% no preference.
- Comparisons of patterns of care in current and previous childbearing experiences: 78% of women are reported to have preferred care offered under the scheme to care received in a previous pregnancy.
- No breakdown for parity; place of care; pattern of care; other confounding factors.

Would women book under the scheme again?
- Yes: 77   (94%)
- No:
Preferred hospital care	2	(2%)
Not planning any more	1	(1%)
Unhappy about GP backup	1	(2%)

Women made a of range of statements relating to potential improvements concerning antenatal, intrapartum and postnatal care. The majority of statements were positive and supportive.

Measures of midwife Satisfaction
Other midwives' perceptions
- All midwives thought the scheme had worked satisfactorily or well.
- Early in the pilot period 57% of midwives said they thought the standard of care had improved: this increased to 80% by the end of the pilot period.
- Midwives indicated that there was a two-tier service for scheme and non-scheme women. Particular concerns noted were: different arrangements on postnatal wards: communication between team and other midwives.

Team midwives perceptions
- Positive aspects of the scheme for women included: increased patient autonomy and patient choice: greater patient satisfaction.
- Positive aspects of the scheme for women included: support from colleagues within team: opportunities to practice, improved job satisfaction and motivation.
- Negative aspects of the scheme included: intense personal commitment required: difficulty of providing on-call: resistance from other midwives to pilot scheme.

Measures of GP satisfaction
Not done.

Measures of management satisfaction
- Patient flow: anecdotal evidence is submitted to suggest that a reduction in the small number of bookings outside of Barnsley can be attributed to women's enthusiasm for team midwifery.
- Limited information is presented regarding early postnatal discharge. No historical or comparative data are available.

Costs of project
- Non-recurrent funding of £38,500 in 1994-5 and £19,000 in 1995-6 from Barnsley Health Authority.
- Estimate of a significant increase in costs of team midwifery compared with pre-existing costs of service.

Conclusions:
Costly scheme: unlikely that it could be developed in its current form to encompass the entire borough.

APPENDIX C24

Wright (1994)

Authors	Date	Study reference	Intervention assessed	Evaluation	Number of women studied	Main outcomes
Wright, B.	Pilot scheme established Feb. 1993 Evaluation reported Feb. 1994	Wright B (1994). The full report of the study is an internal publication from Queen Mary's Sidcup NHS Trust entitled: Caseload midwifery at Queen Mary's Sidcup NHS Trust – the evaluation of a pilot scheme.	• 2 teams of midwives providing antenatal, intrapartum and postnatal care to an identified group of low and high-risk women. • 4 GP practices were identified as the bases for the 2 teams. All mothers belonging to the identified practices were therefore included with some self-referrals from other locations as the scheme became established. • each team consisted of 6.5 w.t.e midwives caring for 250 mothers per annum. • each team midwife worked in both hospital and community.	Evaluation undertaken by the caseload co-ordinator who had planned and implemented the pilot scheme. *Methods* • Informal observation (including staff meetings). • method of data collection for caseload clients' episodes of care not specified. • women's questionnaire: 10 days postnatal. • midwives' questionnaire. • GPs' questionnaire. • method of data collection for health visitors' perceptions not specified.	No. of women cared for = 475. Caseload Midwives: • 4 x G grades. • 7 x F grades (2 more were promoted during the pilot year). • 4 x E grades • 1 x A grade health care assistant.	• Costs • client care on caseload

269

Authors	Date	Study reference	Intervention assessed	Evaluation	Number of women studied	Main outcomes
			• midwives were recruited from within the pre-existing complement and selected by the report's author and 2 existing team leaders.		• A matched sample of non-caseload midwives was also selected to receive the midwives' questionnaire (n=16); matched for experience, grade, work area and number of hours worked. (7 responded) • 17 GPs were surveyed (11 responded).	

Results: Caseload Midwifery at Queen Mary's Sidcup NHS Trust

Implementation:
All staff were asked to complete a 'strengths and weaknesses' form and initial training needs were assessed from these. Experience of community working and antenatal clinic care was provided in the month before initiation of the scheme.

Issues
- Initially many of the women identified as part of the teams' caseloads were not delivering at Queen Mary's but at one of two other local units.
- By the second month of implementation, the teams had been realigned to work with two larger GP practices each and the deliveries per month at Queen Mary's increased.

Staff Reactions:
Informal observations are offered for the following staff groups:
- Caseload midwives
- Obstetric staff
- GPs
- Health Visitors.

Costings:
- Some basic data is provided in relation to start up costs (car lease, sundry equipment, car phones etc).
- A comparison of staff (midwifery) costs for the caseload teams and for midwives of the same grade practising outwith the scheme. The author suggests that 'the running costs for traditional and caseload midwifery are broadly comparable'. Caution is needed in interpreting this conclusion.

Client care on caseload:
- There are some problems in interpreting the data presented as numbers are not consistent and no rationale is given for this.
- No indication of statistical significance is given.

Outcomes:

Type of delivery	No.	%
Spontaneous vaginal delivery	347	76.9
Forceps	22	4.6
Ventouse	21	4.5
LSCS (emergency)	35	7.7
LSCS (elective)	26	5.7
Termination of pregnancy	3	0.6

- It is not clear how the sample of non-caseload women was derived, or how data were collected for the following table.
- Numbers of women in each sample not noted.
- No indication of statistical significance is given.

Pain relief	Caseload %	Non-caseload %
None	6.8	9
Entonox	44	44
Pethidine	23	26
Epidural	12.7	9.2
TENS	6.7	5.6
Other	6.8	6.2
State of Perineum		
Intact	31.4	26.8
Episiotomy	26.8	25.8
2nd Degree	20.3	22.7
1st Degree	8.5	5.3
Labial laceration	7.1	7.8
Other (including 3rd Degree)	5.9	11.6

Client evaluation:
- 356 questionnaires were returned: response rate of 74.9%.
- Bar charts are presented illustrating percentage of women who met a midwife again during their antenatal care, percentage of women delivered by a known midwife, percentage of women who met a midwife again postnatally. (% figures not included for any of these.)
- The length of postnatal hospital stay for caseload women decreased over the duration of the pilot study. No statistical significance stated.
- The number of postnatal visits at home for caseload women increased over the duration of the pilot study. No statistical significance stated.
- The percentage of women who planned to breastfeed and the percentage of women who were breastfeeding at 10 days showed a general trend to increase over the duration of the pilot study. However, the percentage of women who discontinued breastfeeding (not defined) also showed a similar trend. There is no indication of statistical significance for any of these findings.

Midwives' evaluation of caseload
- 15/16 caseload midwives responded to the midwives' questionnaire: only 7/16 non-caseload midwives responded.
- Data is presented for midwives' perceptions about caseload midwifery and about what women want (choice, continuity and control). However, the small numbers make comparison of the percentages in each response category unrealistic.

GPs' evaluation of caseload:
- Over half the GPs were as satisfied with antenatal and postnatal care with caseload as they had been before.
- Concerns were expressed by some GPs about home deliveries and a perceived reduction in their involvement in antenatal care.

Health Visitors' evaluation of caseload:
- Reported to be generally favourable.
- Some concerns were expressed about the delivery of parent education without input from health visitors.

APPENDIX D

Selected Bibliography – Further Reading

Bakketeig, L.S. (1992). 'Methodological problems and possible endpoints in the evaluation of antenatal care'. *International Journal of Technology Assessment in Health Care*, 1, pp. 33–39.

Barron, S.L., Macfarlane, A.J. (1990). 'Collection and use of routine maternity data'. *Bailliere's Clinical Obstetrics and Gynaecology*, 4(4), pp. 681–697.

Bluff, R., Holloway, I. (1994). '"They know best": women's perceptions of midwifery care during labour and childbirth'. *Midwifery*, 10, pp. 157–164.

Bower, H. (1993). 'Team midwifery in Oxford'. *MIDIRS Midwifery Digest*, 3(2), pp. 143–145.

Brown, D.J. (1994). 'Opinions of general practitioners in Nottinghamshire about provision of intrapartum care'. *British Medical Journal*, 309, pp. 777–779.

Browne, A. (1994). 'Are midwives ready for the proposals for change?' *Nursing Times*, 90(47).

Buckley, R. (1995). 'The use of standard setting to improve maternity care'. *Nursing Times*, 91(31), pp. 32–33.

Campbell, R. (1991). 'Choice and chance in low risk maternity care'. *British Medical Journal*, 303, pp. 1487–1488.

Campbell, R., MacFarlane, A. (1994). *Where To Be Born? The Debate and the Evidence*. Oxford: Oxford University Press.

Chalmers, I. (1986). 'Minimizing harm and maximizing benefit during innovation in health care: controlled or uncontrolled experimentation'. *Birth*, 13(3), pp. 155–64.

Clarke, M., Clayton, D.G. (1983). 'Quality of obstetric care provided for Asian immigrants in Leicestershire'. *British Medical Journal Clinical Research Education*, 286(6365), pp. 621–23.

Clinical Standards Advisory Group (1996). *Women in Normal Labour*. London: HMSO.

Cornish, Y. (1996). 'How can clinicians become more involved in commissioning?' *Clinician in Management*, 5(1), pp. 6–8.

Davies, J., Evans, F. (1989). 'The Newcastle community midwifery care project'. *Community Midwifery*, 5, pp. 104–139.

Demilew, J. (1994). 'South East London Midwifery Group Practice'. *MIDIRS Midwifery Digest*, 4(3), pp. 270–272.

Department of Health (1993). *A Study of Midwifery and GP-led Maternity Units*. NHS Management Executive.

Derby City General Hospital NHS Trust (1995). *Changing Childbirth Project: Phase One summary*. Southern Derbyshire Health Commission.

Dimond, B. (1994). 'Midwifery-managed units'. *Modern Midwife*, 4(6), pp. 31–33.

Dowswell, T., Hirst, J., Piercy, J., Hewison, J., Lilford, R., Geddes, A. (1996). *Patterns of Maternity Care*. University of Leeds.

Drife, J.O. (1988). 'Disciplining midwives [editorial]'. *British Medical Journal*, 297, pp. 806–07.

Elbourne, D., Richardson, M., Chalmers, I., Waterhouse, I., Holt, E. (1987). 'The Newbury maternity care study: a randomized controlled trial to assess a policy of women holding their own obstetric records'. *British Journal of Obstetrics & Gynaecology*, 94, pp. 612–619.

Enkin, M.W., Keirse, M.J., Renfrew, M.J., Neilson, J.P. (1995). 'Effective care in pregnancy and childbirth: a synopsis'. *Birth*, 22(2), pp. 101-10.

Enkin, M.W. (1992). 'Randomized controlled trials in the evaluation of antenatal care'. *International Journal of Technology Assessment in Health Care*, 1, pp. 40–45.

Fawcett, H., LaCumber, P. (1995). 'The change in focus of midwifery at Guy's & St Thomas': following changing childbirth recommendations'. *MIDIRS Midwifery Digest*, 5(3), pp. 357–358.

Floyd, L. (1996). 'Community midwives' views and experience of home birth'. *Midwifery*, 11, pp. 3-10.

Forest Healthcare Trust (1995). *Forest Midwifery Group Evaluation: Phase II - Survey of Women*. Forest Healthcare Trust.

Frohlich, J., Edwards, S. (1989). 'Team midwifery for everyone – building on the "Know your midwife" scheme'. *Midwives Chronicle*, 102(1214), pp. 66–70.

Garcia, J., Kilpatrick, R., Richards, M. (1990). *The Politics of Maternity Care*. Oxford: Oxford University Press.

Garcia, J., Renfrew, M.J., Marchant, S. (1994). 'Postnatal home visiting by midwives'. *Midwifery*, 10, pp. 40–43.

Giles, W., Collins, J., Ong, F., MacDonald, R. (1992). 'Antenatal care of low risk obstetric patients by midwives. A randomised controlled trial'. *Medical Journal of Australia*, 157(3), pp. 158–61.

Guthrie, K.A., Songane, F.F., Mackenzie, F., Lilford, R.J. (1989). 'Audit of medical response to antenatal booking history'. *British Journal of Obstetrics & Gynaecology*, 96(5), pp. 552–56.

Hay-Smith, J. (1995). *Early vs Standard Postnatal Discharge from Hospital*. The Cochrane Pregnancy and Childbirth Database (1), pp. 1–7.

Hill, A.M., Yudkin, P.L., Bull, D.J., Barlow, D.H., Charnock, F.M., Gillmer, M.D. (1993). 'Evaluating a policy of reduced consultant antenatal clinic visits for low risk multiparous women'. *Quality in Health Care*, 2, pp. 152–156.

Hillan, E.M. (1992). 'Issues in the delivery of midwifery care'. *Journal of Advanced Nursing*, 17, pp. 274–278.

Hobbs, L. (1993). 'Team midwifery – the other view'. *MIDIRS Midwifery Digest*, 3(2), pp. 146–147.

Hodnett, E.D. (1993). *Birth Room vs Conventional Delivery Settings*. The Cochrane Pregnancy and Childbirth Database (Issue 1):1–7.

Hodnett, S.A. (1996). *Continuity of Caregivers during Pregnancy and Childbirth*. The Cochrane Library (Issue 2):1–6.

Hutton, E. (1995). 'Midwife caseloads – NCT Policy Statement'. *MIDIRS Midwifery Digest*, 5(4), pp. 396–397.

Hutton, E. (1994). 'What women want from midwives'. *British Journal of Midwifery*, 2(12), pp. 608–11.

Kroll, D. (1995). 'Bridging the gap between purchaser and provider'. *Modern Midwife*, 5(8), pp. 25–27.

Kroll, D. (1993). 'The name of the game – team midwifery now'. *Modern Midwife*, 3, pp. 26-28.

Kroll, D., Dwyer, D. (1994). 'Postnatal care: teamwork in the community'. *Modern Midwife*, 4, pp. 10–13.

Littlejohns, P., Dumelow, C., Griffiths, S. (1996). 'Knowledge based commissioning: can a national clinical effectiveness policy be compatible with seeking local professional advice?' *Journal of Health Service Policy*, 1(1), pp. 28–34.

MacKeith, N. (1995). 'One-to-one midwifery practice'. *MIDIRS Midwifery Digest*, 5(1), pp. 23–28.

Mason, V. (1993). *Women's Experience of Maternity Care – A Survey Manual*. London: HMSO.

McGuire, A. (1996). 'Where do internal markets come from and can they work?' *Journal of Health Service Policy*, 1(1), pp. 56–59.

McIntosh, M.B. (1989). 'The team approach to midwifery care'. *Midwives Chronicle* 102(1214), pp. 81–83.

Meldrum, P., Purton, P., MacLennan, B.B., Twaddle, S. (1994). 'Moving towards a common understanding in maternity services'. *Midwifery*, 10(3), pp. 165–70.

Melia, R.J., Morgan, M., Wolfe, C.D., Swan, A.V. (1991). 'Consumers' views of the maternity services: implications for change and quality assurance'. *Journal of Public Health Medicine*, 13(2), pp.120–6.

Meyer, J., Wallace, V. (1995). 'Mother's help'. *Nursing Times*, 91(50), pp. 42–43.

Neil, C. (1985). 'The team from Tooting. Delivering the goods'. *Nursing Times*, 81(5), p. 19.

Newburn, M. (1993). 'Choice, continuity and care'. *MIDIRS Midwifery Digest*, 3(4), pp. 471-473.

Oakley, A. (1991). 'Using medical care: the views and experiences of high-risk mothers'. *Health Services Research*, 26(5), pp. 651-69.

Outram, V. (1995). 'Case study – The Scunthorpe Way' cited in *The Challenge of Changing Childbirth*, section 3, p. 11. Continuity of Care, London: English National Board.

Parsons, L., Day, S. (1992). 'Improving obstetric outcomes in ethnic minorities: an evaluation of health advocacy in Hackney'. *Journal of Public Health Medicine*, 14(2), pp. 183–91.

Paterson, C.M., Chapple, J.C., Beard, R.W., Joffe, M., Steer, P.J., Wright, C.S. (1991). 'Evaluating the quality of the maternity services - a discussion paper'. *British Journal of Obstetrics & Gynaecology*, 98(11), pp. 1073-78.

Prowse, R., Lupton, C. (1996). *Evaluation and Dissemination of Women's Experiences of Maternity Services*. The University of Portsmouth.

Ratcliffe, J. (1996). 'The costs of alternative types of routine antenatal care for low risk women: shared care vs care by GPs and community midwives'. *Journal of Health Services Research & Policy*, 1(3), July.

Reynolds, J.L., Yudkin, P., Bull, M. (1988). 'General practitioner obstetrics: does risk prediction work?'. *Journal of the Royal College of General Practitioners*, 38, pp. 307-310.

Robinson, S. (1993). 'Combining work with caring for children, findings from a longitudinal study of midwives' careers'. *Midwifery*, 9, pp. 183–196.

Rowley, M.J., Hensley, M.J., Brinsmead, M.W., Wlodarczyk, J.H. (1995). 'Continuity of care by a midwife team versus routine care during pregnancy and birth: a randomised trial'. *Medical Journal of Australia*, 163, pp. 289–93.

Royal College of Obstetricans and Gynaecologists (1995). *Report of a Joint Working Group. Organisational Standards for Maternity Services*. London: RCOG.

Royal College of Obstetricians and Gynaecologists (1995). *Report of the Audit Committee's Working Group. Communication Standards in Obstetrics*.

Sikorski, J., Clement, S., Wilson, J., Das, S., Smeeton, N. (1995). 'A survey of health professionals' views on possible changes in the provision and organisation of antenatal care'. *Midwifery*, 11(2), pp. 61–68.

Simic, P., Benett, I.J., Garrod, D. (1995). 'Women's experience of maternity care in an inner city. A team based qualitative study'. *Midwives*, 108(1285), pp. 38–41.

Smith-Hanrahan, C., Deblois, D. (1995). 'Postpartum early discharge: impact on maternal fatigue and functional ability'. *Clinical Nursing Research*, 4(1), pp. 50–66.

Smith, L.F.P. (1996). 'Should general practitioners have any role in maternity care in the future?' *British Journal of General Practice*, 46, pp. 243–247.

Stock, J. (1995). 'Continuity of care in maternity services – the implications for midwives'. *MIDIRS Midwifery Digest*, 5(2), pp. 149–150.

Stocking, B. (1993). 'Implementing the findings of effective care in pregnancy and childbirth in the United Kingdom'. *The Milbank Quarterly*, 71(3), pp. 497–521.

Stone, J. (1994). 'Whose pregnancy is it anyway?' *MIDIRS Midwifery Digest*, 4(3), pp. 367–368.

Swan, M. (1993). 'Team midwifery – The Scunthorpe experience'. *Journal of Management in Medicine*. 7(5), pp. 55–61.

Thomas, H., Draper, J., Field, S., Hare, M.J. (1987). 'Evaluation of an integrated community antenatal clinic'. *Journal of the Royal College of General Practitioners*, 37(305), pp. 544–47.

Towler, J. (1984). 'Midwives' units – wishful thinking or reality?' *Midwives Chronicle*, 97(1152), pp. 3–5.

Turnbull, E., Hodges, S. (1986). 'Continuity of care through improved documentation'. *Journal of Obstetric, Gynaecologic and Neonatal Nursing*, 15(1), pp. 45–48.

Van Alten, D., Eskes, M., Treffers, P. (1989). 'Midwifery in the Netherlands. The Wormerveer study'. *British Journal of Obstetrics and Gynaecology*, 96, pp. 656–662.

Waldenstrom, U., Nilsson, C.A. (1994). 'Experience of childbirth in birth center care. A randomized controlled study'. *Acta Obstetricia Et Gynecologica Scandinavica*, 73(7), pp. 547–54.

Walsh, D. (1989). 'Comparison of management and outcome of labour under two systems of care'. *Midwives Chronicle and Nursing Notes*, 102(1219), pp. 270–273.

Ward, P., Frohlich, J. (1994). 'Team midwifery in Bristol'. *MIDIRS Midwifery Digest*, 4(2), pp. 149–151.

Warwick, C. (1995). 'Small group practices – Part 1: Manager's perspective'. *Modern Midwife*, 5(10), pp. 22–23.

Warwick, C., Kroll, D. (1995). 'Bridging the gap between purchaser and provider 2: The future of maternity care'. *Modern Midwife*, 5(9), pp. 24–27.

Williams, E.M. (1990). 'An integrated midwifery service in Powys'. *Midwives Chronicle,* 103(1235), pp. 358–59.

Williams, K. (1994). 'Home from home'. *Nursing Times*, 90(18), pp. 44–45.

Williamson, S., Thomson, A. (1996). 'Women's satisfaction with antenatal care in a changing maternity service'. *Midwifery*, 12, pp. 198–204.

Wood, J. (1991). 'A review of antenatal care initiatives in primary care settings'. *British Journal of General Practice*, 41, pp. 26–30.

Ongoing Research

AUTHORS/ CONTACT	DATE	LOCATION	TYPE OF STUDY AND AIMS	OUTCOMES TO BE MEASURED
Julia Sanders (Midwife) Deborah Sharp (Professor) David Jewell (Senior Lecturer in General Practice)	Start date January 1996 for 8 months Final report estimated at end of April 1998	Bristol	RCT comparing traditional antenatal care with allowing women to choose the frequency and timing of visits in consultation with their carers. Seven hundred 'low-risk' women will be involved and followed up to three months after birth. Aim: to assess the outcome of allowing women to choose their pattern of antenatal care.	Three questionnaires will be used to assess psychological outcomes A sample of women will be interviewed towards the end of their pregnancy to ascertain their views in more depth. Data will also be collected on any complications of pregnancy that occur.
Carolyn Clark		Brent & Harrow Health Agency	Promoting choices in maternity care with the ethnic and refugee populations.	
Ruth Wrigley	October 1994 – March 1996	Leighton Hospital Crewe Cheshire	To offer informed choice to women to allow them to choose their lead professional. To provide continuity of care by using satisfaction surveys and focus groups.	Official evaluation not yet complete but initial results have indicated: that the travel costs for community midwives in comparison to traditional care is higher. Anecdotal feedback from the women identifies higher levels of satisfaction and midwives expressed greater job satisfaction. The uptake of the midwife – as the lead professional, appears to be high.

AUTHORS/ CONTACT	DATE	LOCATION	TYPE OF STUDY AND AIMS	OUTCOMES TO BE MEASURED
Soo Downe Sheila McFarlane (Research Midwives)	April 1995 – May 1996	Derby City General Hospital NHS Trust/ Southern Derbyshire Health Authority	Changing Childbirth Project One: key intervention: 'All women booked with consultants/GPs/midwives in the pilot sites will be offered a known carer in labour, no matter what their risk status'. Project based on two sites, one urban, one rural, chosen on the basis of GP interest and lack of cross-border flow. Women matched at booking with two women who were not in a pilot scheme area. Semi-structured postal questionnaires sent to women at approx. 36 weeks, 8 weeks postnatally and 3 months after the birth.	Phase 1: 1.1 The change process as experienced by staff 1.2 Maternal experience/satisfaction 1.3 Clinical outcomes 1.4 Financial outcomes (Phase 2 will identify and address staff training needs; Phase 3 will develop a GP contract for the maternity services and assess the impact of the contract on pricing and quality).
Julie Beckwith (Research midwife)	2 year study. Data collection was due for completion end of 1996	Gloucester-shire Royal NHS Trust	Comparative study of two ways of providing care: • an existing community based scheme where women have good continuity of carer antenatally and postnatally and intrapartum care is provided by a hospital based midwife who they would not have met before labour begins • a newly developed scheme where a small team of midwives aims to provide continuity of carer throughout the whole care episode.	Questionnaires to women to provide information re: continuity of care and carer; satisfaction of mothers. Other outcomes: satisfaction of midwives; clinical outcomes; information on working patterns of midwives; financial outcomes; views of GPs (via focus groups). Report will be available shortly. Preliminary results suggest no clinical differences but women more satisfied with the team scheme. Questionable sustainability.

AUTHORS/ CONTACT	DATE	LOCATION	TYPE OF STUDY AND AIMS	OUTCOMES TO BE MEASURED
Alison Holt (Research & Development midwife)	2 year study. Final data collection due Sept 1996	Airedale NHS Trust & Worth Valley Health Consortium	The project aimed to establish a group midwifery practice within a GP led locality purchasing scheme. Objectives included: 75% of women to be delivered by a midwife that they have previously met; choice of lead professional; reduction in the total number of a midwives that a woman sees; increased continuity of carer; reduction in duplication of services.	Four surveys of women: one before start of the project in 1994, and 3 subsequent. Extensive data collection and audit involving both the group practice and a 'traditional care' comparison group. Survey of GPs. Focus groups of midwives conducted by an external researcher.
Cass Nightingale Divisional Manager, Women's & Children's Services	? One year project	Hillingdon Hospital Trust	To investigate whether the role of maternity care assistants can be developed within the community setting, including: breastfeeding advice and support; assisting women in caring for their babies; undertaking basic observations of women; assisting with clerical duties.	Evaluation tool under development.
Helen Spiby CJ Morrell P Stewart S Crowther	Start date 1st June 1996. End date 1st May 1997	Northern General Hospital Sheffield	RCT comparing the effectiveness of postnatal support for women receiving traditional community midwifery care with women receiving visits at home by a community midwifery support worker in addition to traditional midwifery care.	Outcomes include: general health status, incidence of postnatal depression, breastfeeding rates, use of services. Data collection was via: self-completion questionnaires, activity log, interviews, case note review, records of use of resources. Baseline questionnaire within 24 hours following birth. Follow up questionnaire at 6 weeks and 6 months postnatally. Health Visitor questionnaire at 3 months postnatally. GP records audit 6 months postnatally. Support worker activity log during visits.

AUTHORS/ CONTACT	DATE	LOCATION	TYPE OF STUDY AND AIMS	OUTCOMES TO BE MEASURED
P. Rouse B McLachlan (Midwifery manager) R Johanson (Obstetrician)	12 months: 1995-6	North Staffs. Hospital	Area randomized control trial to evaluate 'caseload care' (similar pattern to One-to-One) in comparison with traditional 'shared care'.	• Clinical outcomes (to be reported in first paper due to be submitted soon): mode of delivery, perineal injury, other obstetric interventions. • Women's satisfaction • Midwives' satisfaction